From Chaos to Compliance

Ellis Amdur, M.A., N.C.C., C.M.H.S.

Alan Pelton, M.S.

Communication, Control and De-escalation of Mentally Ill, Emotionally Disturbed and Aggressive Offenders

A Comprehensive Guidebook for

Parole and Probation Officers

An Edgework Book
www.edgework.info

Notes and Notices

From Chaos to Compliance: Communication, Control and De-escalation of Mentally Ill, Emotionally Disturbed and Aggressive Offenders

By Ellis Amdur, M.A., N.C.C., C.M.H.S and Alan Pelton, M.S. © 2011

ISBN: 978-1-950678-02-0

A Message to Our Readers

Edgework is committed to offering the best of our years of experience and study in the interest of professional and public safety. We ask that you express your respect for these intentions and honor our work by adhering strictly to the copyright protection notice you'll find below. By choosing NOT to reproduce these materials, you're supporting our work and making it possible for us to continue to develop materials that will enhance the safety of both the professionals for whom this book is written and the public. We thank you sincerely for your vigilance in respecting our rights!

Credits
Photographs by: Dreamstime.com
Illustrations by: Shoko Zama
Design: Soundview Design Studio
Cover photograph by: Jp Marquis, Wikimedia Commons

Contents

Books by the Author (and Co-Author)

Published by Edgework www.edgework.info

On the De-escalation of Aggression

EVERYTHING ON THE LINE: Calming and De-escalation of Aggressive and Mentally Ill Individuals on the Phone
A Comprehensive Guidebook for Emergency Dispatch (9-1-1) Centers
Ellis Amdur

FROM CHAOS TO COMPLIANCE: Communication, Control, and De-escalation of Mentally Ill, Emotionally Disturbed and Aggressive Offenders
A Comprehensive Guidebook for Parole and Probation Officers
Ellis Amdur & Alan Pelton

GRACE UNDER FIRE: Skills to Calm and De-escalate Aggressive and Mentally Ill Individuals in Outpatient Settings: 2nd Edition
A Comprehensive Guidebook for Health and Social Services Agencies, and Individual Practitioners
Ellis Amdur

GUARDING THE GATES: Calming, Control and De-escalation of Mentally Ill, Emotionally Disturbed and Aggressive Individuals
A Comprehensive Guidebook for Security Guards
Ellis Amdur & William Cooper

IN THE EYE OF THE HURRICANE: Skills to Calm and De-escalate Aggressive and Mentally Ill Family Members: 2nd Edition
Ellis Amdur

SAFE BEHIND BARS: Communication, Control, and De-escalation of Mentally Ill and Aggressive Inmates
A Comprehensive Guidebook for Correctional Officers in Jail Settings
Ellis Amdur & Chris De Villeneuve

SAFE BEHIND THE WALLS: Communication, Control, and De-escalation of Mentally Ill and Aggressive Inmates
A Comprehensive Guidebook for Correctional Officers in Prison Settings
Ellis Amdur & George Galaza

SAFE HAVEN: Skills to Calm and De-escalate Aggressive and Mentally Ill Individuals: 2nd Edition
A Comprehensive Guidebook for Personnel Working in Hospital and Residential Settings
Ellis Amdur

SAFETY AT WORK: Skills to Calm and De-escalate Aggressive and Mentally Ill Individuals
A Comprehensive Guidebook for Corporate Security Managers, Human Resources Staff, Loss Prevention Specialists, Executive Protection, and others involved in Threat Management Professions
Ellis Amdur & William Cooper

THE THIN BLUE LIFELINE: Verbal De-escalation of Mentally Ill and Emotionally Disturbed People
A Comprehensive Guidebook for Law Enforcement Officers
Ellis Amdur & John Hutchings

On Martial Arts

DUELING WITH OSENSEI: Grappling with the Myth of the Warrior Sage
Ellis Amdur

HIDDEN IN PLAIN SIGHT: Tracing the Roots of Ueshiba Morihei's Power
Ellis Amdur

OLD SCHOOL: Essays on Japanese Martial Traditions
Ellis Amdur

In Gratitude for Expert Critique

The following professionals have closely reviewed this book. With each draft, we corrected errors of fact, added new information, and fine-tuned the manuscript. One of the qualities of a good parole/probation officer is the understanding that the task supersedes protecting someone's feelings; therefore, we have appreciated all the direct criticism.

All responsibility for this book, however, must lie in our hands. Any errors, in particular, are our responsibility. Given that lives can be on the line in work such as this, please don't hesitate to contact us if you believe that any part of this book is inaccurate or requires additional material. The book will be revised, if needed, in future editions.

Robin Ingman began working with incarcerated youth in 1999 as a part-time Detention Officer. She now manages the Whatcom County Juvenile Detention Facility, using her firsthand experience to work closely with youth and staff.

Janene Schellhase (Johnstone) has ten years experience in probation with Kent Municipal Probation in Kent, Washington, including three years as supervisor. She is a ten-year member of the Misdemeanant Corrections Association, currently co-chair of the Training and Education Committee.

Preface

As this book has wound its way through the last stages of publication in 2011, the slow economic climb out of the recent recession, although officially ending in mid 2009, continues to confront law enforcement, social services and community health agencies, and government officials at all levels with a dire financial outlook. As a result, local and state legislatures nationwide, faced with reduced revenues and the loss of billions of dollars in federal stimulus funds, are forced to drastically reduce funding for education, community health care, and other vital social services in an effort to balance the books and avoid further deficit spending. Such reductions make the information contained in this book even more important to today's probation and parole officers, as offenders under their supervision find local educational opportunities, social services, and treatment options reduced or eliminated.

The ongoing fiscal crisis has also forced local and state governments nationwide to re-examine the long term economic sustainability of our current system of incarceration, and to begin discussing the possibility of saving some of the billions of dollars currently being spent on building and maintaining the nations prison system(s) by reducing the numbers of low level, non-violent drug offenders sentenced to prison, and increasing the number of mental health and drug treatment programs within the community.

In either event, whether as the result of reductions in available services or the diversion of an increasing number of low level offenders from prison to community corrections, probation and parole officers nationwide can expect to see an increase in the number of offenders under their supervision, many of whom have underlying mental health and/or drug and alcohol issues. Correspondingly, probation and parole officers also face a greater likelihood of confronting an agitated or aggressive offender, and it is the great hope of the authors that the information, strategies, and techniques presented in this book will offer a safe and effective means of resolving such encounters.

Introduction

This book is designed to address the unique challenges facing Probation and Parole Officers (POs) assigned to supervise mentally ill criminal offenders in the community. It is intended to increase officer and offender safety by introducing specific strategies used to recognize and confront threatening or aggressive offender behavior(s) quickly and safely. Just as the supervision of the mentally ill offender requires a specific skill set and specialized training for the PO, so too does their safe de-escalation: particularly, when they are presenting threatening and potentially violent behavior(s) due to mental illness, the influence of drugs and/or alcohol, or very possibly, the combination of the two. The ability to recognize dangerous and manipulative behaviors, as well as honing the ability to de-escalate and control offenders, will make you, as a PO, a safer and more effective officer. With that in mind, the techniques and strategies presented in this book are designed to allow POs to more effectively control the initial chaos of an encounter with a threatening, aggressive, or disturbed offender, contributing to the safe resolution of the encounter and both the short and long term compliance of the offender.

The behaviors of mentally ill individuals can be quite bizarre and hard to understand. What we can't understand is unpredictable, and therefore seems to be dangerous. By learning the meaning of behaviors exhibited by mentally ill offenders you will become more skillful in assessing if such an individual is truly dangerous. In many situations, you will also have the ability to calm them as well. Often, you will find your presence alone prevents a situation from escalating, with offenders complying with directives willingly, some even anxious to meet your approval or gain your respect.

It is the hope of the authors that this book, which encompasses over 50 years of experience in face-to-face encounters with mentally ill, emotionally disturbed and criminal individuals will be invaluable in readying both newer officers and experienced veterans for such encounters.

This book is part of a series of guidebooks for people who must face aggressive individuals. Other books in this series are specific to those who work as 9-1-1 dispatchers, police officers, security officers, emergency medical technicians, inpatient units, and social services personnel. There is also a separate version for families who live with mentally ill family members. Please refer to the website **www.edgework.info** for more information on all of these books.

SECTION I

Crime and Mental Illness
in the United States

CHAPTER 1

The Task Before Us

Probation and parole officers are tasked with a myriad of duties, such as enforcing and monitoring Court imposed stipulations and conditions; acting as conduits between the Court and the social service and treatment agencies where offenders receive assistance; providing guidance to those offenders they are supervising; and collaborating with other law enforcement agencies to reduce recidivism and increase public safety. The demands placed on POs by the Courts and the community, in conjunction with ever increasing caseloads and budgetary constraints, can be overwhelming, and quite often demoralizing. Adding the specialized needs of mentally ill offenders only increases the workload of supervising officers.

Due to the time constraints placed on the PO, mentally ill offenders often receive less than adequate supervision. Even worse, POs trained in the traditional roles of community supervision, i.e., the strict enforcement of Court conditions and swift punishment for non-compliance, often dismiss mentally ill offenders as being too difficult to supervise due to the vagaries of their mental illness, or the misconceptions and assumptions of officers who don't understand mental illness and its relationship with criminality. This can lead to mentally ill individuals being viewed as troublesome offenders, who need to be monitored strictly, without consideration for the limitations their mental illness places upon their ability to comply with the rules and regulations of community supervision. This approach to supervision results in the frequent submission of violation reports for minor technical infractions. Consequently, our nation's jails and prisons are housing mentally ill offenders whom they are not prepared to treat and monitor adequately within the confines of correctional facilities (Council of State Governments Justice Center, 2009).

This approach does little to reduce recidivism or increase public safety, as mentally ill offenders, either poorly treated or untreated while in detention, are released from jail with inadequate support systems designed to facilitate their adjustment to their reintegration into society. Should these offenders then be supervised using the traditional model(s) of community supervision, they will merely get swept up in a vicious circle of misconceptions and misunderstandings that will likely result in their eventual re-incarceration.

The authors understand that the policies and procedures of the various probation and parole departments nationwide may dictate that any and all violations of supervision require the submission of a violation report or in some instances the immediate incarceration of the offender, followed by a court hearing. In such circumstances POs obviously must comply with the mandates of their individual agency and proceed accordingly. However, in an effort to reduce the number of written violation reports and jail admissions for technical violations, thereby reducing the number of violation hearings before the Court, the authors would recommend that departmental directors make efforts to collaborate with their local Court administrators and the judiciary to devise a means of addressing lesser violations within the probation department.

There are a variety of ways in which minor technical violations can be addressed without resorting to the formal court system, such as increased reporting requirements and/or drug screening, admission into treatment programming, or perhaps the offender's placement on electronic monitoring for a period of time. Investing probation and parole departments, and hence individual officers, with greater discretion and autonomy concerning technical violations will result in a significant decrease in the submission of violation reports, jail admissions for minor infractions, and Court hearings. The authors would also submit that POs who have the authority to handle such violations informally can also address the offender's specific needs much more swiftly than the formalized Court process, where an offender may wait weeks, even months, before a violation hearing is scheduled before the Court.

Perhaps even more troubling than being recycled through the system in such a manner is the simple dismissal of the mentally ill offender by overworked POs who often don't find the time to understand this segment of the offender population properly. By ignoring the nature and the manifestations of an offender's mental illness, the desensitized PO can foster a potentially dangerous situation caused by his/her failure to recognize troubling behaviors or signs of impending aggression.

These concerns were cited in a 2009 report authored by the Council of State Governments Justice Center that noted that mentally ill offenders are nearly twice as likely to have their community sentence revoked, and that inadequate or inappropriate responses to this group can heighten risks to individual and public safety. Although the solutions to these overarching policy problems are beyond the scope of this book, the authors can't stress enough the importance of proper training for POs assigned to supervise mentally ill offenders, and the importance of the close collaboration of probation staff, the Court, treatment providers, and other social service agencies that is necessary to safely and effectively supervise mentally ill offenders in the community.

While traditional community supervision practices have been patterned on a more law enforcement oriented approach, today's prison overcrowding issues, and the skyrocketing costs associated with corrections and crime control have called into question the goal of the criminal justice system to reform or punish the offender, particularly in regard to mentally ill individuals. In order to appreciate the specialized needs of the mentally ill offender, probation and parole officers would benefit from a brief review of how we have arrived at the situation in which we find ourselves.

CHAPTER 2

Looking Back: Crime Control
Over the Last 40 Years

Technological and scientific advancements in the fields of communication, medicine, transportation, and even entertainment have improved the quality of life for millions of Americans during the first decade of the twenty-first century. Yet, despite the application of scientific research methodologies and new technologies in many public policy areas, criminal justice policy in the United States is too often rooted in decades-old notions of crime and punishment, shaped by political rhetoric and public misconceptions regarding the true nature of crime, especially as it relates to mental illness. Accordingly, criminal justice policies in the United States are largely reactionary, geared to combat crime after the fact, as opposed to mitigating the myriad causal factors that contribute to criminal activity. As noted by Marion and Oliver (2006), the reactive approach has resulted in the legislation of stricter laws, an exponential increase in prison construction, longer sentences for lesser crimes, and an emphasis on punishment over rehabilitation, despite the fact that research does not support the efficacy of such policies.

Rehabilitation Versus Retribution

Beginning in the late nineteenth and early twentieth centuries, society entered into a period of enlightenment regarding the treatment of criminal offenders. No longer was punishment of the offender the singular objective of the legal system in the United States. Instead, officials in the field of corrections, and more importantly, officials in the legal realm became increasingly concerned with treating the causes of criminal behavior, be they socio-economic in nature, or the result of mental illness.

The beginnings of this rehabilitative movement occurred in 1870 with the National Congress on Penitentiary and Reformatory Discipline, which stated that "the supreme aim of prison discipline is the reformation of criminals ... and the conception of punishment as a defence [sic] to crime has gone into bankruptcy: it neither defends nor deters" (Alshuler, 2003, p. 4). Decision-making in the legal system was now concerned with the long-term benefit to society, as opposed to the short-term benefits of incarceration. To be sure, society benefits when offenders are incarcerated, as offenders can't commit additional crimes while serving a sentence. This reprieve, however, is limited by the simple fact that the vast majority of criminal offenders will be released back into the community, often under the mantle of parole or probation supervision. If the causal factors of the offenders' criminality are not addressed, the likelihood of reoffending is high. Therefore, in order for society to achieve a truly long-term benefit from the criminal justice system, the needs of offenders must be identified and treated correctly, especially for those who are mentally ill.

Time of Change: Getting "Tough on Crime" in the 1970s

The rehabilitative approach to crime control continued throughout the twentieth century, until the 1970s, when a more punitive approach was resurrected following the election of President Nixon in 1968. As a telling precursor of the direction in which the criminal justice system would turn, Nixon, while campaigning for president that year, stated that doubling the conviction rate would do more to control crime than quadrupling federal funding for public programming (Perlstein, 2008). This punishment-oriented approach to crime control is illustrated most clearly by the nation's 40-year long "war on drugs," a phrase coined by President Nixon in 1971, when he declared that drugs were "public enemy number one." Subsequent to this presidential declaration, more punitive legislation was enacted at both the state and federal level, law enforcement agencies were expanded, and the nation's jails and prisons were quickly filled with non-violent, low-level drug offenders, many of whom were suffering from mental illness.

To meet the demands of this "tough on crime" mandate, there was a significant increase in the number of sworn police officers hired, the introduction of mandatory sentencing guidelines, and an explosion in prison construction across the nation. In fact, more than 40 percent of state prisons in operation today were opened between 1979 and 2004 (Daniels, 2004).

The result of these efforts has been an exponential increase in the number of incarcerated individuals in this country, with little evidence of a corresponding decrease in criminal activity as a result of more stringent law enforcement and more punitive sentencing guidelines. Indeed, since the early 1990s overall crime rates have stabilized, and don't continue to decline despite a continued increase in incarceration (Austin & Fabelo, 2004).

Although this strict law and order approach to crime control has proven to be politically popular, it fails to take into consideration how socio-economic factors and untreated substance abuse and mental health issues play so obvious a role in criminal activity. Government officials however, continue to devote precious resources to prison construction and the expansion of federal, state, and local law enforcement agencies, with little noticeable effect on crime rates and recidivism.

Rehabilitative Programming in Prisons Reduced

The confluence of the more retributive approach toward crime control ushered in with the Nixon administration occurred at a time when the American justice system was undergoing a reformation of its sentencing laws with more determinate sentencing guidelines being enacted. Legislators focused their attention on the construction of correctional facilities needed to house the growing numbers of people sentenced to increasingly lengthy periods of incarceration. Additionally, throughout the 1970s, victim advocates were also calling for stiffer sentences for criminal offenders, with the assumption that lengthier prison sentences equated to justice being served to the offender and for the victim.

Lost amid the cries for retribution was concern for those offenders suffering from mental illness. The nation's prisons filled with non-violent offenders whose criminality was related more to their untreated substance abuse and mental illness than to any purely criminal disposition. Precious funding for rehabilitative programming within the prison system and for related social service and treatment centers in the community was increasingly directed toward the construction of new jails, prisons, and penitentiaries.

The Media and Criminal Justice Policy

The media has come to play an ever more significant role in shaping public opinion, and in conveying that opinion to the nation's political leadership. Compounding matters is the fact that the reliance on television and the Internet as prime sources of news and information has blurred the lines between news and entertainment. The public's fascination with crime, in particular, has resulted in a constant barrage of news programming dedicated to crime and justice, as well as entertainment in the form of books, magazines, music, movies, and cable television shows.

Although the media does not set policy, its effect upon political debate and public perception is undeniable. Today's sound-bite media culture can influence the setting of crime policy, as the "inflated reporting of news stories heightens awareness of crime, subsequently creating a false perception of the crime problem among the American people" (Marion & Oliver, 2006, p. 8).

A study, conducted by Beckett and Sasson (2004), and released in their work entitled *The Politics of Injustice: Crime and Punishment in America* illustrates the effect of this increased media coverage of crime:

1. Between 1990 and 1999, the major networks (ABC, NBC and CBS) devoted more coverage to crime than any other topic on their nightly national newscasts. On local television news, crime consumed 30 percent of all news time, displacing coverage of other pressing issues. In comparison to crime, topics like government (11 percent), health (7 percent), education (4 percent), and poverty (2 percent) received far less attention.

2. Nationwide, surges in media coverage of crime and drugs have typically been triggered by increased attention to crime-related issues by public officials and politicians. Because the news media tend to identify government officials as authoritative sources, drug coverage, in particular, increased dramatically on the major television networks and newsweeklies.

3. The rate of violent crime in the United States began what is now an almost two-decade long decline, starting in 1992. Nevertheless, between 1993 and 1994, as the White House and Congress struggled over a new national initiative on violent crime, television and newspaper coverage of the issue increased exponentially. Between 1990 and 1998, a period in which the homicide rate declined by 33 percent, network news coverage of homicide increased by 473 percent.

4. According to one study, although they comprise less than two tenths of 1 percent of all arrests, murders account for between 27 percent and 29 percent of all crimes reported on the evening news. Other kinds of illegalities, such as corporate and state crime, tend to be either reported as "business news" or ignored in favor of violent "street crime."

As a result of this heightened perception of crime, the American public has demanded and accepted, stronger, more punitive criminal justice policies from their political representatives, even though *violent* crime rates have been declining for nearly 20 years. A 2008 Justice Policy Institute (JPI) report found that the United States has seen "a steady drop in violent crimes since a 1992 peak, crime rates remain near a 30-year low ... and the odds of being a victim of violent crime are approximately 60 percent lower today than they were in 1994" (JPI, p. 1). Despite this downward trend, the calls for stiffer criminal penalties, the hiring of more police officers, and the construction of jails and prisons have continued nearly unabated.

The Political Response to Public Opinion

Although law enforcement agencies, the courts, and the corrections industry represent the criminal justice system, the criminal justice policy enforced by these entities is the result of the larger social, political, and economic environment in the United States (Marion & Oliver, 2006). Politicians, never wanting to be perceived as being "soft on crime," have reacted to the public outcry regarding crime and punishment by enacting increasingly more stringent laws, legislating mandatory minimum sentencing guidelines, and providing massive funding increases for the construction of jails and prisons across the nation.

The glaring disparity between the political rhetoric and sensationalized media reports regarding crime, and the factual realities of crime and crime control in the United States, was summarized quite succinctly by Texas State Senator John Whitmire, who noted that "it's always been safer politically to build the next prison, rather than stop and see whether that's really the smartest thing to do" (PEW Center on the States, 2008, p. 18). Coming from a state senator in one of the nation's most "law and order" states, this statement is a rather shocking admission that the current system of crime control is not the most cost effective method of reducing crime and recidivism.

As we shall see in the forthcoming chapters, the media's failure to address the endemic socio-economic factors that have been proven to reduce crime, i.e., an investment in higher education and vocational services, affordable and accessible healthcare, and expanded substance abuse and mental health treatment, while continuing to sensationalize and over-report violent crimes, has undoubtedly contributed to the increase in the number of incarcerated offenders in the United States. This "lock 'em up" approach to crime control has also resulted in placing an unsustainable financial burden upon local, state, and federal budgets, an issue that is becoming ever more apparent in the face of the economic recession that began of 2007.

CHAPTER 3

Incarceration in the
United States

Throughout much of the twentieth century, the rehabilitation of criminal offenders was the primary goal of the criminal justice system, and the ratio of incarcerated offenders per capita remained steady prior to the emergence of the "tough on crime" stance of the 1970s. In fact, between 1920 and 1970 the overall population in the United States nearly doubled, while the number of people in prison increased at just a slightly higher pace. However, between 1970 and 2000, while the general population rose by less than 40 percent, the number of people in prison and jail rose by more than 500 percent (King, Mauer, & Young, 2005).

The unfortunate outcome of ignoring research related to the actual costs and effectiveness of current criminal justice policies has been "crime policy that is rarely about reducing crime, but policy that plays well with the public and the media" (Marion & Oliver, 2006, p. 18). As a result, the United States, the world's wealthiest nation, now has the highest per capita incarceration rate of the world's industrialized nations, with 751 out of every 100,000 individuals being incarcerated in 2008, many of whom are serving sentences for nonviolent drug or property offenses. This number is especially shocking considering the fact that while the United States population consists of just 5 percent of the world's population, prisoners in this country comprise a staggering 25 percent of the world's prisoners (Liptak, 2008). According to a PEW Center (2009) study, 2.3 million prisoners were being held in federal or state prisons or in local jails at yearend 2008.

A study conducted by The Sentencing Project (2005) found that only 13 percent of federal prisoners have been convicted of a violent offense, while 55 percent are incarcerated for a drug offense, and nearly 9 out of 10 (87 percent) had no weapon involvement (King, Mauer, & Young, 2005 p. 7). The result is that a significant proportion of the resources of the prison system are consumed by low-level, nonviolent offenders, with the costs of incarcerating such offenders equal to the costs of incarcerating violent offenders who pose a much more serious threat to society.

Additionally, the incarceration of non-violent offenders may actually increase the chances of these offenders committing violent crimes following their release from confinement as Department of Corrections data show that about a fourth of those initially imprisoned for nonviolent crimes are sentenced for a second time for committing violent offenses. This pattern highlights the possibility that prison serves to transmit violent habits and values rather than to reduce them (Haney & Zimbardo, 1998).

Furthermore, the soaring costs of imprisonment have hindered spending on other vital public programs, such as education and health care, to a degree that many find unacceptable. Indeed, recent polls show a shift in public attitudes toward crime, which has dropped down the list of issues of most concern to voters (PEW Center on the States, 2008, p. 17). Given the economic downturn beginning in 2007, the pecuniary costs of incarceration may be the principal issue in determining the nation's approach to crime control in the twenty-first century. As state governments struggle with reduced revenue streams and budget deficits, while continuing to provide essential services, economic arguments may be the one thing that can derail the belief that prisons are the best solution to crime (Merriman, 2000).

Incarceration is Politically Popular

Notwithstanding recent economic trends, construction and operation of jails and prisons continues to be extremely popular with the nation's political leaders. Indeed, both Democratic and Republican legislators have campaigned successfully on platforms which promote the fear of crime, while offering as a solution the economic opportunities and financial profitability of prison construction. This notion of prisons as an economic engine has been especially popular in economically depressed areas of the country. As agriculture and manufacturing jobs continue to be outsourced, or disappear altogether, depressed communities are only too eager to secure a prison facility in their district. Correctional facilities are a source of jobs, and they provide impoverished communities with increased tax revenues and other implied economic benefits associated with the operation of jails, prisons, and penitentiaries.

As a result, increased funding for prison construction has only led to the continued demand for more prisons, despite the lack of evidence attributing reduced crime rates to increased spending on prison construction. Instead, the adoption of mandatory minimums and stringent sentencing guidelines, which coincided with the boom in prison construction, has resulted in the nation's jails and prisons becoming overpopulated with low-level, non-violent, and often mentally ill offenders. This overcrowding issue then becomes the rallying cry of stakeholders within the prison-industrial complex who call for the construction of even more jails and prisons.

The Financial Costs of Incarceration

From a purely economic standpoint, the cost of operating today's criminal justice system is staggering, as federal, state, and local governments spent an estimated $214 billion in fiscal year 2006 for police protection, corrections, and judicial and legal activities, with $68.7 billion being allocated to the field of corrections alone. By 2011 continued prison growth is expected to cost states an additional $25 billion (PEW Center on the States 2008, p. 11). State criminal justice budgets are going to be further strained as a result of the passage of the 2008 Omnibus Appropriations Bill signed by President Bush on December 27, 2008. This $555 billion domestic spending package included a 67 percent reduction in appropriations (from $520 million to $170 million) for the Byrne Memorial Justice Assistance Grant program that, according to the U.S. Department of Justice (2009a), "allows states and local governments to support a broad range of activities to prevent and control crime and to improve the criminal justice system" (p. 1).

The economic climate caused by the recession of 2007 is cause for great concern to lawmakers at all levels of government. For many state governments, the answer seems to be the continuation and expansion of the privatization of the prison industry, with for-profit companies running an ever-increasing number of the nation's jails and prisons. With both government revenues and corporate profits dwindling, however, what will happen if private prison corporations fail to make a profit? As for profit enterprises, private prison corporations must answer to company stakeholders and companies that are no longer profitable may declare bankruptcy, or even cease business operations, leaving the public to deal with the thousands of inmates currently under the supervision of these private entities.

The continued increases in prison funding and the growth of private sector support services can't be reflected merely in the dollar figure costs of prison construction and maintenance. Expenditures for correctional funding have also been affected greatly by a host of other factors, including Court rulings, unionization of prison staff, and the increased costs of health care for an increasingly aging prisoner population (the issue of rising health care costs for the nation's prisoners is particularly noteworthy given the rancorous national debate over health care reform following the election of President Barack Obama in 2008).

As noted by the PEW Center for the States (2008, p. 12), the average operating cost per prisoner across the nation was slightly under $79 per day, for a total of nearly $29,000 per year (last available figures). Obviously, as the prison population increases, so do the costs associated with housing, feeding, clothing, and providing health care for greater numbers of offenders.

CHAPTER 4

Does it work?

Given the vast amount of resources devoted to the imprisonment of a substantial segment of the adult population in the United States, one would expect to realize a significant drop in the national crime rate, with a correspondingly low occurrence of recidivism (defined as the commission of new crimes) among those offenders released from the nation's jails, prisons, and penitentiaries. According to the *deterrent theory* of crime control, inmates will have learned their lessons and won't commit new crimes because of their fear of future sanctions (Maxwell, 2005). Unfortunately, statistics indicate that the threat of incarceration has little bearing on the overall crime rate, or on the likelihood of parolees to reoffend.

Recidivism Rates

Incarceration has also been shown to have little deterrent effect on the criminal behaviors of those released from prison. This is evidenced by the findings of a comprehensive 2011 PEW Center on the States study that surveyed offenders released from prison in more than three dozen states in 1999 and 2004 respectively. Offenders released from prison in 1999, and found that 45.4 percent were re-arrested within three years of their release, while in 2004 the figure 43.3 percent (PEW Center on the States, 2011, p9). Such high levels of recidivism serve to cast doubt upon the efficacy of incarceration as a means of crime control and behavior modification, which is especially true when considering the mentally ill criminal offender, who receives little in the way of preventative care within the confines of a correctional facility.

The Opportunity Costs of Fighting Crime

In examining the financial outlays necessary for the continued operation and expansion of the corrections industry, in comparison to the actual effects on crime and recidivism achieved, one may become dismayed, even outraged, over the apparent failings of the current criminal justice policies in the United States. This is especially troubling as the cost of prison growth has a direct impact on opportunity costs (the value of something given up to pursue something else). For instance, the monies spent on the construction, operation, and maintenance of correctional facilities could not be spent on other essential public services such as education, healthcare, substance abuse, and mental health treatment. While placing a dollar figure on lost socio-economic benefits due to a lack of sufficient funding for education and healthcare is difficult, a comparison of the monies spent on corrections as a percentage of that spent on education and healthcare is quite sobering, given that research has shown that education, employment, health care, substance abuse, and mental health treatment coincide with lower crime rates (JPI, 2008).

Although the scope and intent of this book does not allow for a detailed discussion of the impact of opportunity costs related to prison growth, a brief look at the disparities of funding for education and health care in comparison to funding allocated for corrections is enlightening. Keep in mind however, that funding for corrections comes not only from cuts in education and treatment related social services, but prison expansion has also been funded by cuts in vocational programming and community revitalization programs. Such cutbacks have led to a reduction in a number of services that are proven to reduce an individual's involvement in criminal activity.

Education

Unlike spending for K-12 education, state spending for higher education and corrections is discretionary, and it is traditionally taken from each state's general fund. This arrangement has resulted in prisons and universities competing for a share of limited state funding. As state prison systems have grown over the last quarter century, the share of the general fund needed to operate and maintain those systems has also risen significantly, leaving less funding available for higher education.

According to the PEW Center on the States (2008 p. 4), in 1987, states collectively spent $33 billion of their general funds on higher education, while spending a collective $10.6 billion on corrections. In 2007, those figures had risen to $72.88 billion and $44 billion respectively. Adjusted to 2007 dollars this equated to a 127 percent spending increase for corrections, while educational spending rose just 21 percent. To compare, during the 30-year period from 1950–1980 the share of state and local spending on colleges and universities doubled, from 3.5 percent in 1952 to 8.0 percent in 1980, while the percentage of spending on corrections remained essentially the same, from 1.5 percent in 1952 to 2.1 percent in 1980 (JPI, 2008).

Healthcare and Treatment Services

The nation's healthcare and treatment systems also receive a mere fraction of the funding allocated to criminal justice services, with an increase of just 482 percent since the mid-1970s, as opposed to the 1,101 percent increase for the corrections field alone (Austin & Fabelo, 2004). In 2007 the federal government spent $1.4 billion on drug-related foreign assistance and another $7 billion on drug-related law enforcement and interdiction efforts both at home and abroad, while spending less than $5 billion on education and for the prevention and treatment programs to curtail substance abuse in the United States (*New York Times*, 2008).

Now what?

In view of the information and statistics presented thus far, perhaps the time has come for policy makers and criminal justice professionals to consider redistributing scarce resources and funding toward alternative methods of crime prevention, punishment, and community supervision, focusing attention on programs designed to reduce the burden on the entire criminal justice system. To accomplish this goal would require a significant amount of current funding to be reallocated toward pre-trial diversion programs and specialty courts, both of which are designed to redirect offenders into treatment programs as opposed to the formal criminal justice system, and reintegration programming for incarcerated offenders. Criminal justice policy focusing on these areas would greatly reduce the number of offenders being cycled and recycled through the nation's prison system.

A recent study released by the PEW Center on the States (2009) indicates that the nation's political leadership may finally be awakening to the realities regarding incarceration as a less than effective means of crime control, especially considering its enormous financial costs. Policy makers are becoming increasingly aware of research-backed strategies for community corrections: better ways to identify which offenders need a prison cell and which can be handled in the community safely; new technologies to monitor their whereabouts and behavior; and more effective supervision and treatment programs to help them stay on the straight and narrow. Taken together, these trends are encouraging policy makers to diversify their state's array of criminal sanctions with options for low-risk offenders that save tax dollars, but still hold offenders accountable for their actions.

Necessary also is a vast increase in funding for probation and parole departments across the nation, departments traditionally overlooked in the rush to hire more police officers and build more prisons. Despite the fact that offenders on probation and parole comprise about three quarters of all people under supervision of the criminal justice system, parole and probation programs only receive ten percent of all correctional funding (Burrell, 2004). By focusing on treatment strategies, reintegration programs, and community supervision instead of traditional retributive criminal justice policies, one can expect to see a corollary decrease in recidivism rates and probation violations, as more offenders receive long-term substance abuse treatment, mental health treatment, educational programming, and job training.

CHAPTER 5

A Redistribution of Resources—
Corrections to Community Supervision

There is no doubt that some offenders are truly dangerous, and need to be incarcerated for obvious public safety reasons. Clear also is the fact that the majority of violent crimes are committed by a rather small segment of the offender population. Unfortunately, our nation's jails and prisons are overflowing with lower risk, non-violent offenders who may actually become further entrenched in the criminal justice system due to their incarceration, as opposed to being deterred from future criminal activity. Some professionals in the field of corrections and criminal justice feel that the nation's current policy of incarceration of many low risk offenders may actually worsen outcomes by exposing low-level offenders to a more experienced and hardened criminal element who may have detrimental effects on their behaviors and views on criminality. Given this concern, as well as the previously discussed untenable overcrowding issues, how can policy makers redistribute funding and resources in an effort to increase public safety, reduce the number of incarcerated offenders, and decrease the rate of recidivism of those offenders under community supervision?

The immediate and obvious answer is an expansion of the funding made available for community supervision, i.e., pre-trial diversionary services, probation and parole agencies, and treatment providers within the community. With adequate funding, the Courts, in conjunction with probation and parole professionals, can determine which offenders pose the greatest risk to society and should therefore be incarcerated, while new technologies and assessment tools allow community corrections officers to supervise offenders placed on probation or released from jail or prison safely and effectively. Successful supervision strategies targeted toward offenders deemed most amenable to change can result in a vast decrease in the number of offenders on probation or parole being returned to prison or jail for technical violations, thereby avoiding additional prison costs and increasing public safety.

Community Supervision: Probation and Parole

By definition, probation is a court-imposed period of correctional supervision in the community as an alternative to incarceration. In some cases probation can be a combined sentence of incarceration followed by a period of community supervision. Following the offender's placement on probation or their parole from a correctional facility, the supervising probation or parole officer is then charged with the concomitant tasks of rehabilitating those offenders who are amenable to treatment, while simultaneously protecting society from those who prove to be dangerous.

Although studies show that community supervision combined with some form of rehabilitative program following a prisoner's release helps reduce recidivism, the majority of paroled offenders are released with few employment opportunities, or the skills necessary for obtaining employment (American Bar Association, 2008, p. 5). Perhaps most deplorable, offenders suffering from mental illness are likely to be released from jail or prison without any formalized treatment plan, or the means to continue their treatment regimen outside the confines of prison. Any disruption in care for these individuals can have a devastating effect upon their ability to reintegrate into society successfully and increases their chances of reoffending greatly.

Policy makers must fund a significant expansion of reintegration programming and community supervision services. Fortunately, as with the aforementioned treatment and education issues, legislators are beginning to recognize the value of reentry programming and community supervision services as a cost effective means of combating criminal behaviors. In April 2008 President Bush signed the Second Chance Act (Public Law No. 110-199), which authorizes $160 million a year for two years to expand assistance for incarcerated offenders, those returning to their communities after incarceration, and children with parents in prison (American Bar Association, 2008, pg 5). As with the Access to Recovery initiative, the funding allocated for the Second Chance Act is miniscule as compared to overall correctional funding. As researchers evaluate the outcomes of this program, it will hopefully be deemed an effective cost saving alternative to incarceration, and future funding will be increased.

Law Enforcement or Social Work: The Role of the Probation/Parole Officer

Probation and parole agencies exist at all levels of government, and one will find a mix of county, state, and federal probation and parole departments nationwide. Although the technical definitions of probation and parole differ, the underlying philosophy of community corrections and the supervision strategies used to monitor (and ultimately change) the behaviors of criminal offenders in the community are the same—the successful rehabilitation and integration of the offender into society.

As officers of the Court, POs are charged with a myriad of duties related to the successful supervision of criminal offenders, such as conducting pre-sentence investigations, submitting offender progress reports, court appearances, mental health screening and risk assessment, case planning, counseling, drug and alcohol testing, visiting offenders in their homes and neighborhoods, cooperating with other law enforcement agencies in criminal investigations, conducting searches of the offenders residence, and at times arresting those offenders found to be in violation of their supervision plans. The advent of new technologies has served to increase the number of assigned duties, increasing the already hectic pace of overworked officers. For example, as medical science has allowed for the introduction of DNA evidence into criminal law, POs may now find that their duties include the collection of DNA samples from felony offenders, and regular Megan's Law registration checks of sexual offenders. Advances in electronic databases and information systems, along with communication technologies, have also been added to the mix, as cell phones, email, and computers allow for instantaneous communication between the PO, the Courts, treatment providers, and other law enforcement agencies. All of these tasks are vital to public safety, but overworked and understaffed probation and parole agencies attend to these additional duties to the detriment of proper community supervision.

The principal objective of community supervision is public safety, leading many probation and parole departments, or individual officers to focus on the law enforcement aspect of community supervision. There is no question that certain offenders on probation and parole do constitute a threat to society, and deserve to be closely monitored and held strictly accountable for actions that violate the conditions of their supervision. An over-reliance on a strict law and order approach to community supervision with all offenders, however, often results in many low-level offenders being incarcerated for minor technical violations of their supervision plan, adding to the burden of overcrowded correctional facilities. This is especially troublesome when the offender in question suffers from mental illness, an illness that may affect the offender's ability to comply with even the most basic regulations of community supervision. Therefore, despite the differences in jurisdiction and in the organizational culture of their respective agencies, probation and parole officers must strike a delicate balance between law enforcement and social work to be most effective.

There are times that the only proper action a PO can take is to incarcerate the mentally ill offender, so they can be stabilized and possibly transferred to an appropriate mental health or residential treatment facility. Given that incarceration for the mentally ill offender can be a devastating experience, it should never be taken lightly. It should never be taken to punish the mentally ill offender, but rather in the interest of increasing public safety, as well as taking into account the offender's well-being. In many cases, the mentally ill offender won't even understand the exact nature and circumstances of their incarceration, adding to his/ her confusion and increasing the chances of a physical altercation.

Supervising officers must take great care in explaining the reasons for each offender's incarceration and the processing of each case through the court system, even as the mentally ill offender is being taken into custody. Such assurances can have a distinct calming influence on everyone involved, lessening the chances of aggression and non-compliance.

Community Supervision: By the Numbers

Forty percent of existing prisons and jails in the United States have been constructed during the last 25 years, resulting in a 274 percent increase in the number of incarcerated offenders (an increase of nearly 1.7 million prisoners), at a cost of billions of dollars in public funds. While these numbers garner the attention of the media and the public, the numbers of offenders under community supervision *also* continues to increase virtually unnoticed, and certainly unremarked upon by public officials.

During that same 25-year period, the number of offenders being supervised in the community grew by an astounding 3.5 million. A recent study by the Bureau of Justice Statistics showed that almost 5.1 million people were under federal, state, or county probation or parole at the end of 2008, as opposed to 1.6 million just 25 years ago. (U.S. Dept of Justice, 2009b, p. 1) As noted by the PEW Center on the States (2009a), 1 in 45 adults in the United States are now under criminal justice supervision in the community, and combined with those in prison and jail, a stunning 1 in every 31 adults are under some form of correctional control; adding up all probationers and parolees, prisoners and jail inmates, you'll find America now has more than 7.3 million adults under some form of correctional control.

As with the prison population, the vast majority of offenders under community supervision are non-violent drug and property offenders (50 percent), while violent offenders comprised just 17 percent of those being supervised in the community. Surprisingly, more offenders (18 percent) were on probation for driving while intoxicated and other criminal traffic offenses than for violent criminal offenses. The percentages remain fairly consistent for paroled offenders also, with 37 percent of parolees having committed drug related offenses and 26 percent for violent crimes (PEW Center on the States, 2009).

The number of offenders being supervised in the community, as a percentage of all criminal offenders, has remained fairly steady during the past quarter century. As noted by the PEW Center for the States (2009), in 1982, 72 percent of offenders were managed in the community, with about 28 percent behind bars, while at the end of 2007, the most recent year for which figures are available, 31 percent were locked up and 69 percent were on probation or parole. Despite the fact that nearly 7 out of 10 criminal offenders are supervised in the community, almost all corrections dollars are spent on prisons.

Costs of Community Supervision

In fiscal year 2008 the average daily cost of supervising probationers and parolees was $3.42 per offender, while the average daily cost of incarceration was $78.95 per offender (PEW Center on the States, 2009). On a national scale, a survey conducted recently by the PEW Center on the States (2009, p. 11), using data collected from 34 states (accounting for 58 percent of total state correctional populations), found that these states spent $18.65 billion on prisons but just $2.52 billion on probation and parole, a ratio of more than seven to one. If the survey states are representative of the nation, one finds that although the incarcerated population has added only half as many offenders as community supervision over the last quarter century, prisons have received almost 90 percent of the new funding. Such an imbalance can't be sustained as states across the nation struggle with the concomitant problems of reduced revenues and overcrowded prisons.

One factor that has kept community supervision from being seriously considered is the lack of political capital to be gained by suggesting an expansion of probation and parole agencies and community based treatment services. No politician has ever run on a platform calling for an increase of criminal offenders living in our communities. This is accompanied by a distinct lack of media coverage of the hard work being put forth by dedicated probation and parole officers across the country. In fact, media coverage regarding community supervision is seemingly reserved for offenders on probation or paroles who commit a criminal offense. Such one-sided media coverage only hardens public misconceptions and strengthens the calls of political officials for stiffer criminal penalties, longer minimum sentences, or even the abolition of probation and parole altogether.

The failure to address the true issues regarding those who commit crimes, in lieu of sensationalized media portrayals, has also led the American public to drastically underestimate (or willfully ignore) the fact that the majority of criminal offenders already live within their communities. As noted by researchers at the PEW Center for the States (2009), many Americans remain unaware that a large number of offenders are not behind bars at all, but receive their punishment in the community.

As America enters into the second decade of the twenty-first century struggling to rise out of the economic morass of a recession, public safety will become tied ever more closely to the constraints of fiscal reality. Therefore, as community corrections agencies continue to supervise nearly 70 percent of the nation's criminal offenders, legislators and policy makers must acknowledge the vital public safety role of probation and parole departments as a cost effective alternative to incarceration. Only after such recognition will the purse holders in state government(s) begin to strengthen and expand sorely neglected community corrections agencies that can offer credible solutions to supervising non-violent low risk offenders and mentally ill offenders who would otherwise be in prison.

CHAPTER 6

Mental Illness and Criminality

Mental illness has been inexorably linked to criminality in the eyes of the public, and often in the eyes of law enforcement officials as well. Certain individuals who commit terrible crimes *are* profoundly mentally ill, and without any doubt, such individuals should be removed from the community. However, incarceration should not be the primary response of the criminal justice system to the majority of mentally ill offenders.

Although there are many factors that may lead a person to come into contact with the criminal justice system (anti-social peer groups, lack of education or employment, drug and alcohol use, etc.), the primary reason for the mentally ill offender is a lack of available community mental health services. When coupled with one or more of the aforementioned criminogenic factors, the chances of a mentally ill individual becoming entangled in the criminal justice system increase greatly. As noted by Marcia K. Goin (2004), former President of the American Psychiatric Association (APA), the lack of funds for community based mental health treatment services means that people who might be able to function as members of society with adequate treatment for their conditions often can't get access to the help they need. Without adequate and accessible care, such individuals are more likely to decompensate, eventually exhibiting behaviors that often result in a police response, even if those actions are not necessarily criminal. The usual outcome of this interaction is entry into the criminal justice system, as opposed to a mental health care facility or hospital, even for minor, non-violent drug or property offenses. The reasons for this outcome are many, including stricter laws, insufficient training for police officers regarding mental illness, and most significantly, the lack of available treatment services within the community.

Further complicating matters is the disruption of care, or the delay of accessing proper mental health services, *caused* by incarceration. Correctional facilities, regardless of their modernity, are hardly conducive to the welfare and stability of the mentally ill, and the likelihood is great that incarceration causes mentally ill individuals to regress. Furthermore, incarceration, even for brief periods of time, can also have a significant impact upon an offender's mental health care due to various prohibitions regarding federal and state laws related to Social Security and Medicare funding. For instance, federal law prohibits state Medicaid programs from using matching federal Medicaid funds for care once a person becomes an inmate of a jail or a prison. As a result, mentally ill offenders released from jail or prison often must reapply for medical funding, a laborious process that may delay treatment for weeks, if not months.

The Deinstitutionalization and Privatization of Mental Illness

Regrettably, public policy enacted during the preceding 50 years has resulted in a structure in which the criminal justice system has become the primary respondent and caregiver for the mentally ill. This unfortunate state of affairs began with the deinstitutionalization of mental illness, a process that began in the 1950s as advancements in medical science and pharmaceuticals altered the traditional approach to mental health treatment. Newly discovered psychotropic medications allowed for the release of many mentally ill individuals from state hospitals and institutions, while also reducing the number of new admissions. Mental health professionals began to proffer the notion that the mentally ill would do better living back in society with a community-based mental health care system in place to handle their needs.

Unfortunately, from their inception, community oriented treatment programs were inadequately funded to meet the needs of the indigent, and today's profit driven private health care providers often fail to provide coverage for mental illness, or cap coverage limits. The inevitable outcome of this lack of adequate public mental health services is that individuals suffering from mental illness often decompensate and behave in ways that bring them into contact with the criminal justice system.

In 1996, the federal government attempted to address the mental health coverage limits imposed by private health care insurers with the Health Insurance Portability and Accountability Act, mandating that annual and lifetime caps for mental health coverage must be equivalent with other physical health coverage. However, the Act does not mandate that insurers sell mental health coverage. Such an arrangement has led the most vulnerable members of society, i.e., the homeless, the indigent, and the economically disadvantaged to rely on the much diminished social safety net of publicly funded mental health treatment services.

Concurrent with the deinstitutionalization of mental illness was the ascendancy of crime as a pivotal political issue. A 1968 Gallup poll showed that for the first time in American political history, crime was the number one concern of the public (Perlstein, 2008). As the nation strove to get tough on crime, and as resources were allocated toward correctional spending, the treatment and care of the mentally ill fell to the wayside. Indeed, a study completed by the Treatment Advocacy Center found a 95 percent reduction in the number of available beds in public mental hospitals from 1955 to 2005 (Bloom, Krishnan, & Lockey, 2008). This institutional shift often left police departments with no other recourse than incarceration when called upon to deal with a mentally ill individual. In effect, states deinstitutionalized the mentally ill individuals from state funded treatment hospitals, only to re-institutionalize them into the prison system. The nation's jails and prisons have become the primary providers of mental health treatment services in the United States, a task for which they are neither intended nor prepared. As a result, one of the most vulnerable, yet treatable, segments of our society languish in punitive institutions where they are likely to receive less than adequate mental health treatment.

Crime Rates of the Mentally Ill

In 2009, the National Institute for Mental Health (NIMH) reported that roughly 1 in 17, 6 percent of adults suffer from a *serious* mental illness, meaning that they fit the psychiatric classification for illnesses such as schizophrenia, major depression, and bipolar disorder. Contrary to popular opinion, however, the majority of those suffering from mental illness are neither criminal nor are they violent. In fact, a study of individuals with psychotic disorders found that those with a mental illness were responsible for only 5 percent of all violent crimes (U.S. Department of Justice, 2006). Of this segment of the mentally ill population, the commission of a violent crime can most often be attributed to individuals experiencing psychotic symptoms at the time the offense occurred, drug and alcohol abuse, and/or a failure to comply with treatment regimens, specifically the failure to take prescribed medications. Much of this, then, is preventable.

Mental Illness and Incarceration

According to the American Psychiatric Association (APA) there are nearly one million criminal offenders in jails and prisons in the United States suffering from mental illness, 70 percent of whom are incarcerated for nonviolent crimes. Of those, 10 to 15 percent suffer from severe mental illness; as noted by the APA, between 13.1 and 18.6 percent of the inmates have major depression, between 2.3 and 3.9 percent have schizophrenia or other psychotic disorders, and 2.1 to 4.3 percent suffer from bipolar disorder (2004). Adding to the difficulties of dealing effectively with this population is the fact that roughly 75 percent of mentally ill inmates also have drug or alcohol addictions.

As correctional facilities are neither designed nor intended to provide adequate long-term mental health care, these facilities often aggravate the mental illness that led to the offender's incarceration in the first place. In a cruel twist of fate, this often leads to mentally ill offenders serving longer sentences than originally mandated (U.S. Department of Justice, 1999, p. 8). Mentally ill inmates in state prisons serve on average 15 months longer than other inmates. Mentally ill inmates are also more likely to be victimized in prison (as in "regular" society also), resulting in fights or other behavioral violations that may lead to further isolation within the prison. Because parole boards are reluctant to release apparently unstable offenders back into the community, parole may be denied due to their prison record.

Overall, correctional facilities are more concerned, and rightfully so, with the safe management of large numbers of criminal offenders than with the needs of the mentally ill. Furthermore, in an effort to maintain the already delicate balance of compliance and control in our overcrowded jails and prisons, correctional officials are apt to *suppress* the symptoms of mental illness rather than treat and manage the illness itself.

The "Catch 22" of these findings is that mentally ill inmates spend more time in prison because they have a more difficult time adhering to the strict rules and regulations of prison life, due to the very nature of their undertreated mental illness. Correctional officers and prison staff are also likely to view mentally ill inmates as being more difficult and problematic. This perception leads to closer scrutiny of these inmates, or their transfer to high security or solitary confinement units. Of course, such isolation, in conjunction with a lack of treatment, results in further deterioration of such offenders' mental illness. The mentally ill offenders are quite likely to leave prison having had little in the way of effective treatment that might reduce their chances of recidivating. To top off their undoubtedly unpleasant prison experience, mentally ill offenders are released into communities that are unlikely to be prepared to meet their treatment needs. In short, without immediate and targeted reintegration strategies, coupled with accessible long-term mental health programming mentally ill offenders' experiences in the criminal justice system may actually increase their chances of reoffending.

The incarceration of the mentally ill also adds substantially to the financial costs of corrections in the United States, with little appreciable gain in public safety or the effective treatment of the mentally ill offender. As noted by the Pennsylvania Department of Corrections, the cost of incarcerating an inmate with a serious mental illness is $140 a day, while costing $80 a day for an average inmate (American Psychiatric Association, 2004).

The mentally ill offender is seemingly caught between the proverbial rock and a hard place, as legislation and public policy enacted over the preceding decades have led to increased rates of incarceration for mentally ill persons, combined with a devastating reduction in the funding and availability of community treatment options. Together, these issues present a unique problem for POs nationwide, for as is often the case, mentally ill offenders placed under the auspices of community supervision require a high level of attention and management. However, the time constraints imposed on today's overworked, understaffed, and underfunded probation and parole agencies, which are already hard pressed to supervise ever increasing caseloads of offenders, don't allow for adequate levels of supervision for the mentally ill population.

Community Supervision of the Mentally Ill Offender

Traditional community supervision strategies don't work well with mentally ill offenders. In particular, strict monitoring of stringent probation or parole stipulations considerably increases the risk of incarceration for technical violations. Consequently, many mentally ill offenders are returned to jail or prison for failure to comply with treatment conditions, as opposed to any criminal activity. The circle of arrest (for a non-violent offense or technical violation), incarceration, revocation, release, and re-arrest continues nearly unabated. The result is that offenders with mental illnesses are nearly twice as likely as others under supervision to have their community sentence revoked, reinforcing the notion that inadequate or inappropriate responses to this group can heighten risks to individual and public safety.

A mentally ill offender often languishes in jail awaiting violation hearings or other court proceedings while their mental condition deteriorates. Therefore, aside from those times when the PO must resort to incarceration for obvious public safety concerns, or as the only available means of getting the mentally ill offender stabilized and into treatment, the PO should make every attempt to arrange for the offender's transfer to an appropriate treatment facility *prior* to or immediately following their incarceration, in an effort to reduce as much as possible the time spent in jail.

An additional consideration is the likelihood that incarceration may result in the termination of the offender's federal or state benefits, creating an added barrier to treatment, as the offender must re-apply for benefits upon their release. Many mentally ill offenders have little in the way of adequate familial or socio-economic support systems to assist in their recovery, and the offender's functional impairments often reduce his/her ability to navigate the labyrinth of the public welfare system successfully, further delaying their access to treatment.

CHAPTER 7

Improving Responses

The underlying issue in regard to the mentally ill offender population is that treatment works: as noted by the American Psychiatric Association (2004), most mental illnesses respond to treatment with recovery rates as high, or higher, than those for many other medical illnesses. Therefore, the first step necessary for improving responses to the mentally ill offender is the recognition and diagnosis of mental illness upon first contact, and the diversion of the mentally ill offender to an appropriate treatment program, either within the community, or if need be, within a correctional facility itself. Modern technologies and treatment modalities now allow for the development of intervention strategies and diversionary programming to better serve the mentally ill at all levels of the criminal justice process, and provide for a comprehensive continuum of treatment and care before arrest, after arrest, and after the offender's release.

Specialized Training for Probation/Parole Officers

Given the important role that POs play in the lives of offenders during the period of supervision, proper training is essential for improving outcomes and increasing safety. In addition to acquiring fundamental mental health training, POs supervising mental health caseloads must also be able to work collaboratively with a wide range of other professionals representing law enforcement agencies, the Courts, corrections, and community treatment providers. Indeed, the PO quite often is the common denominator linking the disparate agencies involved with the mentally ill offender, and as such, all involved, including the offender, turn to the PO for answers regarding an offender's legal responsibilities, benefits, access to medications, and treatment options. Supervising officers are also responsible for gathering all pertinent information regarding an offender's treatment and behavior while under supervision, and presenting this information to the Courts in a clear and concise fashion. In one of the most important innovations in supervision, many departments have developed specialized mental health caseloads, often in conjunction with the development of a Mental Health Court.

Crisis Response and Intervention

Given the probation officer's unique ability to intervene at many different points of contact within the criminal justice and mental health systems, POs are often called upon for consultation when a mentally ill offender is in crisis. The background information that POs can provide can be invaluable to responding police officers and treatment staff.

Probation officers can also initiate consultations with the Court, law enforcement, and treatment providers to determine the most appropriate response to offenders who are not in compliance with their supervision plan, or whom the PO believes may be engaging in criminal activity. For offenders who are not amenable to treatment, or whose mental illness becomes unmanageable in the community, the probation officer can resort to their powers as a Peace Officer and temporarily place the offender in jail for safety reasons. For officers who don't have the direct authority to take an offender into custody an immediate arrest warrant can be requested from the Courts and subsequently served by the local police or sheriff's department. As stated above, the less time people with mental illnesses spend in jail the better, and as soon as they can be stabilized, the offender should be screened and assessed for transfer to an appropriate treatment facility or transitional housing within the community.

In the event that the probation officer happens upon, or becomes involved in a crisis situation regarding a mentally ill offender while conducting fieldwork, the officer should contact the local police department, or call 9-1-1 for assistance. POs should be aware if their local police agency has a Crisis Intervention Team (CIT, comprised of officers who have undergone 40 hours of specific training in working with mentally ill subjects). If there is a CIT in place, a PO should request a CIT officer when dealing with a mentally ill offender;[1] rarely if ever, should the PO attempt to defuse such a potentially volatile situation singlehandedly, and for safety reasons should always attempt to enlist the help of the police, or in some specific circumstances at lower *immediate* risk, an emergency mental health crisis team.

Conclusion

So, what do all of the numbers, statistics, theories, and research presented thus far mean to the PO toiling each day with rising caseload numbers, report writing, court appearances, and any number of additional duties and responsibilities? Quite simply, this information makes clear that POs are going to be responsible for supervising an ever increasing number of criminal offenders who suffer from mental illness; offenders who pose differing degrees of risk, both in the office setting and in the community. As such, the safety strategies and de-escalation techniques discussed in the remainder of this book will become valuable tools for the supervising officer, and will serve to increase officer and offender safety alike. Of course, this book is not designed solely for those POs who specialize in the supervision of mentally ill offenders, and the authors recommend strongly that all probation and parole staff acquire a basic understanding of mental illness and the mentally ill offender. Most of you surely have some mentally ill offenders on your caseload. The ability to recognize the symptoms of mental illness and understand their effect upon the behaviors of the offender will enhance your ability to reduce risk, increase public and personal safety, and improve outcomes.

SECTION II

Core Requirements for De-escalation
and Control of Agitated, Aggressive,
and Mentally Ill Individuals

CHAPTER 8

The Development of a
Safety Mindset

Although the job of a probation and parole officer carries a higher probability for unpleasant human interaction or even danger, there is always the potential of risk to personal safety, whether on the job or off. This is not to say that you must go through your day in a state of hyper-vigilance, constantly on guard against an attack. Rather, maintaining a general awareness of your surroundings, while always being mentally prepared to act to protect yourself and others when necessary, means that you won't have to switch yourself on when you start your working day.

The development of a safety mindset is based upon the following fundamental assumptions:
- Being pro-active about safety issues must be a primary concern of all parole and probation staff: managers, supervisors, line officers, and support staff.
- There needs to be consistency and a common understanding in the application of safety procedures and emergency protocols at all levels of the agency.
- Adequate staff safety preparedness is not a once-and-done training event: a regular review of safety protocols, crisis response processes, physical site safety issues, and ongoing safety training for all staff is crucial.

All too often parole and probation staff forgets the impact your agency's involvement has on offenders and their families. The intrusion of POs into the private lives of individuals has emotionally charged ramifications. Our work is frequently viewed as an implicit accusation of criminality, and is often perceived as demeaning to the offender. There are also times when you must place offenders in custody, which leads to the risk of intense confrontations with an offender, their family, or other involved individuals. Their anger and frustration over their perceived loss of control may result in either a verbal or physical outburst, always with the potential use of weapons.

Although this book centers on verbal de-escalation skills, we must start at a more basic level, because the contributing causes of many critical incidents can be attributed to a lack of attention to fundamental safety precautions, both in the office setting and in the field, and this must begin *before* you start your workday. Explosive acts of violence rarely occur without some type of recognizable behaviors and body language, and an unfocused mind will impair the ability to notice these early warnings signs of potentially dangerous situations. Therefore, officers can't allow personal or familial issues to intrude upon their ability to focus on the job at hand. First and foremost, always be mentally prepared to attend to your duties in a professional manner. The failure to do so can place not only yourself, but also your co-workers and the offender in appallingly dangerous situations. Staff also needs to be mindful that probationers and parolees often don't pose the greatest threat to our safety. Upset family members or complete strangers in the office parking lot or the neighborhoods we visit may well pose a much greater danger.

Figure 8.1 Take a Pro-active Approach

In an effort to avoid creating what they believe to be an atmosphere of fear, some managers attempt to deal with safety concerns by attempting to avoid these issues altogether. This approach is wrong-minded and even dangerous. Experience suggests that heightened awareness and a pro-active approach to safety through planning, developing procedures, training, and on-going communication contribute to a much safer and happier environment.

A variety of issues, including the volume of offenders visiting the office(s), the number of offenders prone to violence, the physical design of the office site, and the proportion of the work done in the field during non-traditional hours or in high-crime neighborhoods, all impact the level of risk. To foster safety and enhance effectiveness, it is imperative that staff members (including clerical and support staff) who engage with potentially confrontational individuals have a sense of control over their situation, grounded in the knowledge that appropriate agency support systems are in place for offenders and staff alike.

A number of factors will reduce the possibility of aggression on the part of an offender, or even other individuals working at your agency:

1. **Solid boundaries.** A predictable and fair set of rules concerning the relationships among offenders and staff, staff and other staff, and the offenders themselves must be established and enforced. Offenders need to know exactly what behaviors are not allowed. Offenders (and staff) need assurance that all relationships will be professional. Staff members must not act in any way that will negatively affect the supervision of offenders.

2. **Adaptability.** Notwithstanding the necessity for a predictable environment and standardized procedures, POs must also be flexible. Staffing constraints, logistical problems, and disruptive offenders require immense creativity. Standardization must never become rigidity, because if the slightest infractions are merely punished in blind adherence to rules, offenders will become either defiant, or in the case of the mentally ill, increasingly deteriorate. However, we must never lose sight of the fact that public safety is the overarching goal of community supervision, and public safety and fair, but strict enforcement of the rules, must take precedence over all else.

3. **Presence and accessibility.** The safest agencies are ones where officers and staff are available to offenders. Boundaries must be kept, but POs can only ensure public safety when they are an *active* presence, aware of their offenders' lives and behaviors.

4. **Good training and regular practice.** POs have a professional and moral responsibility to be well-versed and skilled in de-escalation methods. While this certainly requires an effort on the part of the individual officer, departmental policy must ensure that good training is made avail-

able, and that times are set aside on a *regular* basis to practice these skills. The authors recommend that verbal de-escalation and defensive tactics be integrated into one comprehensive training package.

5. **Integrity.** Beyond all else, officers must be persons of dignity and integrity, who are rightly held to a higher moral and ethical standard. Offenders must also be aware that officers are vigilant in maintaining ethical and moral relationships. Without this, all the de-escalation methods in the world are just empty words.

Staff Meetings Should Always Include a Focus on Safety Concerns

Supervisors and administrators should ensure that regular staff meetings include a focus on safety issues, always building upon existing procedures. The regular discussion of these issues will serve to increase officer morale and foster unit cohesion. While thoughtful preparation can't prevent a critical incident from occurring, an alert and well-trained staff can reduce the impact of such an event through a well-coordinated response.

Debriefing meetings are particularly important in the wake of a critical incident, in the review of a planned action, such as the arrest of an offender, or inter-departmental operations with other law enforcement or social service agencies. Termed After Action Reports (AARs), these meetings are very important in refining or revising existing procedures. AARs aren't to be used as finger-pointing exercises, where some look to lay blame for problems or difficulties during an operation. Even in a successful operation, some things are likely to not go as planned or anticipated, and the means for improvement begins with a thoughtful discussion among those involved. Therefore, AARs must focus solely on what can be done to improve the process and enhance everyone's safety for future operations.

CHAPTER 9

Safety Planning and Risk Reduction
for the Office

Officers often believe, mistakenly, that they will be safe in the office setting. This is far from the truth. According to the Occupational Safety and Health Administration (U.S. Dept of Labor-OSHA, 2002, p. 1) "some 2 million American workers are victims of workplace violence each year. Additionally, some workers are at increased risk including … social services workers such as visiting nurses, psychiatric evaluators, and probation officers." Although being on your home ground does provide some comfort, failure to attend to safety concerns in the office may result in serious incidents.

Physical Site Safety

Your office is an extension of yourself, and although officers and staff should be comfortable, safety should not be sacrificed for convenience. A well-designed office will enhance security, while simultaneously leaving the offender with fewer opportunities to act aggressively. Ideally, your personal office (or the dedicated interview room) should have a minimum of furniture and clutter. You should also position yourself closest to the door in case you need to exit quickly. Although privacy issues may be of concern to the offender, the authors recommend that officers never close their office door when conducting an interview. Not only will a closed door prevent others from detecting an escalating situation, closing your office door will simply present a barrier to anyone helping you. Furthermore, being sequestered with an offender leaves the officer open to potential claims of impropriety or misconduct.

Figure 9.1 One Author's Experience

Years ago the author was supervising a young female offender whose mental instability did not become apparent for some time. During the course of her probationary period, this offender developed a detailed fantasy complex regarding law enforcement officers, claiming not only to having been romantically involved with any number of police officers, but also made claims of sexual assault and abuse by various law enforcement officials. None of these claims were true. To prevent any such claims of sexual impropriety this offender was always interviewed in an open office setting, and all officers and support staff were made aware of her propensity toward flights of fancy in the event that the supervising officer was not available at the time of her office visit.

Establishing a secure office site may be compromised due to architectural design limitations, as well as the financial constraints of your agency. For example, the installation of modern security and video surveillance equipment can be prohibitively expensive. However, there are many ways of enhancing office site security that are relatively free of cost, requiring only that officers and staff be alert to safety issues and communicate with one another. Listed below are just a few of the issues to consider regarding physical site security:

1. Control ingress and egress to the office proper. A secure reception area should be established to control the flow of offenders and other individuals into the office. Ideally, the receptionist, or the officer manning the front desk, should be situated behind a secure partition with a pass-through window for report forms and other documents. The door leading from the reception area into the office itself should remain locked at all times, and officers must escort each offender into and out of the office. Never allow an offender to wander unescorted through the office.

2. Security doors must remain locked if they are to be effective. Propping a security door open, or leaving the door unlocked to facilitate officer and staff movement negates its intended purpose.

3. Dedicated interview rooms should be established and used to conduct all offender interviews. Such rooms can remain free from any extraneous clutter, office equipment, and furniture, leaving the room free of many potential weapons. Furthermore, officers can then feel free to place personal items or family pictures in their individual offices, which are not accessible to the offenders.

4. Any object on your desk or in your office can become a weapon:
   - Pens, pencils, staplers, paper punches, and other office equipment can be used as weapons if a situation is escalating. Keep desks free of such items, particularly in an interview room.
   - Are picture frames or corkboards secured to the walls? Any item that can be removed from the walls or picked up easily is a potential weapon.
   - Loose chair parts and light furniture can be used as weapons as well. Make sure that all necessary office furniture and equipment is in good condition and in proper working order. When designing an office, or acquiring new furniture, safety must be considered in addition to comfort and aesthetics.

5. Personal photographs of family members and loved ones should not be able to be viewed by offenders; they could be imaged and used inappropriately. Not only will they attract the interest of the predatory offender, such photographs may exacerbate the envy of the "failure in life," who, seeing the picture of your good fortune, wonders why you get to be so "lucky" and they are not. One of the authors had to intervene in a case where such an individual began planning to burn down the house of his therapist, (who offered sessions in a home office) because "I want to see how much you'll still be smiling if your wife and daughters burn to death in front of your eyes." Finally, personal items also encourage the offender to talk about *your* family, hobbies, or other interests. Don't unwittingly invite the offender into your personal life.

6. Outside your personal office space, give consideration to all hallways, stairwells, staff and public elevators, parking and storage areas, and the reception area. Are there adequate sight lines to see who is entering the reception area? Is the lighting adequate in hallways, stairwells, and parking areas?

7. If your department authorizes the use of weapons of any kind, make sure that they are in a locked cabinet or drawer when not in use.

8. Use wands to screen for weapons, and require offenders to remove bulky overcoats, "hoodies," and outerwear that can easily conceal weapons.

9. If possible, install panic buttons at the front desk and in each office or interview room. Drills should be conducted regularly to ensure that these panic buttons actually work, and that designated officers actually respond when an emergency button is pressed.

Safety Response Planning

Even the most secure office site can't prevent an offender from becoming agitated or even aggressive. There are many situations where the offender must be informed of something that is potentially upsetting, i.e., being told to leave a living situation, returning to court to address certain violations, or being taken into custody; any of which may escalate into a potentially dangerous situation. No matter how skilled one may become at verbal de-escalation on an individual level, many situations are best handled by a team, and officers should enlist the help of others whenever possible, rather than trying to resolve a dangerous situation on their own. Therefore, officers and staff must also have a workable safety response plan in place, allowing for an appropriate response with a minimum of confusion and delay.

However, the willingness to assist a fellow officer is not enough. Officers and support staff must know *how* to help if things do go wrong. Regular drills are second only to clear and concise communication in the development and implementation of a safety response plan. Each officer and staff member must be fully aware of their designated role in the overall safety plan, and possess the skills and training necessary to carry out their assigned duties. Individual officer limitations or liabilities must be taken into account when preparing a safety plan, and duties and responsibilities should be assigned accordingly. For instance, an officer may be better suited to being the designated communication officer; responsible for establishing and maintaining effective communication with emergency responders or other agencies. In fact, having one officer assigned to communication will lessen confusion and allow other team members to focus on their assigned tasks. Other officers may be much better suited toward the tactical and physical aspects of the response plan, such as the arrest or detention of aggressive offenders, or the establishment of physical site security pending the arrival of emergency responders.

Figure 9.2 Importance of an Arrest Team

An arrest in the office is undertaken in a much more controlled environment than an arrest in the field, with the resources of the entire office ready to respond. However, officers should never dismiss the possibility of resistance, either verbal or physical, and any arrest must be approached with due caution.

In order to safely take any offender into custody, an arrest team must be incorporated into the office safety response plan. Arrest teams should consist of a minimum of 3-4 officers, all of whom have undergone the appropriate training, including verbal de-escalation, empty-hand control tactics, handcuffing, and pat down procedures. If possible, all officers should be trained in arrest tactics and be prepared to assist their fellow officers should a designated member of the arrest team be unavailable.

> Arrest teams must also practice regularly and keep their tools on hand so that they can respond with a minimum of hesitation and delay. Given the wide variety of local, state, and federal Probation and Parole Departments nationwide, officers should refer to their individual agency's policies and procedures for detailed information regarding the arrest of offenders under their supervision.

Regardless of individual assignments, ongoing communication among officers and staff must be considered one of the most vital aspects of office safety. POs have a professional responsibility to inform fellow officers and staff members that a confrontation may occur when a particular offender reports to the office, or that an arrest will be taking place at the office due to outstanding warrants or other violations. Of course, not all potential emergencies can be foretold, but many can be anticipated, and an appropriate response can be planned accordingly.

An officer who anticipates an aggressive encounter should never "surprise" their co-workers with a last minute request for assistance *after* the offender has already been admitted into the office proper. Notifying other officers and staff as to the potential for an emergency situation takes but a moment, and can be accomplished while the offender remains in the reception area. Failure to do so is a guaranteed formula for escalating an otherwise manageable encounter into a critical event. Therefore do the following beforehand:

1. Alert staff to the possibility of an emergency, and have intervention procedures in place.
2. Consider who should be present in the room. The assigned officer is the lead and will direct the offender and other officers in regard to the situation. If an arrest is planned, then the arrest team should be assembled and advised of the reasons for the arrest, the offender's propensity for resistance, and who will be doing what in the room.
3. Strategize how best to communicate the disturbing news to the offender.
4. Be prepared to call law enforcement for assistance and transportation of the offender to jail or prison.

Depending on the location of your department, i.e., rural versus urban agencies or field offices, local police departments may not be able to respond quickly to requests for non-emergency assistance, such as the arrest of an offender for technical probation and parole violations. In some jurisdictions, police officers will respond only after the offender has been taken into custody at the Probation Office, at which point local law enforcement provides transportation of the offender to jail or prison. However, in the event of a true emergency, probation staff must not hesitate to call 9-1-1.

Figure 9.3 Use of Personal Vehicles for Transporting Offenders

The safe transportation of an offender presents challenges. Of particular import are insurance and liability concerns should an officer become involved in a traffic accident while using his or her personal vehicle to transport an offender. There are also the serious concerns of contraband or weapons being hidden in the officer's car, only to be found later by friends or family. For these reasons, the authors recommend that officers enlist the help of their local police department for the transportation of offenders. The scope of this book does not allow for a detailed discussion of all issues and concerns related to the transportation of an offender, therefore, officers should refer to their agency's policies and procedures.

The following should also be considered when developing a safety response plan:

1. Develop an emergency communication plan. Emergency numbers, including 9-1-1 (or your country's equivalent emergency dispatch number), should be programmed into the office phone system or posted nearby each telephone extension in the office. Whenever possible, use a land line to call for emergency assistance. In North America, and in many other countries, your address will automatically be available to 9-1-1 call takers, letting them know your location even when you can't speak freely. POs should also enter all emergency contact information into their cell phones, including numbers for local police departments, treatment centers, and their home office.

2. Two officers should be designated as the primary and secondary communication officers. These officers will be responsible for maintaining an open line of communication with all of the agencies and departments involved in an emergency response. The authors recommend the use of line officers for this important role, so that the office supervisor remains free to take direct command and control of the scene, liaise with arriving emergency responders, and to relay vital information to departmental headquarters as necessary.

3. Install emergency call buttons that trigger an audible or silent alarm, even including a light over the doorway of the room where the crisis is occurring.

4. Develop and implement emergency code words or phrases that will activate emergency procedures, including a show of force within the office, or a call to law enforcement, if necessary. Officers may find themselves in a situation where they need to summon help without alerting the offender that they are doing so. The use of code words or phrases over your office phone, in conversation with a fellow officer, or over the public address system, will trigger an appropriate response.

5. Develop and implement the use of critical incident reports, which are to be completed following the resolution of the emergency or critical incident. The authors recommend that POs fill out a critical incident report any time they feel that their safety has been threatened or jeopardized, both in the office and in the field, no matter how hard it might be to define just what was of concern. For example, grooming behavior to set you up for a possible assault or blackmail can be an investment of considerable time on the part of an offender. It is sometimes only revealed when a PO has noted subtle behaviors that concern him/her that, taken as a whole, reveal a pattern.

6. Supervisors should compile a list of emergency contact numbers for each of their officers in the event of an emergency. Supervisors should keep a copy of the emergency contact list at home as well as in the office.

With proper planning and attention to detail, many potential emergencies can be curtailed before they develop into harmful situations. Of course, even the best laid plans won't prevent an emergency from arising, which is why regular practice of the safety plan is a requirement for the safety of all concerned. Regular practice will also highlight areas of the response plan that need to be modified and improved upon, *before* a true emergency occurs. Officers and staff who have developed a safety mindset will foster a safer and more cohesive office culture, one where safety is paramount.

Figure 9.4 Use of Code Words

Whenever the agreed-upon code word or phrase is voiced, no matter what the <u>apparent</u> context of the call, the recipient knows that the designated safety response plan must be initiated. For example, "I'm in the second conference room. Would Mr. **HOLMES** get me our information on convicted felons having contact with other adjudicated offenders." In this case, the use of the name **HOLMES,** by prearrangement means, **"I need help right now."**

Figure 9.5 Example: Safety Plan in Action

Not all emergencies are the result of aggressive, non-compliant offenders, or criminal activity. The following incident occurred in the office of one of the authors and is offered here to indicate the flexibility and adaptability of a well-prepared response plan.

While conducting a routine officer performance review, the officer in question began to suffer from a seizure. He began to shake uncontrollably and was gasping for breath. I immediately yelled out to the officer in the next office to call 9-1-1, and called for assistance from other available officers to render aid and assistance to the stricken officer until the EMTs arrived.

This call for assistance triggered the emergency response plan in the office, with the officer who called 9-1-1 becoming the communication officer. He relayed all of the necessary information to 9-1-1 personnel, and remained on the line until help arrived on scene. Another officer rushed outside the building to meet the EMTs and lead them into the office (this officer also held the elevator doors open so there was no delay in getting the paramedics to the correct floor). Other officers controlled access into the office itself and cleared the area. With my officers in control of the immediate situation, I was able to contact the headquarters office to advise them of the situation and began taking steps to contact the officer's immediate family members. Meanwhile, emergency personnel arrived within mere minutes of our call to 9-1-1. As a result the fallen officer was attended to properly, and after a period of recovery, was back on the job.

CHAPTER 10

Field Safety

Figure 10.1 A Note on Field Safety

Conducting fieldwork presents its own set of unique challenges and risks to the PO.

The information provided below is offered in order to cultivate the development of a safety mind-set as it relates to fieldwork, which can be quite different from our discussion regarding office safety. Note that the authors don't address the use of weapons or firearms directly; and the reader should refer to their individual agency's policies and procedures regarding their use.

Fieldwork is an essential element of successful community supervision. The PO must have a solid understanding of the offender's living conditions, the daily dangers and difficulties they face merely by living in certain inner-city neighborhoods, housing developments, rural communities, and public transportation issues which may hinder the their ability to attend treatment, or the dearth of available treatment programming in the community. All of these concerns are especially important for the safe and effective supervision of the mentally ill offender who may not be capable of overcoming the negative influences found in many of our nation's cities and towns.

However, no goal of effective community supervision can be reached, if POs are not safe. Officers must keep in mind that the offender they are visiting may not be the one that becomes aggressive. The offender's family, friends, and neighbors may be cause for greater concern, due to what they perceive as your unwarranted intrusion into their lives.

Fieldwork: What is the purpose?

Fieldwork must be undertaken in a serious fashion and with a specific purpose; an officer should never simply drive aimlessly through the streets and neighborhoods, intending to "drop by" available offenders, or make field visits only to those who are most compliant and accessible. In fact, most fieldwork should be reserved for those offenders who are not compliant with their supervision plan(s) or who present a threat to public safety. Listed below are the primary reasons for conducting fieldwork:

- to verify an offender's address;
- to verify compliance with conditions of supervision;
- to investigate probation and parole violations;
- to conduct a search of an offender's residence;
- to arrest an offender.

Preparations for Conducting Field Work

As noted in Chapter 9, officer safety does not confine itself to formal work hours, and therefore, field safety should begin before leaving your home or office. Officers must make sure that they are mentally and physically prepared to conduct fieldwork. If you are not feeling well, or are temporarily disabled due to a physical injury that could hamper your ability to defend yourself, then perhaps you would better utilize your time that day by staying in the office and catching up on paperwork (as we are all too familiar, there is always paperwork that needs to be done).

In many probation and parole departments, including that of one of the authors, POs primarily conduct fieldwork alone. Unlike police officers, POs don't have the luxury of radios with which to summon backup quickly, nor is there likely to be a substantial number of other POs in the immediate area who can come to your assistance in the event of an emergency. Consequently, the preparations made prior to "hitting the streets" are vitally important to officer safety.

POs can reduce their risk in the field significantly by conducting a bit of preparatory research regarding the background of their offender(s) before making a field visit. Officers have the ability to obtain a substantial amount of information by accessing various criminal justice related informational and database systems which will allow the officers to:

- Acquire a recent photograph of the offender.
- Conduct a criminal background check to note any crimes of violence or weapons-related charges.
- Check for outstanding warrants or pending criminal charges.
- Check local jail records for a history of admissions.
- Review pre-sentence reports and/or case notes related to the offenders previous periods of supervision.
- If your offender is a military veteran, contact the Department of Veterans Affairs Police, who will have records of criminal behavior within the military and in military hospitals that may not be part of their civilian record.

If your agency has issued officers laptop computers, such background investigations can be conducted relatively easily in today's digital office environment or in the field. The information you gather can be especially important prior to visiting unknown offenders recently assigned to your caseload, for many of whom the field visit may be their first encounter with the PO.

In a nod to the technological capabilities of some offenders, POs may also wish to conduct online searches of social networking sites such as Facebook or MySpace. You may be surprised at how many offenders have an online presence, and also the information that can be gathered from such sites. Conversely, POs should also take appropriate measures to secure their own online presence, as some offenders will undoubtedly attempt to conduct online a search of their assigned PO.

Figure 10.2 Safety and Local Law Enforcement

If a PO has a legitimate concern regarding a certain offender or venturing into a particular neighborhood, then go as a team, or solicit the assistance of local law enforcement.

- In general, officers should have already introduced themselves to local law enforcement authorities and developed professional working relationships with all of the police departments in their geographic area of supervision.
- Whenever operating in their jurisdiction, POs should notify local law enforcement agencies of their presence in the area as a professional courtesy.
- Local law enforcement must be notified beforehand of any planned arrest or searches being conducted in their jurisdiction. If possible, local police will honor your request for their assistance to provide backup and scene security when affecting an arrest of your offender.

Figure 10.3 Author's Experience Regarding Online Investigation

In 2008, an offender under the supervision of one of my officers had an online "blog," which he used as a forum for spewing all sorts of reprehensible speech, tinged with racially motivated and hate filled diatribes, as well as the offender's dislike of law enforcement. While such writings are vile, they are also protected speech under the First Amendment. In fact, the offender made no secret of his online postings, and even bragged about his protections under the First Amendment. However, this particular offender, convinced of his First Amendment protections, also posted several pictures of firearms on his blog, along with pictures of him firing certain weapons, and discussions regarding his experience with them.

After consultation with the District Attorney's Office it was determined that the pictures indicating his possession of firearms, not his speech, was a potential violation of his supervision plan. In fact, the nature of the offender's conviction precluded him from possessing or owning any firearms.

We assembled a search team and enlisted the backup of the local police department. The offender was instructed to report to the office for a routine visit, at which point he was taken into custody, and the search team proceeded to his residence. What the officers found was chilling. The offender had a large number of firearms of all types placed strategically throughout the residence; inside cabinet drawers in the kitchen, sitting in plain view on end tables, and within easy reach of the chairs and sofa in the living room. He even had a pistol under his pillow and a shotgun placed underneath the sheets of his neatly made bed.

The offender was subsequently arrested and indicted in federal court for his illegal possession of the firearms and ammunition. One hesitates to think of what may have occurred had this offender's PO made an unannounced field visit alone. Fortunately, the officer's attention to detail, along with a little online sleuthing, resulted in the safe arrest of the offender and the confiscation of a large number of guns and ammunition.

After assembling a list of offenders to be visited in the field, POs must ensure that all of their work tools, such as cell phones, laptops, flashlights, handcuffs, Oleoresin Capsicum OC spray, electroshock weaponry (TASER), firearms, etc., are readily available to them and in good working order. One's personal safety should never be jeopardized because of something as preventable as an uncharged cell phone or dead flashlight batteries.

Are you dressed appropriately? Will your choice of clothing and footwear impede access to your work tools or prevent safe flight should a situation develop? When conducting field work in inclement weather, outerwear should be chosen not only for climate control, but also for freedom of movement and access to your work tools.

In an effort to increase officer safety, many probation and parole departments have adopted a dress code that prescribes the types of allowable clothing and accessories, including what kind of jewelry officers can wear, or have adopted and/or encouraged the wearing of uniform clothing that readily identifies one as law enforcement.

Out in the Streets: Conducting Field Work Safely

While your previous attention to detail will have reduced several risk factors, officers must maintain a heightened sense of awareness of their surroundings while contacting offenders in the field. Officers must also display a proper sense of authority and professionalism when visiting offenders in their homes and neighborhoods, particularly as they will also very likely be coming into contact with the offenders' associates, neighbors, and families.

Effective contact with offenders as well as those associated with them begins not with what you say, but with your demeanor. Often the first impression is the most important in establishing good working relationships with the offenders and their families, and sets the tone for future interactions as well. A common mistake that new officers often make is to create a crisis for themselves by *unnecessarily* exerting or overusing their authority. Therefore, try to present a calm, confident look, both relaxed and professional.

Entering the Neighborhood

Figure 10.4 Your Car is a Work Tool

Conducting fieldwork safely is dependent upon your vehicle being in good working condition. Whether using an agency supplied vehicle or your personal car, proper maintenance is a key ingredient to officer safety. Is your vehicle likely to overheat on a hot summer's day, or fail to start on a cold winter's day? Are all lights and signals working properly? How about windshield wipers and tires? Do you have enough gas? Are you insured adequately in the event of an accident?

In addition to vehicle maintenance, officers should never leave their vehicles running while unattended, even for a brief period of time, and electronics such as cell phones, laptops, and GPS units should not be left on the seat or dashboard where they are readily visible.

Drive around the area to familiarize yourself with one-way streets, cul-de-sacs, and traffic conditions. Get a sense of what kind of neighborhood you are in, and be alert for any obvious safety concerns, such as ongoing street activity, the nature of local businesses (for instance, a neighborhood filled with bars and pawn shops should certainly raise a red flag), the condition of the homes and apartment buildings, and ease of access to your offender's residence. Note the location of local police departments, fire stations, district courts, hospitals, and other potential safe havens.

Such scouting also applies to neighborhoods with which you are familiar, as something might have changed since your last visit. POs are encouraged to pay attention to local news media as a source of information regarding criminal activity in a particular neighborhood. Has there been any notable recent criminal activity in the neighborhood, a rash of gang related violence and shootings perhaps? Has there been an incident involving the police department that would set the neighborhood on edge, making your presence unwelcome?

Remember, as with your chosen attire, local weather conditions also play a significant role in field safety. On hot summer days, there are likely to be many more people on the streets, gathering at intersections and local storefronts, or in front of apartment buildings and housing developments. Conversely, during the winter months POs may have to navigate untended sidewalks, walkways, and staircases made treacherous with a covering of snow and ice. Regardless of weather conditions, POs should never forget that their presence in the neighborhood is noticed immediately, and they are likely to be under the surveillance of any number of eyes, both seen and unseen.

Approaching the Residence

After briefly scouting the neighborhood, if at all possible, you should park your car pointed in the direction you wish to exit. Don't box yourself into a narrow space that may be difficult to exit quickly. Until you become more familiar with an offender and their family, don't park your car directly in front of their residence or in their driveway. Many people are territorial and may become aggressive towards you for a perceived encroachment onto their property.

Before exiting your vehicle, check to see that your cell phone is turned on and is in range of service; test your phone while still in your car. Officers should have their cell phones pre-programmed with emergency contact numbers and information, including having 9-1-1 (or the emergency number used in your country) on speed dial (See Chapter 9).

Officers should also verify the address before leaving their car. If you must call 9-1-1 (or the identified emergency number in your country), the first thing you should do after identifying yourself is to state your location, and the nature of the emergency. You must also inform the call-taker if you are carrying a firearm, so that responding police officers are aware of your weapon. By remaining calm and giving precise, yet succinct information, 9-1-1 dispatch should have all of the relevant information needed for a police response in case you have to terminate the call or drop your phone.

In the event you are out of cell phone range, extra precautions must be taken, including a consideration of whether to cancel the field-stop altogether or until you can secure back-up. If the situation seems unsafe for any reason, don't continue to the offender's home! Return to your car, and either leave the area or call for assistance as the situation warrants. In some situations, simply telephone the offender and instruct them to meet you elsewhere.

After exiting your vehicle, continue to survey your surroundings as you approach the residence on foot. Note potential escape routes, safe havens, and blind spots. Be aware of other individuals in the area and how they react to your presence: distinguish between curiosity, hostility, and outright menace. Listen for sounds of conflict emanating from both the immediate area and the residence itself. Pay particular attention to the presence of pets, notably large dogs. If you notice a length of chain with links the size of your fingers bolted to the side of the house, then there is probably a rather large dog somewhere on the property (Chew toys strewn about the yard, or the presence of feces will also alert you as to the presence of a dog.).

Moving with Purpose and Intent

A PO should also be ready for "street interviews." Potential aggressors in the neighborhood may approach, engaging you in conversation to distract you or to gauge your susceptibility to being victimized, all the while subtly invading your personal space. They may sexually harass you, say threatening things, or merely give you hard looks, all with the goal of noting your body language and defensive capabilities. *DON'T dismiss any feelings of trespass or danger.* On the other hand, don't act like a victim either, by shrinking in fear or puffing up, in an attempt to look tough. Act preemptively by leaving, taking evasive action, or confronting the potential aggressor, as appropriate.

Officers should also keep in mind that many, if not all, such encounters can be avoided by being easily identifiable as a law enforcement officer. The use of uniform-style clothing and visible identification not only identifies you as such, but also inhibits others from approaching too readily.

There may be times, however, when POs don't wish to present themselves so visibly, such as when visiting an offender's place of employment, a treatment facility, or related social service agencies. Even in plain clothes, you can reduce your chances of being approached or victimized by walking with purposeful intent, conscious of your surroundings. One does not need to look tough, just aware. Not only will you become aware of potential danger, but also the predators *surveying you* will see someone who moves in a confident and self-aware manner. This makes you unappetizing as a victim. Like most predators, they are likely to wait for someone frailer, more confused, or less aware to come along, because someone surely will.

As a final safety tip, officers should not walk through the neighborhood or approach the offender's residence with their arms full. Leave your cup of coffee in the car, and don't burden yourself with unnecessary paperwork or other items. If you prefer to carry a field book with you for note taking purposes, the authors recommend that POs carry a small, all weather notebook which can be placed in a pocket and accessed easily, or an aluminum hardcover notebook, which won't only serve to protect your notes, but could also be used as a defensive weapon.

At the Residence

Don't lower your guard when you have arrived, even if you have visited this particular residence in the past. An offender's home is not a safe haven. You need to be most aware when you enter the offender's home. Field visits are usually made unannounced, and officers may be interrupting an ongoing domestic dispute or other criminal activity when knocking on the door or ringing the doorbell. This is especially true for new offenders whom you have not yet met. Remember, you NEVER know who might be behind that door.

Knock on the door or ring the doorbell with safety in mind. Check the hinges to see if the door opens outward or inward, and from which side, the right or the left. In either case, the authors recommend that you stand back and to the open (non-hinged) side of the door. If the door opens outwardly (toward you) this will prevent the door from being slammed into you and will also place you out of the immediate line of fire. This position will also give you the earliest view of who is opening the door and a better sight line into the residence. If the door opens inwardly (away from you), step back and stand on the handle side, so that if the door is yanked open abruptly you are again, not in the immediate line of fire. Does the residence have a screen door? If so, officers may consider placing their foot up against the bottom of the door, on the handle side, to prevent any dogs from nosing the door open, and rushing outside when the inner door is opened.

Figure 10.5 PO Safety—Doors and Gates

Does the residence have a security fence or decorative gate at the sidewalk or pathway leading to the front door? Officers should never close any such gates or access doors behind them as this will impede escape should flight become necessary. Some officers keep a small roll of duct tape to tape the latch open if the gate is spring loaded to automatically shut. The tape can be removed upon departure.

Entering the Residence

Figure 10.6 Field Visit Safety

Field visits are not social occasions, and they should not be used to conduct in-depth interviews or interventions with an offender. Officers should be wary of spending too much time in the offender's residence, especially when alone. If an in-depth interview, intervention, search, or arrest is to be conducted, then the PO should arrive at the residence with sufficient backup to do so safely.

When you enter the offender's house, note exactly how the door closes and locks. POs should never allow the offender to lock the door behind them. Should the offender attempt to lock the door, either calmly explain the need to leave the door unlocked or leave the residence altogether. POs should insist on this as a condition before the interview can go any further. The authors recommend that POs limit their entry to within a few feet of the door, never venture too deeply into the residence, and always leave an escape route.

Even from your limited vantage point in the entryway, POs should remain alert and survey the immediate area for anything out of place, such as weapons, indications of recent drug use, or contraband. If you notice such things, remove yourself from the residence and take appropriate action. For obvious criminal or technical violations, the PO should contact their supervisor to arrange for a search team to arrive, or contact the local police department if immediate action is needed for personal or public safety reasons.

Officers should also ask the offender if anyone else is present in the home. How many people? Who are they? If someone appears after you have been told that no one is there, leave the residence, or confront the offender as appropriate. Officers should never enter any rooms that they don't have to enter, or allow themselves to be led further into the residence, particularly with unknown or potentially dangerous people present. However, should you find yourself in such a position, remember that the most dangerous rooms of the house (besides, of course, a basement) are the kitchen, because of the numerous weapons of opportunity, and the bedroom, because of the fantasies your presence may arouse for certain offenders.

The authors also recommend that POs turn down an offer of a soft chair or sofa, or the offer of a soft drink or cup of coffee. Aside from the offered seat possibly being the seat of authority in many homes (you will have, thereby, usurped their place in the eyes of their family), such chairs are difficult to get out of quickly, and all too often are infested with bugs, such as fleas or lice. Simply decline the offer politely by telling the offender that you have been sitting most of the day driving, and appreciate the opportunity to stretch your legs for the moment, that you have had your daily allotment of coffee already, or you have a coffee in your car.

Figure 10.7 A Note on Safety

The scope of this text does not allow for a detailed discussion of the concerns and recommended tactics regarding the arrest of offenders in the field. The authors recommend that officers refer to their individual agencies policies and procedures as related to the arrest and detention of offenders under their supervision.

CHAPTER 11

Threat Assessment

Figure 11.1 Proper Risk Assessment

Proper risk assessment of any offender entails a balanced mixture of objective and subjective data. Paradoxically, "objective" data is not objective until it has undergone a subjective review. In short, risk assessments must be qualitative: highlighting what is unique about each situation and each offender.

Intake: Gathering Critical Information

Some probation and parole departments have rather extensive intake procedures, and newly assigned cases will contain many pieces of information vital to the supervising officer. Newly received case files *should* include a complete set of court documents, a copy of the original arrest report, and any presentence reports submitted to the court prior to sentencing, a current photograph of the offender (either attached in the file or available on the agency's electronic database), personal identifiers such as the offender's FBI and/or state identification number and date of birth, a Record of Arrests and Prosecutions (RAP) sheet, and previous periods of supervision and confinement.

All too often, due to the lack of resources allotted to probation and parole departments, and the unrelenting pace of offenders being paroled or placed on probation, many officers receive cases containing a bare minimum of information. In these instances, officers must conduct their own background checks via the informational database systems available to them prior to making that initial first contact with the offender. This objective data will allow the PO to conduct a preliminary risk assessment prior to their first meeting. Indeed, this preliminary information may dictate the time, place, and method of that initial contact.

Regardless of your agency's intake procedures and capabilities, officers are encouraged to obtain and review as much hard data as possible before scheduling an offender for an office meeting, or making an unannounced field visit.

Threat Assessment: Triage and Case Assignment

Many probation and parole departments have implemented a tiered system of case supervision in order to supervise the ever-rising numbers of offenders under community supervision more effectively. Although there are a variety of viable risk assessment tools available, the overall intent is the same, that each offender receives an adequate level of supervision based on their perceived risk to society. Offenders are most often assigned an initial risk value during the intake process. This value is based on the offender's age and available data regarding their criminal history, specifically their number of arrests both as a juvenile and an adult. This will determine the offender's initial placement in the low, medium, or high-risk category, and their case is then assigned to the appropriate unit within the agency.

A more detailed assessment will be conducted by the supervising PO during the initial interview process, taking into consideration the offender's education level, family support systems, peer groups and associates, employment history, drug and alcohol use, mental health issues, and treatment history. Subsequent to this more detailed risk assessment, the offender may be moved up or down the risk scale, receiving the level of supervision deemed necessary.

This secondary assessment process is where officer experience and intuition can play a valuable role in assessing the offenders risk level. The officer may override the offender's statistical risk value and recommend a more intensive level of supervision. This is especially true for offenders suffering from mental illness, as their illness alone may dictate a more comprehensive level of supervision and case management. Of course, those offenders adjudicated through Mental Health Court, or similar specialty courts, will automatically receive a more detailed supervision plan regardless of their calculated risk value based on merely objective data.

In order to more fully understand any offender's true level of risk, POs should attempt to elicit from them information based on the items listed below concerning the offender's potential for aggression or violence. The information in this section is not a mere checklist that you should tick off, item by item. All information has a context. For example, you may become aware that an offender used to own several knives. That fact, in itself, tells you little. You need to know why he owned them: for cooking, for a collection, or as part of his rape kit. You need to know if he has ever used them and in what context, and what the weapons mean to him. Another offender, a woman, is depressed. Because this can be a risk factor in physical child abuse, any information about her own personal history of victimization, suicidal behavior, or violence may prove vital in helping to determine if her children are in danger. More helpful information is listed below:

1. **A past history of violence.** This is one of the most important factors. A capacity for violence is both innate and learned: the more it is used, the easier it is to use, and the more likely it will be chosen as a preferred "problem-solving" activity. Furthermore, it is rewarding for many people; power over others is the best experience of their lives.
2. **History of bullying or intimidation**. This is the psychological counterpart of physical violence.
3. **Prior arrest**. Any arrest is a heightened risk factor, even if it was for a non-violent crime. The offender may be terrified or outraged at the idea of being arrested again, or even at the idea of having more contact with law enforcement. Furthermore, with the prevalence of physical and sexual assault within correctional institutions, the non-violent arrestee may have come out a very different person than they went in.[2]
4. **Possession of weapons, fascination with weapons, past history of using weapons.** Officers should be concerned when the offender has a history of brandishing or using weapons, or talk-

ing about weapons and their use in menacing terms. Depending on the nature of the offender's current offense or criminal history, they may be prohibited from possessing weapons of any type, specifically firearms. If an offender admits to having weapons in their residence, the PO needs to determine ownership and the offender's access to those weapons. If necessary, the weapons will have to be removed or the offender may not be allowed to reside there any longer. This can get tricky depending on who owns or controls the residence, and of course, on what type of weapons are involved. There is a qualitative side as well. A fascination with weaponry, or fantasizing about them in a pathological manner, even if they don't possess one at the present time, is very definitely a heightened risk factor.

5. **History of physical abuse or the witnessing of physical abuse and violence.** Beyond a history of personal victimization, it is particularly traumatic to have witnessed abuse of a family member. The victim of abuse often hates his own weakness, and begins hating weakness in others as well. Once this occurs, it is a natural move for some people to begin victimizing what they hate: the weak.[3]

6. **Head injuries. These are associated with impulse control problems.** Many of our young soldiers are coming home from twenty-first century combat with closed head injuries. It is also endemic among violent felons; some proportion of them may have hair-trigger tempers and difficulty controlling negative emotions.[4] Law enforcement officers from all parts of the Western world are noting an increase in aggressive encounters with ex-military as well as those still serving. A war-zone is not just a place; it is inside of you as well.

7. **Dementia.** Elderly people with Alzheimer's disease or other degenerative brain illnesses can show some of the same impulse control problems of those with traumatic brain injuries. Although not a major portion of a PO's case-load, one will occasionally have elderly offenders, released after many decades in prison. Some of them develop dementia.

8. **Fear of attack or invasion of personal space.** Paranoid and fearful offenders may lash out in defensive violence. If you are properly "tracking" the offender, you should be aware if they become increasingly stressed when in close physical proximity to you.

9. **Low frustration tolerance.** Inability or unwillingness to tolerate limit setting: "I want what I want and I want it now, and you'd better not keep me from it." This is something that the subject will often verbalize.

10. **Recent stressors and losses.** Bereavement, separation, divorce, job loss, incarceration, etc., can make an offender more willing to become violent. In some cases the offender may feel as if they have nothing left to lose.

11. **A feeling of victimization and grievance.** Certain offenders may feel victimized by society in general, or hold a grudge with "the system," in which their current predicament is always someone else's fault. In some instances the PO becomes the "face" of the system for the offender, and as a result, their feelings of anger or victimization may be targeted directly toward them.

12. **Almost all intoxicating substances can be disinhibiting.** Intoxicants tend to "dissolve" the internal barriers that hold us back from our base desires, among them aggression. Note that more and more offenders are abusing prescription medications that may have been originally prescribed for a perceived medical need.

13. **Physical pain or discomfort (particularly chronic).** This also includes the side-effects of certain medications, or withdrawal from drugs and alcohol. Unfortunately, many medications that help mentally ill people can have very nasty side-effects, particularly when the patient is inadequately monitored, something that happens both in corrections setting and in the community.

14. **The offender has already given up.** Some offenders expect every interaction to be difficult or negative. Their response can be, "What the hell. Nothing will help. If I'm aggressive, at least I can make my mark on the world . . . or on you."

15. **Severe psychopathological symptoms:**
    - **Rapid mood swings.** Such offenders are unpredictable, and can escalate into a rage unexpectedly.
    - **Hallucinations**, particularly command hallucinations and/or auditory hallucinations may be telling the offender to do something terrible. If you think someone is hearing voices, ask what they are hearing.
    - **Mania.** This is a state of excitement, typified by rapid speech, grandiose thinking, very poor judgment, and impulsive behavior. It is a behavior we see in people with bipolar disorder (manic-depression), intoxication on stimulants such as methamphetamine or cocaine, and not infrequently, alcohol.
    - History of **predatory or manipulative behaviors**.

16. **Interactional factors between the aggressor and victim.** Particularly in domestic violence situations, the aggressor views the victim as having power over them, views them as being inflexible or controlling, or denying the aggressor his due. In short, the aggressor usually believes himself to be the victim. All of this can also occur in the interpersonal dynamics between an offender and a PO.

17. **Religious and cultural clashes.** Culture is any set of rules and customs that orders the relationships between people. Officers should avoid any religious, political, or cultural debates. However, POs should also make an attempt to be aware of the cultural mores and religious practices of their offenders, so they won't inadvertently insult them. Be aware that some cultures sanction violence and these cultural rules may be different from one's own mainstream culture.

Review of Aggressive Encounters with Mentally Ill Offenders on Your Case Load

Take some time to reflect on the aggressive and/or violent incidents that have occurred in the past with offenders in your case load. Try to learn more about the patterns of behavior that might have preceded their aggression, as well as any actions on your part that were either unhelpful or contributory towards an offender becoming violent. Note the following:

1. What were the circumstances that led to the aggressive encounter?
2. What was the *first* sign that indicated that the situation was getting volatile or dangerous?
3. Remember what the offender said and did in the moments just before the aggressive incident.
4. Generally, people are able to control their verbal signals better than their non-verbal signals, so recall the offender's body language prior to the incident. Tension can also create a change in the quality of the voice such as rate of speech, pitch, and/or volume.
5. Consider what you felt, physically and emotionally, at each stage of the encounter. The sensations evoked within the context of an encounter with another person are physical expression of

intuition. When you next experience that same sensation, it is an early warning sign that a similar situation may be developing.

6. What do you believe you should have done differently?

7. What planning did you do in regard to that offender subsequent to the aggression? How happy are you with that plan?

8. Did you report the encounter, and to what degree do you believe your agency backed you up? Officers are encouraged to report any incident in which they felt threatened in any fashion. Over time, these reports will provide the data for a general representation of the more common threats that officers face when performing their duties. Safety protocols can then be fine tuned to concentrate on the most common threats.

Core Questions Regarding Potential Violence

Mentally ill offenders are sometimes too decompensated or overwhelmed to undertake a comprehensive interview. However, whenever possible, ask the offender direct questions about their previous history of assaults and their potential for violence. POs can review the offender's official criminal history rather easily, and this information can be used to ascertain the offender's truthfulness in response to questioning.

Officers should convey, without verbalizing it, that they are asking for information to better understand them, not because they are afraid. POs are also trying to convey that they are able to handle anything the offender might mention, even angry or threatening statements. Therefore, POs should be sure to stay calm and relaxed, offering a direct gaze. Remember, the *quality* of the offender's answers, their tone of voice, body language, and facial expressions, are as important, if not more so, than the specific answer they give. Questions to offenders can include, but are not limited to the following:

1. "Have you hit anyone within the last six months?" "How about the last year"? "Have you ever been arrested for assault?" "How about for fighting with someone?" Notice the nuanced levels of the questions. You are able, here, to assess the offender's familiarity with the legal system, (What if they deny assault, but endorse an arrest for "fighting"?). By asking "six months," you may get a more manipulative person, who otherwise might lie, to say, "Not in six months," because they think that is all you care about. Or, they deny assault, but endorse fighting, which indicates that they went through an entire trial without either paying attention to the charges, or with no particular interest in the proceedings. Or, the offender will launch into a long story of how they were the actual victim of the assault, or that their action was blown far out of proportion, and they only pled guilty to get out of jail.

2. "Tell me what happened?" "Why do you think this situation occurred?" "Was there anything you could have done to avoid such a confrontation?" The context of why offenders were assaultive, what it meant to them, why they thought they had no other options, or why they chose violence first, not last, is vital information to the supervising officer.

3. "What do you do when someone really makes you angry?" "What kind of thing might someone say that would make you mad?" Among other things, this gives you advanced warning of what the offender's triggers are. Predatory intimidators sometimes seize this opportunity to try to say something vaguely menacing, like, "Oh, you don't want to know."

4. "If you got mad at someone here, what would you do?" "How would you handle it?"
5. "If you did get mad, how could I help you calm down?"

Each question is a gateway to further questions. Furthermore, the context of the situations in which a person became aggressive is all-important.

Figure 11.2 Examples of Context

Let us imagine two offenders, both of whom served time in prison for a life-threatening assault on another person. The first smirks and describes how he fractured the skull of a rival drug dealer. He airily says that he'd never do anything like that again, "because I'm not in the business anymore." The second describes, in a tone of outrage, how he went to a club with his wife, and while he went to pick up their drinks, returned to find a man mauling her sexually. He broke a glass and slashed the man's face, blinding him. Which man is more dangerous? **We don't know**. We do know, however, that the context of their aggression is poles apart. Furthermore, they tell their stories in very different ways. One obviously savors the opportunity to recount his violence and probably savored the act as well. The other is horrified by what he did, but still feels justified in doing it. Not only are their triggers different, but it also suggests that they need quite different case plans and interventions, were either of them to become enraged.

(NOTE: This is not a complete list. These are just a few examples to help understand the scope and nature of the open ended questions you need to use.) By asking open ended questions which require more than a simple yes or no answer on the offender's part, the PO can gather quite a bit of critical information. These types of questions can also be used to get the offender thinking about their patterns of behavior and their triggers.

Figure 11.3 Record Keeping is Crucial

Good record keeping is crucial to safe and effective community supervision. In fact, poor record keeping or illegible notes in the offenders file can be considered professional malpractice. Clear and concise case notes are essential to the safety of your fellow officers, who may at times have to interview the offender in your absence. Critical information should be highlighted, or written in red ink in the case of handwritten records, so that anyone opening the file is immediately aware of the risk factors involved.

Handwriting is not an issue in agencies were electronic databases are used. However, critical information should be noted on the face page of the offender's electronic file, either through the use of a color-coding system or visible "alert" tabs.

The authors also recommend strongly that any PO tasked with interviewing the offender of a fellow officer take a few minutes to review the case file, noting any special conditions or alerts contained therein. In fact, all officers should take a moment to review their offender's case file before conducting the interview to remind them of previously noted information. An officer should never feel rushed to begin an interview. Review prior to the interview the offender's case history. This should become a routine aspect of supervision.

Don't Let the Abnormal Become Normal

We can't underscore how important it is to check out your concerns and intuitions with fellow officers, and sometimes with professionals outside your office. Don't only consult others when you are concerned about an individual. **You should also consult when you *should* be concerned and aren't.** Some POs become so familiar with pathology that the abnormal becomes normal. The officer no longer reacts in a natural way, tolerating or not noticing covert aggression, boundary trespass, or grooming behavior. Officers can easily become complacent when dealing with familiar offenders. Note that just because you have not been hurt (yet) does not mean you are doing a good job of keeping yourself safe.

Supervision Planning to Reduce Risk

A thorough risk assessment, such as the Level of Service Inventory-Revised (LSI-R) will assist the PO in constructing a detailed supervision plan, which targets the offender's need for appropriate treatment, housing, education, employment, and/or job training programs, as well as highlight criminogenic factors. Offenders processed through Mental Health Court (MHC), or a similar specialty court, will already have a detailed treatment and supervision plan developed prior to adjudication, as part of the MHC plea process. The POs assigned to supervise MHC caseloads will often have had a hand in preparing the offender's supervision plan, in conjunction with various other stakeholders in the system, and the offender will likely be in treatment prior to being actively supervised.

Supervision planning should take place *without* the offender present, and should result in a clear and unambiguous plan that will be offered to the offender as a condition of supervision. Of course, any supervision plan must be flexible enough to accommodate both the offender's successes, as well as the inevitable setbacks due to relapses or continued criminal activity.

Once the supervision plan has been developed, the supervising PO must clearly explain the details of the plan to the offender, along with the rules and regulations of community supervision, including the consequences of non-compliance. In certain cases, the offender will be accompanied to the Probation Office by their social worker or mental health case manager, another member of their treatment team, or a family member who can help reinforce the supervision plan. Both the PO and the offender are then required to sign a dated copy of the rules, including the specific stipulations of the supervision plan, and an acknowledgement that these topics were reviewed with the offender. The offender should also be provided with all relevant phone numbers, addresses, office sites, and schedules related to their supervision.

Following the initial interview, the PO may find that they need to regularly reinforce the rules and regulations, as well as details of the supervision plan with certain mentally ill offenders. This is often due to their inability to retain or comprehend complex information, rather than to deliberate resistance to authority.

In order to reinforce this information with the offender, and to better protect the community, the PO must be in regular contact with the other members of the treatment team to discuss the offender's compliance, effect changes to the supervision plan, and/or notify the Court of any violations. This will enable the PO to monitor the offender closely, and allow for a timely response to any non-compliant behaviors.

When developing a supervision plan, ALL of the involved stakeholders must recognize their individual responsibilities and professional duties as related to the reporting of non-compliant behaviors on part of the offender. Social workers and treatment staff must be informed of the rules and regulations of community supervision, and the violation process for non-compliant offenders, and the requirement that they present the PO with timely and truthful information regarding the offender's compliance with treatment. One of the authors has had the unfortunate experience of having social workers and treatment specialists omit critical information regarding the offender's behavior from their reports to the PO; minimize or dismiss the offender's criminal behaviors and technical non-compliance as mere manifestations of their illness; obfuscate information presented to the court; and even attempt to hide an offender for whom we had an arrest warrant! We must be perfectly clear in explaining to social service workers and treatment specialists that the primary responsibility of the Probation Department is that of promoting public safety, and if necessary, the offender will be taken into custody and placed in jail or prison, accordingly.

Conversely, POs must remember that, although they have a hand in the development of the supervision plan, their responsibility is to monitor the offender's compliance with treatment, and not make any detailed recommendations as to the actual treatment process, i.e., the number of sessions required, individual or group therapy, inpatient versus outpatient treatment, and/or changes in medication(s). In order to best serve the offender and the public, each member of the team must attend to their professional responsibilities, while also keeping all other team members "in the loop" so that no one is taken by surprise, including the offender.

Figure 11.4 Confidentiality and the Health Insurance Portability and Accountability Act (HIPAA)

In most states, there are rules stipulating when collaboration and sharing of information between mental health workers and law enforcement is a **requirement**. In other cases, it is forbidden. There are also occasional conflicts between Federal HIPAA laws, and individual state and local laws and ordinances governing confidentiality. Consult with your legal advisor to ensure that you are fully in compliance with the laws governing confidentiality and that you are also able to hold others to those same statutes.

Medication

The use of psychotropic medications to treat and control the symptoms of mental illness has become standard practice in the twenty-first century. The chances of mentally ill offenders under your supervision being on some type of psychotropic medication(s) regimen are quite high. Although POs are not in the position to recommend any specific medications for a particular offender, they do have a professional responsibility to familiarize themselves with the medications most commonly prescribed, which illnesses they are intended to treat, their intended purpose, and any side effects. Additionally, while POs are also not in any position to dispense medications, they may consider requiring the offender to present their prescription bottles at random intervals in an attempt to monitor the offender's intake by simply counting their pills. What then should POs know about their offender's medications?

- Name of medication(s), both generic and brand name
- Date prescribed and expiration date
- Number of pills prescribed
- Prescribed dosage
- Number of refills
- Purpose of the prescription
- Common side-effects
- Side-effects that the offender may be experiencing
- Palliative measures taken to deal with any side-effects
- Potential interactions with other medications
- Potential interactions with illicit substances and/or alcohol
- Offender's history of discontinuing medications

The authors recommend that every unit in every probation and parole department be supplied with Mosby's Drug Guide for Nurses[5] or a similar guide, in order to help familiarize officers with the various medications available, and to help identify any pills that may be taken from an offender during a search or an arrest.

Why do they stop taking their medication?

There are many reasons offenders resist taking their medications, discontinue them, or take them intermittently. As noted in Chapter 5, the lack of affordable, accessible community health care is a major impediment to treatment for many offenders, whose lack of insurance and medical coverage prevents them from filling their prescriptions, as well as the byzantine nature of the federal and state regulations regarding Medicaid and Social Security/Disability funding. Other than these bureaucratic obstacles, however, there are several reasons an offender may wish to quit taking their medications:

- **Unwelcome side effects.** Among possible side-effects are muscle spasms, intolerable itching/crawling sensations in the limbs, tongue thrusting, tremors, impairment of sexual functioning, dry mouth, weight gain, weight loss, skin disorders, even life-threatening disorders that must be monitored through such invasive procedures as regular blood-draws, to name but a few.
- **No effect (or so it seems).** Many psychiatric medications are not "felt" beyond their side-effects. They don't make the offender "high," or even "better." Apart from the side-effects, the offender

simply feels like "him/herself." Feeling good, therefore, one draws the natural conclusion that the drug has done its job, or in other cases, does not work, and therefore can be discontinued.

- **No effect (in truth).** Many of the medications simply don't work. They may have had very high hopes that the medications would have helped, even cured them. All that they got, instead, were the sides-effects.

- **The illness is better than the cure.** Sometimes, even apart from noxious side-effects, the illness can feel better than the "cure." Many psychotic individuals find that the medications muffle or suppress hallucinations, but they don't make them disappear. Furthermore, the medications don't touch the belief system around their delusions. Life on medications, for such people, is like living under a sodden blanket. What is reality to them may be muffled, tranquilized, and constricted, but not otherwise changed. For such people, the medications may help them live a more stable, uneventful life, but just as we shake off constricting bedding when we are too hot and constricted, psychotic individuals may discontinue medications, simply to have, in their view, air to breathe.

- **Mania, the "up-side" of manic-depression.** This (Chapter 40) can be a state of high-energy and ecstasy. Medicated life, on the other hand, can be flat and boring.

- **Discontinuing medications.** The offender's use of illicit drugs and/or alcohol leads them to discontinue their prescribed medications.

- **Self-Medication Impossible.** The offender is simply incapable of taking medications by themselves every day.

CHAPTER 12

Dealing on the Phone With
Offenders in Crisis

The major differences between speaking with someone on the phone, as opposed to face-to-face, are in the mode of perception and the distance separating the PO and the offender. Although you are unable to assess the body language or facial expressions, you can become sensitive to the changes in the offender's tone and pace of speech that might suggest they are in crisis or becoming angered or enraged.

Mentally ill offenders in a state of crisis are unlikely to communicate their concerns clearly, or may seem to be speaking utter nonsense due to their psychotic state. The PO can best control the situation by remaining calm and thinking clearly. POs must not respond angrily or be dismissive of the offenders just because of the impersonal distance across the telephone lines; they must retain their professionalism and gather as much information as possible in order to assess the actual nature of the crisis. If the PO does not believe that the call represents an actual emergency, they should contact the other members of the treatment team to apprise them of the situation, and possibly arrange for a field visit to be made to the offender's residence to check on their well-being.

In the event of a true emergency, the PO should remain on the line with the offender, if possible, while another officer calls 9-1-1 to request a police response to the residence. Should a police response be necessary, the PO must relay as much relevant information to the responding officers as possible, including obviously the offender's address, age, immediate mental state, level of risk, the possibility of weapons being involved, and the nature of the offense(s) for which the offender is under supervision.

The following are things that might be useful in obtaining as much relevant information as quickly as possible:
1. Ask for a detailed description of the problem, and then ask further questions to understand the context.
2. Ask direct questions to ascertain if there is any threat of violence or suicide.
3. Ask if the offender has access to weapons, and what type, particularly if a police response or field visit is necessary.
4. Ask if the offender or anyone else present is currently using or has recently used drugs or alcohol.
5. If there is any sense of chaos, violence, or danger, ask if anyone has been hurt. If so, ask how. Get specific.
6. If you have any sense that the offender is being circumspect or unresponsive because a dangerous person is listening to the call, say, "If you are in danger right now and don't want someone else to hear what you are saying, just say yes or no in response to my questions." This may be most common in a domestic violence situation.
7. In some situations, ask to speak to others in the residence to get a better picture of what is going on.

CHAPTER 13

Training Your Intuition
to Pick Up Danger

A sense of spatial awareness, of potential escape routes, likely weapons, and access to help should become a natural part of the PO's personal and professional life. This routine attentiveness is often referred to as "having street smarts;" however, the truth is that some folks are naturally street smart, and others are not. This applies equally to POs and offenders. This section offers a method to teach probation and parole officers to pick up danger on an intuitive level if that is not something that comes naturally. As a PO you need to gain insight into the thinking patterns of an aggressive offender when he enters your territory or when you enter his.

Go to your office early one morning before anyone else arrives. Enter a room with a predator's mind and a predator's movements: slowly, gracefully, with calculation. Imagine that you are going to hurt the next person who comes in that room. How would you cut off their escape routes? What could you use as a weapon? Where would you position yourself to attack? How could your victim best escape? If POs are in the habit of noting potential dangers (items that can be thrown, sharp objects, etc.), they will have a greater likelihood of avoiding harm when it is offered.

Do the above exercise on an occasional basis. Consider it a refresher course on the mind of a predator. Done over time, you will start to develop the ability to automatically scan any room to see if there is anything there which makes it a place of danger, as well as switching your mind on to picking up predatory or other dangerous behaviors on the part of offenders.

Figure 13.1 Author's Experience

I entered the apartment of an elderly woman, reportedly demented. She began screaming at me to get out, but my job as a mental health assessor required me to be there. The apartment was not messy, but it was filled with all sorts of small objects, the collection of about 80 years of living. My eyes picked up something sticking out of a beaded curtain. I walked quickly over, past the woman, and found two large butcher knives jammed into the window frame. I pulled them out and put them on top of a cabinet, telling the woman I would return them when I left.

As it turned out, she was acutely psychotic, and believed that she was being harassed by Satan. She decided that Satan would come in the front door, so she planned to back up to the curtain, grab her knives and disembowel the "Lord of Darkness." My habit of scanning, trained through the above exercise, very likely saved me and an accompanying social worker from a very difficult situation.

Intuition: That Small Voice to Which Officers Must Listen

There must be a free exchange of information, including respect for each other's intuitions. Such "gut feelings" are sometimes vague, but they are often the *first* signs that one is in a dangerous situation. Not only should experienced officers be sure to voice their intuitions at staff meetings, but newer officers, too, must not be hesitant to relate their concerns and ask questions. As with physical "hands on" self-defense training and verbal de-escalation skills, officer intuition should not be overlooked as a valid means of increasing safety:

- Officers should not minimize their gut feelings and intuitions when exchanging information. Don't begin by stating "I know it's nothing, but...." In doing so, the officer may lead others to minimize the situation as well.
- Officers should not be hesitant because they don't have "hard evidence" to support their concern.
- Veteran officers or senior staff members must not belittle other officers' or support staff's intuitions of danger. Even the most senior officer has not experienced every possible contingency.
- Differences among officers and staff must be discussed respectfully, particularly in regard to questions of safety. If one person's idea or intuition is discounted or dismissed, he/ she may cease to speak up, and vital information regarding everyone's security will be lost.

Figure 13.2 Experience of Lifesaving Intuition From One of the Authors

Once, on a mental health outreach requested by a landlord, some internal sense commanded me not to knock on the resident's door and to retreat to my car. I literally backed down the steps, not taking my eyes from the house. Returning to the office, I wrote in the person's new chart in huge red letters "Something is wrong. Don't go to this house without police back-up."

Thankfully, a co-worker heeded my "irrational" advice, and several days later, she and the police found a floridly psychotic woman waiting with a gun behind the door. In a previous psychotic episode, she had been attacked by two men intent on raping and murdering her. She held them off with a gun and was eventually rescued by police. Now, some years later and again in a psychotic state, she was waiting with her gun, having seen me approach the house.

It is probable that only my <u>not</u> knocking on the door saved my life. When my co-worker went to the house with the police (her "rescuers"), she willingly turned over the gun. What did I perceive? Was it a stirring of the curtains, a soft click of the bolt of an automatic weapon being pulled back, or was it ESP? To be honest, I do not care. What matters is that we, and anyone we work with, respect such intuitive commands.

CHAPTER 14

Honing Intuition Through
Awareness of Personal Spacing

Communicating with mentally ill offenders is often difficult, particularly when they are becoming agitated. Suppression of all anger should not be your goal. POs must develop the ability to differentiate between true aggression, with the very real possibility of physical attack, as opposed to allowing the offender to get something off their chest: expressing their frustration with the court system, their personal difficulties, treatment issues, and the like, all while remaining ready to respond to a physical confrontation.

While there is no sure fire method of predicting future behaviors (such as an impending attack), the information gleaned from the offenders criminal history and previous risk assessments plus an awareness of "tells" that the offender is exhibiting in the moment, will enable the PO to reasonably predict the likelihood of the offender escalating to physical aggression. The manifest behaviors of aggressive offenders will be discussed in detail in Chapter 50. This chapter will focus on developing the ability to *sense* when a potential aggressor is beginning to escalate.

Comfort Zones and Physical Spacing

Agitated people lose the ability to accurately listen to what you are saying, much less maintain a coherent train of thought in their own right. Instead, they will be tracking other aspects of communication: your muscular tension, the amount of physical space between you, the positioning of your hands, and the quality of your voice. You should be doing the same.

As the offender becomes more agitated, the PO must take care to remain calm and prepare mentally for the possibility of a physical confrontation, while simultaneously maintaining focus on verbally de-escalating the situation. **Most importantly, the PO should not feed the anger!** This is a trap that many POs fall into during a confrontation. It only makes the situation worse. **Many people can't sustain their anger for more than a couple of minutes, so if you can keep your composure you can maintain control.**

Although the basic emotions are physically expressed in pretty definitive ways, irrespective of culture, non-verbal behaviors can be idiosyncratic: not only do people often have their own ways of physically expressing their emotions, but they also have their own ways of interpreting (or misinterpreting) yours (Ekman, 2003).

It is not enough, therefore, to learn a list of the typical behaviors that aggressive people are likely to display. POs must also hone their intuition to detect subtle warning signs that a dangerous situation is developing. The leading edge, so to speak, of intuition, is a sense of personal space. This is not just a matter of feet and inches. Simply asserting that you keep an arm's length and a half, or two arms' length apart between you and a subject is not enough. How much space would you want if the person has a blade, or is twice your size, and half your age?

Our attitude can also affect our sense of space. For example, the more relaxed you are in the company of someone you trust, the less personal space you require, something that manipulative aggressors try to take advantage of. When you are uncertain or suspicious of someone, you instinctively move to get more distance from them. If you are having a bad day, you need more space to tolerate anyone's proximity. Of course, POs should remember that every culture has its own definitions regarding personal space that define day-to-day interactions. For those unfamiliar with the cultural norms of their offenders, you may inadvertently cause offense due to either your own proximity to the offender, or by your reaction to an offender who unwittingly enters into your own personal space.

Figure 14.1 Two Cautions Concerning Personal Space

1. DON'T knowingly step inside someone's personal space, unless doing so helps you establish a clear tactical advantage.
2. DON'T accommodate anyone by allowing them to stand too close to you.

You MUST be aware of the physical sensations of someone in your "zone." When you set such a limit as "Johnnie, I very much wish to hear what you have to say, but you are standing too close. Move back five feet and then we will continue to talk."

The reply you get will be great threat assessment information. You are dealing with very different individuals when one, told to step back, responds with profuse apologies compared to someone who smirks and says, "What's the matter, are you nervous around men?"

The Brain Wants to Survive

There are parts of the brain that are solely concerned with survival. These parts of the brain don't care about being polite, politically correct, or intellectualizing why someone is the way they are. These parts of the brain don't use words. They perceive by recognizing significant patterns, and signal their recognition through physical sensations and reactions. The survival section of the brain is fast, about half a second faster than the thinking brain. About to step on a squiggly shape on the ground, the adrenaline hits and you jerk back your foot even before the rest of your brain thinks, "SNAKE!"

Inter-personal space has a kind of "texture" that we perceive through both physical and emotional reactions. One can train intuition through becoming more aware of the signals your body sends to you. Paradoxically, many of us get "skilled" at tuning out those signals, treating them as a kind of unwanted noise. Being mindful of the space between you and others can give you an early warning system that a situation is becoming potentially explosive. Thus, if someone is aggressive, psychotic, excited, depressed, menacing, hateful, or is trying to con you, or any other "strong" interaction, the survival brain recognizes a pattern and reacts. Be aware that there are no rules to these physical reactions: they are individual to you. For example, when in proximity to the scared person, perhaps you feel warmth in your chest, but with the con-man, your lips compress and neck tightens. With psychotic people, you feel a sensation of cold in your stomach and your hands and jaw clench with aggressive people.

Some of your physical reactions may be unpleasant or unflattering to your own self-image. For example, let us imagine that you get somewhat sick to your stomach when facing an aggressive person, or experience a subtle, but real sense of revulsion when dealing with someone who is depressed. You don't need to change this reaction. When you are a person of integrity, your feelings and emotions convey information, but they don't *demand* that you act. For example, you may be talking with an offender and you notice that previously mentioned sense of revulsion. Although he is smiling, perhaps talking fast, you know that this physical sensation happens to you very often when dealing with depressed and despairing individuals. So you shift the conversation to assess if he/she is depressed, because a sense of hopelessness and helplessness, the hallmarks of that state of mind, can lead to either suicidal or homicidal thoughts, and at minimum, can jeopardize their parole or probation plan.

If you continue to hone your awareness in this matter, you will develop a form of conscious intuition called **MINDFULNESS**. Mindfulness is the ability to be consciously aware of what is going on in your interactions with another person.

Figure 14.2 Developing Intuition

It is very easy to train yourself to become more mindful. Carry a small notebook in your pocket. If you encounter an individual who interacts with you in a significant way (aggressive, manipulative, depressed, etc.), note down (later) how your body reacts.

IMPORTANT NOTE: We should be far more concerned with physical sensations than what we normally refer to as "feelings," our description of emotional states. For example, you have a sensation of high energy, with tension in your stomach. Some would call this "anxiety," while others would call this "anticipation." If you think that a sense of anxiety does not "fit" the situation you are in, you will tend to ignore the physical sensation. If, on the other hand, you merely associate a physical sensation with a situation, i.e., "Every time someone tries to con me, I get a little smile and tension in my neck," you will notice your physical reactions without biasing them based on what you think you *should* feel.

Where these reactions really come in handy is when someone is trying to hide their intentions—smiling, for example, while trying to get close to you to stab you. Let's say, in this case, it is a woman whom you helped when her baby choked on food. Your "thinking mind" tells you, "She wouldn't want to hurt me! I saved her baby's life!" But your eyes are tightening and you are getting the same tension in your lower back that you have had on every occasion when someone has assaulted you in the past. Don't talk yourself out of it! Danger, and a very sharp point are about to hit you right in the gut. **By taking notes on sensations, you are training yourself to recognize the patterns, consciously, that your survival brain notices unconsciously.** Instead of surmising "I was having a lucky day. Something told me not to knock on that door," you say, "I had that feeling in my hands I always get right before a fight. I knew something was going to happen, so I went around the back and looked in the window and saw him standing behind the door with a piece of angle iron."

Figure 14.3 Author's Experience When Intuition Was Not Heeded

An individual once thanked me profusely at the end of my encounter with him. Instead of the warm pride I get when I've helped someone (and I HAD helped him), I had a very strong reaction that I always have when someone overtly threatens me. I mentally brushed it aside, thinking, "I'm being an idiot. The man just complimented me." Sometime later, he poisoned me. I am only alive today because he chose to degrade me by contaminating my food rather than putting something lethal in it. I learned in the ugliest way possible to always pay attention to what my body "tells" me. As we said above, the body is linked to the most primitive areas of the brain, structures that serve to protect us from danger through pattern recognition rather than verbal cognitions. To treat our bodily reactions with disrespect is to disavow that which has kept humanity alive for eons.

SECTION III

Centering—Standing With Strength
in Crisis Situations

CHAPTER 15

Introduction to Centering

Supervising offenders who may be mentally ill, drug dependent, victims of traumatic events, struggling with developmental disabilities, brain injuries, personality disorders, poverty, or a lack of education can be an honorable calling. You will be in daily contact with the most unfortunate members of society, as well as the most virulently anti-social offenders.

Such work can also be terribly demanding. Being frightened, confused, or intimidated by an offender can be debilitating and can result in poor decision-making. Even more troubling is the realization that your reactions to the offender sometimes make things worse. Internalizing feelings of frustration can lead to burnout, a state of being which could be summed up in the phrase, "I don't want to see any more of this." One way to think of burnout is "slow motion post-traumatic stress." Burnout can cause you to not pay attention, at moments when awareness is most necessary.

The strategies in the following chapters of this section revolve around maintaining self-control and about mentoring other officers. Mastering methods of self-control is a way for you to role model proper behavior to others. This is the ability to adapt to circumstances. Not only will this make you more able to roll with the problems that the mentally ill present, but also, it will make you more effective in crisis situations.

Figure 15 Centering—It's All About Tactics

We had a small dilemma with this section. Given that this section includes tactical breathing methods, and an awareness of triggers that an aggressor could use to set you off-balance, we have been concerned that some officers might interpret this as "touchy-feely" stuff. It's not. Consider the PO who approaches the residence of a high-risk offender who has just violated the terms of his parole. He will be arrested. The PO uses breathing methods to stay absolutely calm so that he/she can accomplish the task. Or consider an offender screaming at your receptionist and you are running down the hall to protect her, all the while using a tactical breathing method so that you are ready for anything (and breathing smoothly!) when you arrive on the scene. Pretty much all of the tactics in this book are dependent on being centered. You can say all the right things, but if you aren't "lined up right," they will be of no use. So we kept this section. Given that an aggressor, be they mentally ill or not, is potentially attacking you, the more control you have over "you," the more certain you will do the right thing and the more certain your victory in the event that the situation becomes physical.

CHAPTER 16

A Fair Witness: Peer Support
is a Survival Tactic

There may be nothing worse than feeling helpless or shamed after experiencing a physical or emotional attack. This is especially so on our jobs, because if an offender is verbally aggressive or even physically violent toward us, our own professional pride is violated as well. One often feels terribly alone when under assault, even with others present. This sense of isolation gets far worse if there is no one with whom we can discuss what happened to us. Some of the things that most powerfully affect POs are so ugly or appalling that officers are reluctant to discuss them in detail with their spouses or other family members. To do so would be inviting violence or obscenity into their home, and POs don't wish to pass the burden of grief or horror on to a loved-one.

In such circumstances, you need fair witnesses, people, often fellow officers, who know you, who respect you, and who are willing to hear you out. Such peer support can include strategizing sessions, (debriefings) or tactical review, but we must underscore that there are times that this is the last thing you need. A fair witness informs you, often simply by being there, that you are still a part of the human family, a valued member of the organization, despite the negative emotions that may have been engendered by the traumatic event you just went through.

Figure 16.1 Safety is more than stopping violent attack

This chapter may seem far from a discussion on safety to some of our readers, but when we talk about someone "getting our back," it does not only mean that they are with us while going through the door. If we don't have an assurance that someone will be there after we come back out, it's a lot harder to go through the doorway in the first place.

Many probation and parole agencies have formalized the fair witness process through a system of peer support, commonly referred to as Critical Incident Response Teams (CIRT), Critical Emergency Response Teams (CERT), Critical Incident Stress Management (CISM), or Critical Incident Stress Debriefing (CISD). A critical incident is an extraordinary event that forces a PO to face vulnerability and mortality during the course of their official duties. These incidents typically occur without warning, and jeopardize one's physical safety or emotional well-being. Incidents such as being victimized in an assault or engaging an offender in a lethal force encounter can overwhelm the probation officer's stress capacity. A prompt and structured departmental response can reduce the negative consequences of such incidents and help restore the affected PO's physical and mental health.

CIRT members (CIR – Critical Incident Responders) are fellow officers who are trained to respond to critical events within the agency, and provide the affected PO with emotional support and assistance. In the event of an emergency, CIR report to the scene as soon as possible where they will assess the POs physical and mental condition, request that emergency medical services and police be dispatched to the scene if necessary, or serve as a liaison to law enforcement and other first responders already present. The CIR will also accompany the affected PO to the hospital if necessary and attend to any number of related duties, such as contacting the POs family.

Following the incident, CIR will consult regularly with the affected officer's immediate supervisor and recommend services (counseling, for example) for the individual as deemed necessary and appropriate. They will also assist with any necessary paperwork that must be completed by the affected officer. Typically, the CIR will contact the affected officer once a week for at least one month following the incident, and remain in contact with them until they are confident that the affected officer's physical and emotional needs have been addressed.

Figure 16.2 The Debate Concerning Documentation in CIRT

Some CIRT protocols recommend submitting a critical incident report to the administrative unit for the purpose of collecting information necessary to provide short and long-term assistance to the affected officer and to document activities, services, and progress.

A potential problem can be that although this report is not intended to be used as an investigative tool, it can be. As an official record, it may also be subpoenaed in a lawsuit or other legal proceeding. Therefore, many CIRT protocols, particularly those associated with police departments, recommend that nothing should be put in writing. This helps the affected officer feel like he or she can talk more freely. Written records should be confined to formal after-action reviews.

On the other hand, a written report by the CIR can make a case for counseling, leave, and/or other services without those in headquarters feeling like they must interview the officer as well. Agencies should weigh both options and come to a decision regarding this point.

CHAPTER 17

It's Not Personal
Unless You Make It So

Probation and parole officers must take care to not personalize any disagreements or altercations with offenders, no matter what the provocation. Responding to an offender, perhaps mentally ill, on a personal or emotional level will cloud an officer's judgment, while distracting him/her from legitimate safety concerns.

At any rate, although their attacks on you might *seem* personal, that is only true if you make them so. If the attack is untrue, what is there to be upset about? And if what the offender said is valid, then you are reacting in anger when someone tells you the truth. You knew it anyway, so what are you upset about?

- They call you fat? Well, you knew that already, didn't you?
- They called you a Nazi? Well, you aren't, so why are you taking it personally?

Probation and parole officers must also remember that personal feelings of revenge, of "getting even," are unacceptable in the true professional, and your actions must be the result of unbiased decision-making, based on the facts at hand. Offenders can't be violated simply because of a personal vendetta or hurt feelings, and recommendations to the court at any violation proceedings must be relevant to the offender's actual behaviors.

Some people use obscenity and verbal violation to get you distracted, focused on what they are saying rather than what they are doing (such as edging their chair a little closer so that they can attack you). Others are just spewing nasty verbalizations and suddenly realize that you, upset at what they just said, have lost focus and are open to attack. Still others suddenly perceive in your response to what they said that *you* have "lost it," and they "attack you back first," because they believe you are about to react. Others challenge you by trying to offend you or by making you explain yourself. Provocative challenges are for the purpose of getting leverage on you.

No One Will Own Me

The verbal aggressor is trying to "push your buttons," often in an attempt to elicit an unprofessional or off-centered reaction. As previously described, the brain is organized to respond to danger through pattern-recognition. A large object moving rapidly towards us, a sudden pain, or a violent grab initiates a cascade of responses—fight/flight/freeze/faint—that are geared to keep us alive in the worst of circumstances. At lower levels of danger, particularly that presented by another human being, we are provoked into posturing—dominance/submission displays—that serve to maintain or enhance our position in a social structure.

The curse of being human, however, is that these survival responses are precipitated by any noxious stimuli, particularly those that shock or surprise us. When someone unexpectedly violates our sense of right and wrong or verbally assaults us, we often respond by automatically shifting into those aforementioned primitive responses, even when survival is not truly an issue. **When our buttons are pushed, we react as if we are threatened with bodily harm.** When this happens, we end up losing our dignity and our integrity, a reaction that ill-serves the PO at establishing effective control of the offender.

Bracketing: Naming Your Hot Buttons

Anything that puts us off-balance puts us at risk. Therefore, it is important that we are aware of what our buttons are. Beyond that, we use a technique called *bracketing* to make it harder if not impossible for others to even get to our buttons. Bracketing is a technique that entails facing your vulnerabilities head on, so that no one can use them against you. Bracketing is a ruthless self-inventory to make yourself fully aware of what your hot buttons are. It takes guts to examine yourself and say, "Here are my weak spots." Doing this will give you greater strength. Not doing so will make you more vulnerable to attack.

You might think that a fair witness could be of great assistance in helping you to stay truthful and strong. However, talking about such difficult issues with another person often results in them trying to reassure or comfort you, reframing the "bad" as "not so bad," or giving you an excuse to explain why you are the way you are. To really identify your vulnerabilities, POs must face the worst without the refuge of a comforting friend or witness.

Here is a worksheet that can help you name and bracket your own hot buttons. (You may photocopy it to work on.) Some example statements may include:

1. I can't stand it when someone attacks or demeans <   >, because that's something I love and treasure.
2. I feel outraged when someone demeans <   > because it is something I believe to be unquestionably right and good.
3. People get me defensive when they say or point out <   >, because, to tell the truth, I hate it in myself (or, it is a flaw....).
4. When people say or do <   >, I lose it because it's as if they are taking control of me, or disrespecting me.
5. They better not say <   >. That's the one word I won't take from anyone.

Statement	Why Does this Get to Me?
EXAMPLE: When people say or do < >, I lose it because it's as if they are taking control of me, or disrespecting me.	

Taking Inventory

Not surprisingly, we are most likely to lose our temper (our flexibility and strength) when we are blindsided. Sudden emotional shock elicits the same responses in the nervous system as a physical attack. For example, if someone you trust suddenly insulted your race, religion, or gender, it is very likely that you will shift into a response using those parts of your brain, the limbic system that expresses raw emotions. The limbic system is not concerned about the truth, about negotiation, or how to make peace. Instead, it views the world as one at war, with the other person trying to destroy one's position of strength.

To avoid this, you must do the equivalent of checking your kit before going out into the field. **Every morning, upon waking, and maybe even a few times during the day, you simply run an inventory, as if flipping through a set of cards, and call to mind each of your emotional triggers.** By bringing them to consciousness, you prepare yourself for the possibility that someone may try to set you off that day. Some people might find this sort of inventory depressing, but this is no more valid than complaining about being required to check your mirrors before backing out of your driveway. When (not "if"), an aggressor tries to push one of your buttons, you are not surprised or caught off guard. You expected it without being anxious about it. If you take inventory, you center yourself for another day, ready for the worst without it tearing you down.

CHAPTER 18

Circular Breathing—Be the Eye in the Center of the Hurricane

Aggression and violence can smash through a previously peaceful day with the suddenness and force of a hurricane. Chaos doesn't only take over the day, but also it may overtake you. However, when you can respond by stepping coolly into the worst of situations, you embody the eye of the hurricane, with all the chaos coalescing and revolving around you. The root of this skill lies in breath control. Using a method called "circular breathing," where you breathe slowly, with focused attention, you regain control of your physical self. When you control your body, you control your life. Then you are in a position to take control of the crisis as well as the person causing it.

Figure 18.1 A Clarification from an Author

Lest there be any confusion: this is NOT a "time-out" where you take a few deep breaths and then return to the subject, refreshed. That is ridiculous. You can be moving very fast while breathing very slowly. You are training your body and mind to go into this breathing as a response to danger and stress. It is a trained response that should be instantaneous.

As someone who has practiced the following technique for over thirty years, I can assert that it has become automatic. Unlike my younger days when the adrenalin would hit and I'd start breathing fast and high in the chest, my breathing usually slows down in emergency situations. You are practicing to develop a "pseudo-instinct," a trained response so bone-deep that you don't even have to think about it, anymore than you have to tell yourself to yank your hand from a hot stove.

Two Variations

Circular breathing is derived from East Asian martial traditions and was used to keep warriors calm on the battlefield. There are two variations. Try both, alternating between them, until you know which one works best for you. From that point on, exclusively practice the one you prefer. *If you train regularly, it will kick in automatically, rather than being something you must think about.* In essence, your breath itself becomes your center, not your body posture, not the situation in which you find yourself, or whatever is going on between you and the aggressor.

Circular Breathing Method #1 – Initial Practice Method

- Sit comfortably, feet on the floor, hands in your lap.
- Sit relaxed, but upright. Don't slump or twist your posture.
- Keep your eyes open. (As you practice, so you will do. If you practice with your eyes closed, your newly trained nervous system will send an impulse to close your eyes in emergency situations. If you want to use a breathing method for closed-eye guided imagery or relaxation, to get *away* from your problems, so to speak—use another method altogether.)
- Breathe in through the nose.
- Imagine the air traveling in a line down the front of your body to a point 2 inches below the navel.
- Momentarily pause, letting the breath remain in a dynamic equilibrium.
- As you exhale, imagine the air looping around your lower body, between your legs and up through the base of your spine.
- Continue to exhale, imagine the air going up your spine and around your head and then out of your nose.

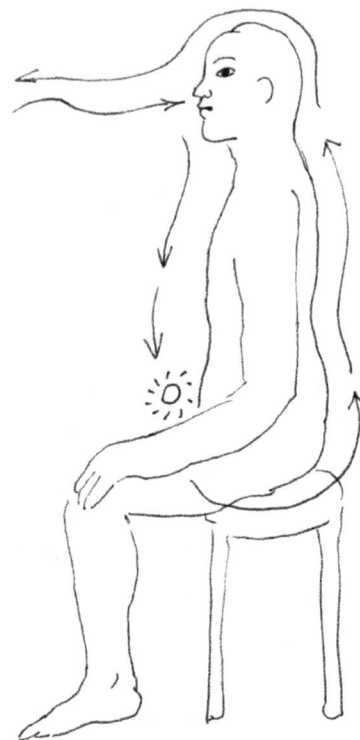

Circular Breathing Method #2 – Initial Practice Method

- Sit comfortably, feet on the floor, hands in your lap.
- Sit relaxed, but upright. Don't slump or twist your posture
- Keep your eyes open. (As you practice, so you will do. If you practice with your eyes closed, your newly trained nervous system will send an impulse to close your eyes in emergency situations. If you want to use a breathing method for closed-eye guided imagery or relaxation, to get *away* from your problems, so to speak—use another method altogether.)
- Breathe in through the nose.
- Imagine the air going up around your head, looping down the back, falling down each vertebra, continuing down past the base of the spine to the perineum, and looping again, this time up the front of the body to a point 2 inches below the navel.
- Momentarily pause, letting the breath remain in a dynamic equilibrium.
- As you exhale, imagine the air ascending up the centerline of your body and out your nose.

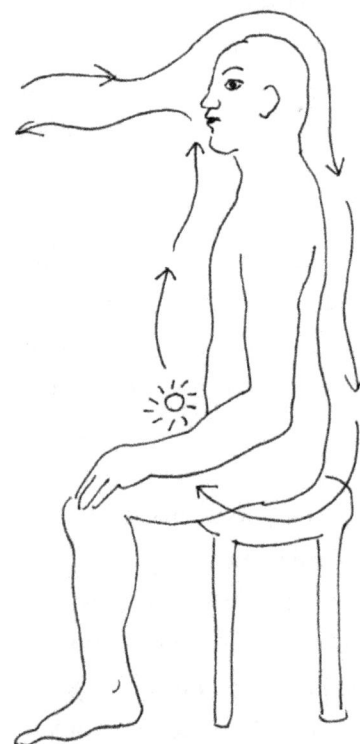

How to Practice Circular Breathing

Some people find that imagining their breath has light or color is helpful. Others take a finger or object to trace a line down and around the centerline of the body to help focus their attention. Again, choose which of the variations works better for you.

When you first practice, do so while seated and balanced. Once you develop some skill, try circular breathing standing, leaning, or even while driving. Most people find that after a short period of time they don't need to visualize the circulation of the breath. You literally will feel it, a ring of energy running through your body. You begin to feel balanced and ready for anything.

Once you are comfortable with your chosen pattern of breathing, experiment with it in slightly stressful circumstances, like being caught in traffic, or sitting through a meeting as a supervisor drones on about new paperwork requirements. When you can better manage yourself in these slightly aggravating or anxiety-provoking situations, you are ready to use it in an emergency situation. If you have practiced enough, you will naturally shift into this mode of breathing when the crisis hits. There will no longer be a need to tell yourself to "do" circular breathing. It will become reflexive, automatic, replacing old patterns of breathing that actually increased anxiety or anger within you.

Remember, this is a skill to be used during emergencies, not for relaxation or meditative purposes. Instead, you are trying to enhance that ability to do whatever is needed to fight, to dodge, to leave, to think gracefully and intelligently, whatever is required for the situation at hand.

When to Use Circular Breathing

The way you organize physically affects your thinking. For example, if you assumed the posture and breathing of a depressed person (slumped body, shallow breathing, sighing), and maintained it awhile, you would actually start to feel depressed. Similarly, if you clenched your fists, and start glaring around you with a lot of tension in your body, you will start to feel angry. (You have probably observed a number of individuals working themselves up from anger through rage into an attack in just this way.) Similarly, circular breathing creates its own mindset, one adaptable and ready for anything, equally prepared for an easy conversation and for a fight, yet fixed on neither.

This method of breathing is very helpful when you are anticipating a potentially dangerous situation, anything from driving towards someone's residence to serve a warrant, to seeing potential danger down the street and moving in that direction. This breathing activates the entire nervous system in a way that enhances both creativity and the ability to survive.

Even in the middle of a confrontation, particularly a verbal one, there are many times when this breathing will have a very powerful effect. Not only do we get more stressed or upset in the presence of an upset person, but also we become more peaceful in the presence of a calm one. People tend to template their mood to the most powerful individual close by. We are sure that you know officers who, when they walk onto a scene, often calm it down before they have said a word. You have probably seen the opposite as well. Using this breathing method is a vital tool in making you the former type, a man or woman of quiet power.

Use this method of breathing after the crisis as well. You will need to regroup to go on with the rest of your shift. Circular breathing will bring you back to a calm and relaxed state, prepared to handle the next crisis, should one occur.

If we bring feelings from a crisis situation back home, we carry violence back to our family. Therefore, before entering your home, sit quietly in your car or even in the yard, and practice this breathing for a moment or two. The only thing that should come home is "you," not the crises you weathered.

Circular Breathing to Ward Off or Even Heal From Trauma

Figure 18.2 Note on Circular Breathing as a method of dealing with Trauma

Although the material in this section may seem a little to "therapy" oriented, it is invaluable if you ever find yourself having difficulty dealing with a traumatic reaction and, for one reason or another, help is either not available, or you can't or should not avail yourself of the help that is offered. Keep this in reserve for those times when you need it.

Post-Traumatic Stress Disorder (PTSD) is not defined by how horrible the event sounds in description. It is defined by the victim's response to the event. PTSD is not exactly a problem of memory, it is a problem because the event has not fully *become* a memory, and the event is still primarily experienced as if it is happening right now. When an event is fully a memory, it is experienced as something in the past, over and done with. Another way to think of it is a scar, it may not be pretty, and it certainly is a signpost that something significant happened to the person, but it no longer hurts. A trauma, on the other hand, is an open-wound. It is an *experience*. It is not in the past, and in fact, may be affecting every moment of the person's life, or emerge suddenly, when evoked by something that elicits a sense that the event is happening again.

In PTSD, the person's nervous system is set to react as if there is an emergency whenever the trauma is recalled. This can be anything from an explicit memory to a small reminder. For example, although he does not consciously know why, a soldier gets anxious every time someone coughs. This is because one of his squad coughed right before an improvised explosive device (IED) went off.

Because trauma affects the brain at the deepest levels associated with survival, logical interventions (anything from reassurance to cognitive therapy) offer only equivocal success in helping people emerge from trauma. Image-associated breathing techniques, which affect the brain as a whole, can assist people in realizing that the event is over and no longer a part of present experience. The following should be helpful in handing PTSD:

- Let us imagine that something very upsetting has happened to you. Perhaps you even recall an old trauma that still plagues your mind.
- Whenever you think about it (or it forcibly intrudes into your consciousness), your body tenses or twists in various ways. Your breathing pattern often changes.
- If this is your situation, go someplace where you won't be disturbed for a while. Make the mental image of that trauma as vivid as you can tolerate. This takes some courage, because most of us simultaneously avoid-as-we remember traumatic events. Rather, if only for a moment or two, meet it head on and re-experience it. If you physically organize (with your breath, muscular tension, posture, etc.) *as if* something is happening, the brain believes that it truly is occurring right now. Notice, in fine detail, how you physically and emotionally react. As difficult as this may be, it is important to establish for yourself what your baseline response is to the trauma. You must clearly experience what it "does" to you when you recollect it.
- Now take a couple of deep sighs. Sighing breaks up patterns of muscular tension and respiration. This is like rebooting your computer when the program is corrupt.
- Mentally say to the ugly experience: "Hush. You move right over there to my right (or left). I'll get to you in a minute." For some people, it is even helpful to make a physical gesture, "guiding" or "pushing" the experience off to the side. You won't be able to *force* yourself to stop thinking about an experience if it has psychological power. Instead, move it aside, as if you are guiding a wounded person to a waiting room while you organize yourself to properly deal with it.
- Now initiate your preferred method of circular breathing.
- As the memory creeps back in (and it will), just breathe and center yourself, again placing the memory off to the side. Once again say, "Hush, I'll get to you in a minute." You can't fight it, so don't try. Just ease it aside until you are ready.
- When your breathing is smooth and your body is centered, you will be relaxed like an athlete, ready to move but with no wasted effort.
- Now, deliberately bring that ugly memory or trauma into your thoughts and imagination. Now, as you find yourself reacting, continue circular breathing, trying to bring yourself back to physical balance even while you focus on the traumatic memory.
- Bit by bit, in either one session or a few, you will notice that you are increasingly able to hold the image with a relaxed body and a balanced posture. You are now able to re-experience the memory without the same painful, tense, or distorted response you had in the past. You are, metaphorically speaking, turning the open wound into scar tissue.

Think of how you hold babies so that they are safe: you don't drop or squeeze them so tightly that they are frightened or uncomfortable. To be strong in the face of trauma is very similar in that you internally hold the memory with all the grace and strength with which you hold babies so that they are safe, whether asleep or struggling to see over your shoulder. You are not wiping the slate of memory clean. Rather, you are placing it in a proper context—something that happened to you, but does not define you.

Figure 18.3 The Value of Circular Breathing Imagery

What is particularly valuable to many POs who use circular breathing imagery is that it allows one to take power back on one's own. There is no doubt that counseling, sometimes, is invaluable. However, it is sometimes hard to find a good counselor who understands a PO's situation.

Furthermore, ongoing litigation, in which confidentiality can be threatened by subpoena or court order, can sometimes force POs to forego counseling that they might really need. This particular breathing method offers an option when counseling is either not an option, or something that the PO does not want.

Furthermore, if you can, on a daily basis, "inoculate" yourself against stressful, even potentially traumatic experiences, life will continue to be enjoyable, or will become enjoyable once again, even as you continue to work in a highly stressful environment. You will begin to develop something David Grossman calls a "bullet proof mind." The goal is not trying to restore some kind of mythic "innocence," that one had "pre-trauma." The goal is to relegate the experience to its proper place— something ugly that happened sometime in the past.

CHAPTER 19

The Intoxication and Joy
of Righteous Anger

Most people consider anger to be a harmful emotion, one that upsets the angry person as well as the recipient. This is not true for everyone. There is a subset of people, including POs, who don't mind fighting whatsoever, particularly when they believe their cause is just. These individuals go off-center in an interesting way, becoming calm, even happy, when someone offends them. As a boxer once stated in regards to an opponent, "When he gets hurt, he wants the round to be over. When I get hurt, I get happy." Such people, when functioning in a professional capacity, have an especially difficult task. They must recognize that when they feel *good*, they are in danger of becoming part of the problem. Instead of imposing calm, they escalate the situation, not minding it in the least.

Circular breathing (Chapter 18), for those who are anxious, stressed, or frightened, provides a real sense of peace and relief. However, if confrontation feels good to you, such calming breathing may seems like the last thing you would like to do. You think, "Center myself? Hell, no. I'm right where I want to be." If this description fits, your task is to recognize the special joy that comes with righteous anger, and act to center yourself to a calm state of mind, even though in the heat of the moment, it feels like a loss rather than a gain.

The righteously angry PO may be known for this type of reaction, but he/she is the one most likely to *not* recognize this, and *not* believe they need to do any breathing or calming. If this is you, recognize it. This is not about becoming some sort of Zen sage, never angered, never off-balance. Of course there will be times when you will be angry, and it may even help keep you alive if you ever need to fend off an attack. However, the real issue here is the PO who reacts angrily to even the slightest provocation, or worse, one who treats every offender, in every situation, with anger. Such officers simply serve to escalate minor situations into serious ones, heightening the chances for a physical altercation with the offender, placing everyone involved in danger unnecessarily. And such officers are particularly ineffective with mentally ill offenders.

Protecting Your Family From What You Otherwise Would Bring Home

Another type of righteous anger is that evoked when someone does something so clearly evil that one feels annihilation of the perpetrator is the only justifiable response. Returning to the subject of the last chapter, this is a particularly important example of how such breathing can protect your family. Both of us (authors) have had the experience of feeling utterly contaminated by being in the presence of the perpetrators of child abuse or sexual assault. Having done our job well, so that, for example, we have gotten a confession, evidence to make a case, or ensure that an abusive parent never had access to the child again, we each have left the room feeling a failure because we did not take his/or her throat between our hands and squeeze the life out of them.

Both of us made sure that we never brought this feeling home. We would sit in our car, running the breath around our body, maybe going to a quiet place in the house or yard and working through the images in our brains so that when we walked into the presence of our wives and children, the only thing we ever brought home was ourselves. No child molester or other evil doer will ever walk into the house with us.

SECTION IV

Dealing With Those With
Unusual, Intense, and Eccentric
Communication Styles

CHAPTER 20

Overview

What is a mental illness anyway? Is it any odd or eccentric behavior, or should we not confine the term for more serious disturbances of behavior and thought. It sometimes seems that we lump together mental phenomena that are as disparate as the distinction between a common cold and lung cancer. Yes, both may be troublesome, and make breathing difficult, but they are very different disorders.

Probation Officers should not feel it incumbent upon themselves to diagnose what an offender may be suffering from, even in the most general way. We must emphasize that this book focuses on behavior, not on illness. It is not your job to figure out why, or even what. However, if someone behaves in a way that makes it difficult to communicate with them, or even more problematically, enacts disruptive behaviors, then the PO (you) should be prepared with several skills, among those are the following:

- The ability to recognize said behavior as showing a pattern.
- The knowledge of best practice communication strategies to respond to a person who is displaying said pattern, whatever the cause of the behavior may be.

Not everyone who needs to be calmed or de-escalated is aggressive. However, those who display unusual or eccentric patterns of behavior are more difficult to communicate with, and when the ability of people to communicate breaks down, the risk of aggression increases.

CHAPTER 21

Rigid Personality: Asperger's Syndrome and Other Similar Disorders

People with Asperger's syndrome are frequently socially withdrawn, often very intelligent, sometimes outcasts, who may live their lives mostly in an online environment. Such individuals are becoming more involved in computer crimes, particularly hacking. When convicted of such crimes, however, judges are presented with credible evidence that their disorder plays a significant factor in their criminal activities, and also that these offenders are not suited for life within the confines of prison. Therefore, they are increasingly being placed on community supervision.

Despite what can be formidable intellectual abilities, often sectored in one area of knowledge, offenders with Asperger's syndrome often have tremendous difficulty in negotiating social interactions. They find other people to be incomprehensible, confusing, and/or threatening, and to make matters worse for them, they find it very difficult to know from your facial expressions, body posture, and vocal tone, what you are feeling or thinking. Other offenders, particularly some schizophrenics, often show a similar combination of "cluelessness" and rigidity in communicating with others. Because it is not the PO's task to diagnose your offenders, we are using the term "rigid personality" to designate people with this pattern of behavior, whatever their actual diagnosis may be.

Such rigid personalities become fixated on their own preoccupations, and may imagine that everyone else shares them too. As one child with Asperger's syndrome said when asked what the bully who beat him up was thinking, "Oh, he was thinking of Lewis and Clark." When asked with astonishment why he would be thinking of that, the child replied, "What else could he be thinking about? Lewis and Clark took the greatest journey...." It was a good ten minutes before the therapist got him off the subject. Such rigid individuals can also be very literal (concrete) and can get "stuck" on certain thoughts and behaviors (obsessive). Others are simply not interested in or aware of other people's feelings, which can lead them to be very blunt or brutally honest.

Figure 21.1 Two Examples of Socially Clueless Statements by an Offender Displaying Rigid Personality Traits

1. "What is the bump on your face? It's quite ugly. You know, it could be a melanoma, which could cause your face to simply rot away, or it could infect your brain and then you'd die. I've seen photos of tumors that have actually eaten right through a person's cheek and you can see their teeth and tongue out the side of their face."

2. "You've gained a lot of weight in the last year. I don't mind, but many men don't think that is attractive."

There is no malevolent intent here. Other people's feelings—unimaginable and incomprehensible—are simply not a relevant bit of data to a person with these personality traits.

Such a person often does not appear to be mentally ill. Rather, they are stiff and socially awkward people, who are always a little out-of-sync. Their voice may be too loud, and they may sound odd. Their eye contact may be "off," or non-existent, and they are sometimes physically uncoordinated. They do not pay attention to the effect that their actions or appearance might have on others. They are frequently insensitive to body spacing. Because they find people unpredictable and unreadable, they frequently experience high anxiety. As a result they use self-soothing movements like flapping their hands or rhythmically tapping an object and/or body part to help distract them from what stresses them out.

If you are dealing with such an offender, stating or reiterating the rules is the first method of intervention. Consider this, if an individual had difficulty figuring out what someone, a probation officer, for example, wants them to do, and the officer's body language, tone of voice, and facial expression is incomprehensible, the rules, clearly stated, would be very reassuring. Attempts at validating their feelings will often merely result in the offender becoming increasingly confused or upset. State each rule in a matter-of-fact way, as if simply providing information. Follow this up with a logical sequence of steps to resolve their problem. You must be as concrete and literal as they are. State the obvious. Below is an expanded list for dealing with an offender with rigid personality traits.

- In a matter of fact tone, explain the rules. She says, "Why should I lower my voice? I am angry!" Your reply should be, "Because it is the rule here to speak about grievances with a quiet voice." "That's a stupid rule," she replies. "Nonetheless," you return, "it is the rule."
- Give them a logical alternative way to follow-up on their grievance.
- Even more than with other individuals, try to avoid physical contact. Many folks with rigid personality traits detest touch and can react violently. Only touch them if you are taking physical control of them (defensive tactics).
- If they continue to be non-compliant, you may have to physically require them to comply with your lawful order, but take the extra time in the manner we suggest whenever possible.

- If they are displaying a physically repetitive movement, such as flapping their hands, understand that it is for the purpose of calming themselves down. Nonetheless, if the movement (hand flapping near the waist or chest) could resemble a move towards a weapon, order them to stop, by telling them that it is "against the rules to wave your hands around while standing near a probation officer." When they ask why, simply repeat that it is against the rules. When they ask if it's alright while speaking on the phone, say that it is alright in that circumstance, but not face-to-face. Understand that their incessant questions are an attempt to try to figure out just what they can and cannot do. It is not game-playing. They feel the need to cover all possibilities. After a too many questions, however, you should take over and give a general policy that, hopefully, will cover all variations.

Figure 21.2 De-escalation of an Individual With Rigid Personality Traits

Pavel. I can't go to court tomorrow. I saw seven spiders in my house, and that is bad destiny.

PO. Pavel, you are required to go to court, no matter the number of spiders you have seen.

Pavel. But this could mean a disaster for someone. Seven spiders are terrible.

PO. The rule is that offenders must appear in court when ordered, and this applies even when the offender believes that there are unlucky signs.

Pavel. Destiny, not bad luck.

PO. It is still the rule, destiny or not. The rule has no deviation.

Pavel. How about if a meteor hits the courthouse.

PO. Pavel, the rule is ironclad. If you are scheduled to appear in court, you must appear, unless I call you and inform you that court is cancelled.

Pavel. Something bad will happen—it's destiny.

PO. Nonetheless, you will be there at 10:00 A.M. It is the rule.

Figure 21.3 Review: Dealing with Rigid Personality

You will recognize the offender with a rigid personality because they get stuck on subjects that seem rather odd in the circumstances. They seem unaware of their effect on others. Their emotions, if they are even displaying any, are not those you would expect in the given situation. To deal with this type of individual do the following:

- State the rules in a matter-of-fact way, as if simply providing information.
- Follow this up with a logical sequence of steps to solve their problem.
- Discussion about their feelings will be counter-production. Tactical paraphrasing (Chapter 56) or other ordinary tactics to deal with an angry person tend to make things worse.
- No physical contact unless it is part of defensive tactics or physical control.
- Don't get deflected from your task. Like a parody of a lawyer, they may bring up possible exceptions to your order. "Step through" the objections and simply state that they are required to follow the rule.
- Please note, this type of offender is relatively uncommon, with most of their crimes in the high-tech field, or physical assault in family or school settings. Use this type of strategy only when it is clear that this is the type of offender you are trying to interact with: rigid, stiff, concrete, and socially out-of-sync. Think of Data on Star Trek—and perhaps include in your imagination what Data would look like while mad—either coldly logical, or if that didn't work, frustrated, and out of control. In the latter case, as always, control based on the mode of rage they are displaying (Section XI).

CHAPTER 22

Tell it Like It Is:
Communication with Concrete Thinkers

Concrete thinkers have a lot of difficulty, or even a complete inability, to understand metaphors, slang, or imagery. Instead, they take everything you say literally.

Figure 22.1 How Concrete Thinking Causes Problems for an Offender

One of the authors was speaking to a case manager at an inpatient treatment facility regarding an offender's failure to abide by the house rules of the facility. Although his transgressions were not aggressive or threatening, they were nonetheless disruptive to staff and to the other patients, and nearly resulted in his premature discharge from treatment. This behavior would have resulted in a violation hearing for this individual and a possible incarceration, all for a peanut butter and jelly sandwich.

Just before the lunch hour the case manager found the offender in the kitchen area, about to eat a bowl of cereal. The former explained that, as it was nearly lunchtime, the offender could not have a bowl of cereal, and he would have to eat lunch with the rest of the group. The case manager then locked the cabinet containing the boxes of cereal and momentarily left the room. She returned just a minute later to find the offender eating a peanut butter and jelly sandwich. When asked why he would do such a thing after being told that he could not have a bowl of cereal because it was nearly lunch time, and he was to eat lunch with the group, the offender, very upset and confused, replied, "You told me I couldn't have a bowl of cereal. You never said anything about peanut butter and jelly!" The offender was not playing games. He honestly thought he was complying with the directive.

When communicating with concrete thinkers, POs should use short, clear sentences, using simple, yet specific words that are easy to understand. Remember, they will understand what you say in a very literal manner. They can comply with the specific, but not even understand the general principal. Speak in a firm manner, and refrain from showing too much emotion. If you become angry or frustrated the offender will react to your emotions, not your instructions.

Figure 22.2 A Non-emergent Dialogue Between a PO and an Offender Showing Concrete Thinking

PO. OK. So you don't have to worry anymore.

Concrete Person. I wasn't worried. I was upset.

PO. Oh, OK, you were upset. Anyway, the ambulance is coming, and will be here shortly. I want you to sit tight.

Concrete Person. How do I sit tight? Should I wrap myself in a blanket?

PO. <Sigh> No, you don't have to wrap yourself up. I meant you should sit quietly and….

Concrete Person. You mean I shouldn't talk?

PO. <Aghhhhhh> No, you can talk! I want you to talk! It's a figure of speech!

You get the idea. In the last example, what might be a better way to accomplish the task? Imagine this just from the PO's side:

- The ambulance is coming.
- Sit in the chair right here.
- Yes, sit where you are right now and keep talking to me. No, you don't have to wait by the door.
- Yes, I can hear them too. No, sit in the chair until they come in the house.

Figure 22.3 Review: Concrete Thinkers

You will recognize concrete thinkers because they take what you say literally. Therefore be sure to:

- Use clear, short sentences, with a firm, calm voice.
- Give directions using simple words that are easy to understand.
- Show a minimum of emotion. Don't get irritated when the offender does not immediately understand you. They respond much more to your tone of voice than to what you say.

CHAPTER 23

Information Processing and Retention:
Consolidating Gains

Many mentally ill offenders develop the ability to "fake normal." People around them may do frightening things, but they don't show their fear. Other people may anger them, but they smile and pretend everything is all right. Conversations and ideas may be too complex, too fast, or irrelevant to what is going on inside them, but they have learned to pick up the rhythm of other people's speech, nod at the right moments, smile or laugh when needed, and agree with the tag lines that invite such agreement.[6] Therefore, never assume that a mentally ill offender understands what you have told them just because they nod their head at the right moment. You need to verify that they understood you.

In dealings with the mentally ill the following points have been proven helpful:

- **The least effective method is to repeat using other words.** If they have either tuned you out, or did not understand you the first time, they may fake understanding again. This is different from the repetition you must do with the disorganized offender, when you DO repeat yourself when giving instructions, with the intention of "getting through" to them. *Here, you are checking to see if what you said got through.* However, simply repeating yourself and assuming the offender understood what you said is often a mistake.

- **Have the offender repeat your instructions.** However, some offenders echo what you say, so this, too, does not prove that they actually understand or will follow through.

- **Open-ended questions are more helpful than yes/no questions.** If you say, "So you will call your doctor tomorrow, won't you?" they may agree with you, hoping to make you happy. Instead, ask, "What are you going to do tomorrow?"

- **Another method is open sentences.** For example, "So, Diane, if I've got it right, I will call your lawyer tomorrow and explain the problem. And you will…." You expect (hope) that the offender will complete the sentence.

- **Write down the most important points.** Many mentally ill offenders don't assimilate a lot of information that they hear, no matter how hard they listen. The PO may find that writing the most important points of the conversation or agreement down on the back of a business card or a 3 x 5 card is quite helpful. Remind the offender to check the card if they have any difficulty remembering what they are supposed to do. Have them type the card near their phone or keep it in their wallet. (We are aware that there are many circumstances where this strategy would be out of the question, but both of us have used it on occasion.)

Figure 23 Review: How to Best Consolidate Gains

- The least effective way is to simply repeat yourself, hoping that the reply really mean that he/she understand you.
- Have the offender repeat back your instructions.
- Use open sentences and questions, allowing the offender to fill in the blanks.
- Have them write down the most important points on a card.

CHAPTER 24

Coping with Stubborn Refusals

There are many occasions when, despite having treated an offender with clarity and respect, they refuse to comply with directives, violations, and/or sanctions notwithstanding. Of course, if you have been bossing them around, patronizing them, or treating them with disrespect, it is not surprising if they resist you. All people, mentally ill or not, have pride, and no one likes another person talking down to them or controlling their lives, but once you are clear that it is not your approach that is creating the problem, what, if anything, can POs do to elicit compliance, without having to resort to the violation process?

Figure 24 Steps Toward Compliance

- **Focus on the task.** POs should never take an offender's non-compliance personally.
- **Clarify the message.** POs must be clear on what the offender is required to do regarding their immediate supervision plan. Don't bring up previous examples of their non-compliance, such as "the last time this happened," or "you always," or "remember when you." Stay very concrete.
- **Control the interview.** Stay on topic and don't allow the person to divert your attention to unrelated issues.
- **Use a strong and calm voice.** Keep your tone of voice strong, but not demanding or aggressive.
- **De-personalize your role.** Remind the offender that as the PO you are merely enforcing the orders of the Court, and that any violation proceedings, revocations, or incarcerations are the result of the offender's behavior.
- **State the consequences.** POs should be very clear in explaining to the offender the consequences and possible sanctions that may be imposed for non-compliance. This should be provided as "information," rather than threat, the same way you inform a child on a cold winter day, "If you stick your tongue on that metal pole, you are going to get stuck." Offenders may be placed on restriction in a treatment facility, made to report more often, placed on house arrest, or be returned to jail for continued non-compliance.
- **Place the power in the offender's hands.** Without handing over one iota of your authority, allow the offender to be the "decision maker," and clarify their role in complying, or not complying, with their supervision plan. Perhaps say something along the lines of "It looks like you've got something to decide. You have a couple of choices. You can be taken before the judge and you can tell them why you don't feel like complying with the Court's order; or, we can just take you to jail instead, because that is the penalty for non-compliance." Don't threaten the offender with jail, or anything else, if you know that is not a viable option. Simply state the facts of the consequences for non-compliance.

CHAPTER 25

Stuck: Coping With Repetitive Demands, Questions, and Obsessions

Sometimes offenders will make repetitive demands for information, for permission to deviate from their supervision and treatment plans, or to impose their own conditions for their supervision, such as, "program hopping" in order to find a treatment program that is to their liking.

1. Sometimes an offender becomes "stuck" with an obsessive thought or idea. No matter how many times you answer their question, they have to ask it again. This is often a sign of Obsessive-Compulsive Disorder (OCD), which is frequently missed by forensic evaluators, because offenders become skilled in covering up such a humiliating problem. Such people experience unbearable anxiety when they don't give in to the obsession or compulsion. The PO may be the first to really notice OCD behaviors when an offender gets stuck on things and can't "let go." The PO may recommend a further evaluation and/or treatment of this specific disorder.[7]

2. An offender may obsess as part of another disorder like schizophrenia, developmental disability, or other serious impairments of cognition. Their repetitive questions or obsessing on a single point may be due to information processing errors (Chapter 23).

3. Sometimes an offender repeats a question *intending* to be irritating or challenging. In a bland tone of voice, simply say, "You already know the answer to that," or otherwise calmly point out that they already have the information, and <u>move on</u>. By disengaging, you are saying, "I'm not participating in the game." If they persist, let them know that continued game playing will only make their life more difficult.

4. Mentally ill offenders sometimes *perseverate*, meaning they are stuck on a subject and feel like they have to talk about it, often at length. This behavior is slightly different from the almost automatic kind of locked-in quality of the OCD offender. These offenders simply get stuck on a subject. In this case, the PO may say something like, "I know this is very important to you, and you want to talk about this and ask me questions. But you also know you and I have a lot of work to do, so I will make you a deal. At each meeting we can talk about this for 3 minutes and 30 seconds, and no longer. So, it's your job to think carefully about what you need me to know about the subject, because when the time limit is reached, that is it. Any further information will have to wait until our next contact." Note that the reason for the "odd" number of minutes is that it sounds important, as if it has been calculated down to the second.

Figure 25.1 Author's Note

A mental health officer in my department found it quite helpful to put an egg timer on his desk, which he set to a specified time limit when he began his interviews with certain offenders. This established a definitive time frame for the interview and was rather effective in keeping some of his more disorganized offenders focused on what was being discussed.

Figure 25.2 Examples

- Bob has Huntington's Chorea. People with this disease often have no sense of proper body spacing, and frequently ask repetitive questions and make repetitive demands. He knows it aggravates the officers who have contact with him, but he can't modify his behavior.
- George, on probation for a number of alcohol related misdemeanors, has OCD and he has an incessant obsession that he will, one day, choke his baby daughter to death. He has no desire to do so and is horrified by the thought, but he can't escape it. In his search for help, he calls crisis lines, and talks to counselors, and they, understandably contact law enforcement because they can't be sure that he is not simply mentally rehearsing a crime. He is now divorced, has had two psychological evaluations, an extensive law enforcement investigation, and the PO keeps getting calls with demands that she get her offender under control.

CHAPTER 26

The Need for Reassurance

Some people are quite anxious by nature or circumstances. For others, intolerable anxiety is either their primary illness, or one of the most troublesome symptoms of their mental disorder. Anxiety is living as if something of which you are afraid might happen, is happening right now, or living with feelings of imminent doom. For instance, one particularly anxiety ridden offender believed that each and every emergency siren he heard *had* to be the police coming for him, even though he knew he had done nothing to attract their attention. This same offender would contact his PO regularly to ask if there had been any warrants issued for his arrest, and needed constant reassurance that he had nothing to worry about. Despite these assurances, the offender's anxiety would cause him to repeat this behavior nearly every time he heard the siren of an emergency vehicle. While such a pattern of behavior can be quite frustrating to the PO, the few moments the officer spent talking to the offender were met with extreme gratitude, and this offender was otherwise compliant with all of the other aspects of his supervision.

Imagine you have an offender on your caseload who has been traumatized, either before he/she was incarcerated, or as often happens, during their period of imprisonment. Despite what may be considerable sympathy that you have for the offender, don't coddle them. If you treat him/her like they are weak, they will probably believe you. They may think that something awful is going to happen and that is why you are talking in such careful tones. At the same time, don't affect a cheerful, "ain't no big thing" tone of voice. This kind of falsity will make the person either uneasy or irritated. Instead, speak in a matter-of-fact tone. Take their unease into account, but speak with an expectation that they are strong enough to manage their anxiety.

Figure 26 The Anxious Offender
When the anxious offender needs reassurance, use a confident voice that makes them feel stronger for listening.

CHAPTER 27

Dealing With Mood Swings

These offenders' behaviors are sometimes referred to as labile. They can be verbally abusive, provocative, complaining, passive-aggressive, blaming, apologetic, ingratiating, and friendly all in the space of an hour or less. POs will commonly see such behaviors among those offenders diagnosed with borderline personality disorders, bipolar disorders, or those who have damaged their brains with long-term substance abuse. They can be very difficult to communicate with, much less de-escalate, because just as progress is made with their current mood, they shift into another mood. They often try to get control of others even when they have no control over themselves.

Coping With Mood Swings

Rather than respond to the offender's specific moods with body language or words that manifest one's own anger or frustration, the PO has to remain balanced and emotionally non-reactive. <u>A PO can influence them by being exactly what they are not.</u> The more the PO is unaffected by an offender's emotional storms, the more likely that the offender will calm down (Section III).

Figure 27 Review: Mood Swings

Offenders with mood swings shift emotions rapidly, with no particular relationship to the situation they are in. When interviewing or de-escalating these offenders remember:

- Don't mirror the individual's emotional state or lose control of your own emotions.
- Control them through controlling your own emotions. Remain powerfully calm.
- Speak in a firm, yet calm and controlled manner.
- Because they display any emotion you can imagine, use general de-escalation tactics, as described throughout the book, as needed.

CHAPTER 28

They Aren't Moving: What to do?

You have surely been in situations where you tell the mentally ill person to do something and they stare at you vacantly, voice a million questions, express misgivings or anxiety, or drift off into a monologue about something completely different.

Other mentally ill offenders seem to lack motivation; they just won't do what *we* think is good for them. We are referring here to the offender whose mental illness impedes their ability to accomplish the things they are required to do.

A word of caution here, some offenders, and even their family members or therapists, will use their mental illness as an excuse for their failure to comply with even the most basic rules and regulations. Mental illness becomes their "fallback" position for their non–compliance, so that they never accept any *personal* responsibility. POs should not do things for the offender that he or she can do for themselves, other than perhaps scheduling certain appointments (and this is done primarily so the PO knows the appointment was indeed scheduled), or helping them navigate some governmental bureaucracy or another.

You must ask yourself if the offender is truly capable of complying with the stipulations of the supervision plan, or if they even understand what those stipulations are. Perhaps an indifferent judge simply imposed the same series of boilerplate conditions that they impose upon every offender that comes before their Court, with little regard for the offender's actual needs or condition. In other cases, the Court was influenced by promises of compliance made by the offender and their defense attorney at the time of sentencing.

Either way, the PO must assess the offender's actual ability to comply, and use their discretion when determining what constitutes an acceptable level of compliance, or at least a concerted effort at compliance on the offender's part. In the event that the offender is incapable of complying with the Court's order *due to mental illness*, the PO should bring this to the Court's attention, and request a modification of the supervision plan.

If the offender is non-compliant despite their ability to do so, the PO can resort to the official violation process and bring the offender back before the Court for a violation hearing, revocation, or possible incarceration. The violation process is incredibly motivating for some offenders, even if their new-found compliance is made in an effort to impress the Court prior to their violation hearing. POs should not be reluctant to file a violation report against a mentally ill offender or overlook their non-compliance because of their illness. Mentally ill offenders must still be held accountable for their actions, and public safety concerns will certainly outweigh any exigent circumstances related to the offender's mental capacities.

Finally, POs should take note of just how they attempt to motivate the offender. Do you like the sound of your voice? Are you overly threatening? Or conversely, are you pleading with them? POs must retain their dignity when trying to motivate their offenders. Give directions in a firm tone of voice: don't cajole, or sound like a "cheerleader" in an attempt to try to get them to comply. When you are dignified, your offender will respect you more, sometimes in spite of himself. Offenders are far more likely to be compliant for POs that they respect.

Figure 28 Review: They Aren't Moving: What to do?

1. Don't do for them what they can't do for themselves.
2. Don't require them to do things that they are incapable of doing.
3. If they are truly non-compliant, use the violation process for motivation (or sanction if they continue to refuse).
4. Act with dignity. Don't try to "cheerlead" them into compliance, berate them, complain, or any one of a number of actions that compromise your integrity in the interests of getting them moving.

CHAPTER 29

Should a PO ever apologize?

Some offenders store up grievances, allowing feelings of persecution and perceived personal slights to affect their entire worldview. With mentally ill offenders, these feelings can be more problematic, because their memories may be distorted or even delusional. Frequent complaints about old history can become a significant barrier to an offender's compliance with their supervision and treatment plans; not to mention being extremely aggravating to the harried PO who must continually turn the offender's attention to immediate issues and future concerns.

Unfortunately, you as a PO, represent the last stop along the offender's journey through the criminal justice system. Feelings of animosity toward the arresting police officer(s), perceptions of civil rights infractions, dissatisfaction with their legal representation, and bitterness toward the sentencing judge; all of these highly upsetting and emotional experiences are now directed toward you, the PO. After having been arrested, convicted, and perhaps incarcerated, the offender has to deal with *you,* yet one more authority figure that is intruding into their life, and telling them what they can and can't do.

As with disorganized and labile offenders, POs must refrain from reacting emotionally to the offender's inability to move beyond the past, even as you try to redirect their attention to the present situation. Above all, don't personalize the offender's complaints or their feelings of prior injustices. POs can hardly be expected to bear the emotional burden for the entire criminal justice system, or feel responsible for any actual mistreatment or improprieties surrounding the offender's case.

1. **Acknowledge their concerns.** Quite often offenders merely need to express their frustrations or feelings of helplessness regarding their case, and they view the PO as the only available outlet to do so. Sometimes, allowing the offender to express their feelings (as long as they do so in an appropriate manner), and acknowledging their viewpoint may be enough to alleviate their anger. Don't agree or disagree with them, or otherwise reinforce their feelings of persecution, just recognize their complaints and then move forward. <u>Don't however, allow the offender to revisit the issue at every interview; this should be a "one and done" event.</u>

2. **Apologize.** When your offender complains, yet again, about something directly concerning you, think about it very carefully. Perhaps, in this instance, you were wrong. If so, apologize sincerely and fully. In some situations, this is enough. However, the authors can't stress strongly enough that POs should be wary of apologizing to an offender as a means of moving them off of a specific subject or grievance. An apology may lead the offender to believe they are now in control of the relationship, and that the PO will act cautiously so as not to upset the offender in the future. The best thing for the PO to do is to act ethically and professionally at all times.

By staying calm and in control a PO is much less likely to say or do anything for which they would need to apologize.

3. **If an apology is not enough.** POs may say to the offender, "You are still upset about this. You want to talk about it again, don't you?" Notice that you don't ask the offender—you merely state your understanding. This gives them the opportunity to correct or adjust your understanding so that if their complaint is legitimate, you are able to effectively put it to rest.

4. **Complaints as their own reward.** Certain offenders are never satisfied, because the complaint becomes a "rewarding" activity in itself. Others bear a pervasive resentment toward their POs, an institution, or even life itself. For them, complaints are merely a way to express hostility or an attempt to control the interview by getting you, their PO, to talk about things on their agenda. In these cases, simply take the issue off the table, forever. Remind each of your offenders that you have already addressed their complaint, so that there is nothing more to discuss. If necessary, terminate the interview if an offender persists in discussing the past.

Figure 29 Review: Should a PO ever apologize?

*   If they have a general grievance towards their situation and the criminal justice system, acknowledge their complaints in a "one-and-done" manner, as long as you neither apologize for things that are not your fault or responsibility and you don't compromise your authority.

*   If you have wronged the offender, if it does not put you in danger, and if it enables you to assume tactical strength, then you should apologize.

*   If the offender is stuck on the issue, say, "You are still upset about that," or something similar, giving them an opportunity to clarify why it is still a problem for them.

*   If the offender is using the grievance or complaint to get control of the exchange, distract you, or simply complain for the sake of complaining, shut it down. Call them on their game and don't allow it to continue.

CHAPTER 30

Useful Tactics for Dealing With Symptoms of Paranoia and Persecution

> **Figure 30.1 This Chapter Focuses on the Paranoid Attitude,**
>
> This chapter focuses on tactics specific to paranoia. Rather than the delusional state, which we will discuss in Chapters 38 and 39, we are here discussing an attitude, with the following characteristics: a sense of being persecuted, blame of others for any problem, and a hair-trigger sensitivity to being vulnerable. The delusional paranoid individual has this attitude complicated by fixed false beliefs and even hallucinations. We are here talking about something much more common: a character trait.

Supervising a paranoid offender can be exceedingly difficult. Their motto of life could be summed up in a phrase: "If there is a problem here, it's your fault." The paranoid world is one of dominance and submission: the paranoid tries to dominate the people in his/her life, and is terrified or enraged at being forced to submit.

We are not only referring to a psychotic or delusional state, but also the far more common paranoid character, in which the offender (without delusions) has a consistent *attitude* of blame, resentment of authority, fear of vulnerability, and an expectation of being betrayed by people they trust. Stimulant users, notably those addicted to methamphetamine and cocaine, frequently display these behaviors. It is also a very common "solution" that criminals arrive at to excuse any failure. Paranoid offenders are, at core level, terrified that they will be made vulnerable, but they are aggressive toward that of which they are afraid. One helpful image of the paranoid offender is an angry porcupine, all quills, with a soft underbelly, hunched over, ready to strike in hair-trigger reaction. Character traits and behavior patterns of paranoid offenders include:

- **Paranoid offenders interpret relaxation as vulnerability.** Therefore, they become more paranoid when you, their PO, begin to establish rapport with them. Friendship means letting your guard down—for this reason, paranoid people are particularly volatile within their families.

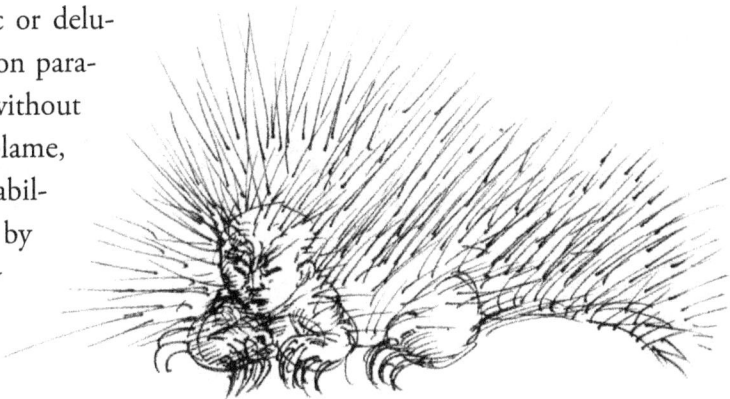

Don't be surprised if paranoid offenders suddenly flare up with suspicion or accusations during times that are uneventful or even, within professional limits, friendly.

- **Being mistaken or wrong is another form of vulnerability.** Rather than admitting wrongdoing or mistakes, paranoid individuals reflexively *project* negative feelings on the other person. If they feel hate, they believe, "You hate me." If they forgot to go to an appointment to get medical assistance, they will claim, "You set me up. You knew I couldn't get there on that day."
- **Paranoid offenders live like detectives.** They continually search for evidence to prove what they already know is true. They have *ideas of reference*, in which they believe that other conversations, glances, or actions are directed at them. They assume that others are conspiring about them, talking about them, laughing at them. Ironically, their reactions, in response to their paranoid ideas, frequently cause others to act in exactly the way the paranoid person expects.
- **Paranoid offenders make others uncomfortable or afraid.** Because of their aggressive or standoffish behavior, they can make other people uncomfortable or afraid. If they sense fear in you, they expect you to attack, and they "attack you back first," fear driving their own aggression.

Try to Let Them Know What Is Going On

Because paranoid offenders are so suspicious, they will often question your actions and instructions. Whenever you can, tell them what you are doing. Although you would do this with any other offender, it is especially important with these individuals. Clearly and explicitly explain the rules and regulations of their supervision plan. POs should also make clear their expectations of compliance, and explain the violation process, as well as the potential consequences of non–compliance. Even if you must arrest them or get them committed to a hospital, explain what you are doing and why, once they are secure. You will be dealing with them again, and if they have a sense that you have treated them in good faith, things are more likely to go well next time. However, you should not accept being quizzed incessantly. You are not required to explain every action. It might be a tactic to throw you off guard or distract you.

Personal Space: Physical and Psychological With the Paranoid Offender

Many paranoid offenders are preoccupied, even obsessed, with fears that they will be invaded, violated, or controlled in some fashion. The more severely psychotic can be afraid that they will be molested or otherwise sexually violated. Some of the following are, of course, relevant when dealing with any offender, but they are doubly important when an offender is paranoid.

- **Maintain the angle.** Whether standing or sitting, turn your body at a slight angle, so that physical "confrontation" is a choice rather than a requirement. If you directly face a paranoid offender, you *force* them to turn away if they do not want to face you. Do NOT, of course, turn away from them, so that you are no longer aware of what they are doing.
- **Mindfulness.** Never let your own guard. You are in an avalanche zone, and anything could set off another slide.
- **Differentiate.** Paranoid offenders feel safest when you differentiate yourself from them, so that you are not interwoven with their delusional fears. It is better to be somewhat emotionally distant rather than too warm and friendly.

- **Too friendly is as dangerous as a threat.** Try to be aware when things are getting too relaxed. It is not only about you maintaining awareness. If the paranoid offender relaxes, they may suddenly startle, realizing that for a brief moment, they let their guard down. They may respond by exploding to make sure you do not "take them over."
- **Cover your triggers.** Paranoid offenders will try to provoke you. If you lose your temper, they will feel justified in whatever they do to you, and it may just as well key into their terror-based aggression. A slang expression for this is "fear biters." They bark and snarl and when you react, they attack as if you went after them first.

Is There a Specific Paranoid Rage or Violence?

There is no specific "paranoid rage." Instead, paranoia is an "engine" that drives rage in all its various forms. De-escalate the offender using tactics specific to the mode of rage they are exhibiting (Section XI) rather than de-escalating "paranoia" itself. Paranoid offenders can exhibit traits of fear, frustration, intimidation, and manipulation. With their focus, however, they are rarely disorganized. Even so, some disorganized offenders can experience an "omni-directional dread," a pervasive terror that is inescapable. Unlike paranoia, however, this pervasive sense of terror has no target (Chapters 65 & 66).

Figure 30.2 Review: Paranoia and Persecution

The paranoid offender has an attitude that if anything is wrong it is another person's fault. Whether delusional or not, they see others as conspiring against them or persecuting them.

- Depending on what will prove useful, paranoid offenders use any of the standard tactics that delusional people use.
- De-escalate based on the behavior, not the paranoia.
- Let them know what's going on.
- Speak in formal tones. Do not be too friendly.
- They will try to provoke you so they can "hit you back first."
- Be aware of both physical and emotional spacing. Maintain a correct distancing, neither too close nor too far.
- Differentiate by not being too friendly, and if they are delusional, clearly separate yourself from their paranoid ideas without getting into an argument with them.
- Maintain your calm, the paranoid offender is usually assaultive when they feel under attack, when they perceive you as controlling them, or when they perceive that you are afraid.
- If you do take them into custody, or otherwise control them, let them know what is going on and why, once you have them secured. Paranoid offenders are most likely to become dangerous when they base their actions on their imagination rather than on reality.

SECTION V

Recognizing the Strategies of Opportunistic and Manipulative Offenders

CHAPTER 31

Divide and Confuse:
Borderline Personality Disorder and Splitting

Figure 31.1 Author's Note

Individuals with borderline traits frequently display suicidal and para-suicidal behaviors. These behaviors will be discussed in detail in Section VII.

Character disorders, also called personality disorders, are habitual patterns of behavior that sometimes cause an offender, and almost always others associated with them, considerable distress. Most types of personality disorders don't cause behaviors that significantly affect safety. One that does, discussed previously, is the paranoid personality (Chapter 30). However, POs will also find themselves supervising offenders with another type of character disorder, borderline personality disorder. In essence, such an offender believes that whatever feeling they are having right now is the only possible reality. For example, road rage is a borderline reaction. Someone cuts a person off while driving, it makes them mad and instead of cooling down, they chase after the offender and smash into their car. On the flip side, they meet someone attractive in a bar, and within five seconds, they know that it is the love of their life.

Figure 31.2 Examples of Borderline Personality Disorders

The two main characters in the movie, *Monster*, starring Charlize Theron and Christina Ricci, are portrayals of women with two types of extreme borderline personality disorders. Theron plays Alicia Wournos, a woman who came from a horrendously abusive background, drifted into prostitution, and then murdered six "johns." She had the emotional stability of a toddler, shifting from sweetness and trust to hair-trigger rage. Whatever she felt at that moment was her only reality. Some of her murders, at least, were based on the threat and abuse she *felt* she was experiencing from the johns.

The Ricci character was a woman of almost no character at all. She templated to whomever she was with at the time. Rather than an "active" borderline like Wournos, she was passive. Like Wournos, however, all her actions, too, are based on feelings alone, not on any rational evaluation on what was good for her, in this case, bonding with a dominant, violent individual, and then, later, betraying her to her law enforcement interrogators.

Any of us can be overcome by feelings that seem beyond our control and make emotional decisions that are not in our own best interest. Sometimes we are impulsive, and sometimes we get angry, even enraged.

For us, however, such experiences are an aberration, while for the offender with borderline personality disorder they are an everyday occurrence.

Those on the mild end of the spectrum will be quite emotional, over-reacting to things that others could take in stride. For those whose disorder is more severe, it is as if their nervous system, at least that part which regulates emotion, seemingly lacks any protective sheathing. Imagine trying to live your daily life with two layers of skin peeled off. On an emotional level, that is borderline existence. One's current emotions are inescapable. The borderline person lives with the intensity and the emotional resilience of a toddler. They experience the world and the people in it as good and bad, perfect and foul.

Because of this combination of character traits, offenders with borderline personality disorder frequently find themselves in various crises. Among them are genuine suicide attempts, para-suicidal acts (self-mutilating behaviors or repeat suicide "gestures" staged for discovery and attention Chapters 46 & 47), impulsive acts of assault (particularly those involving family members or others close to them), and brief psychotic episodes. Among them are offenders whom POs call "frequent fliers:" offenders who drain enormous amounts of time and resources from the criminal justice system.

Figure 31.3 Borderline Personality: a Female or Male Disorder

The stereotypical individual with borderline personality traits is a woman. Examples of the type of individuals we usually think of in this light are those in Figures 31.2 and 3.4. However, just as many men as women have borderline traits. Many men have the kind of problems we expect when thinking of this dysfunctional pattern of behavior: dramatic crises, impulsive relationships, drug abuse, suicidal and para-suicidal actions, etc.

There is another pattern of borderline behavior that is predominantly, but not exclusively male. In this case, their destructive behavior is directed outwards rather than inwards. Rather than suicidal or self-mutilating acts, these individuals hurt others, particularly in domestic violence, or other sudden flare-ups into rage and violence. To be sure, Alicia Wournos, remarkable for a number of reasons, not the least of them that she was female, represents the far end of this spectrum. There are hundreds of thousands, if not millions of people, however, who shift between periods of calm into a downward spiral of emotional misery and then an explosion of violence, the so-called "cycle of abuse." In short, you will have many people on your case-load who actually have a borderline character who, because they do not conform to the "drama-queen," largely self-destructive stereotype, fall below the radar. An understanding of their unstable character structure may assist you in better maintaining them in community supervision as well as determining the best services to keep them from being incarcerated again.

Finally, an awareness of this set of character traits will also serve to keep you mindful that they may flare upwards into rage at the slightest pretext, just as a toddler does, something that makes them as adults very dangerous indeed.

In reaction to these events, the PO may discover that many of the people associated with the offender, including their therapist(s), will disagree over the most appropriate course of action in regard to their treatment, even to the point of arguing about whom is at fault for the offender's current crisis. In particular, those involved in a therapeutic relationship with the offender often lean to contextualizing, explaining, or excusing the behavior, especially when the offender has a previous history of trauma or abuse. When the individuals associated with a borderline individual get tangled up in intense disputes about what is best for the offender this type of conflict is called *splitting*.

Splitting doesn't happen in a vacuum. The offender, although not really conscious of what they are doing, is at the center of the conflict, presenting a different facet of their personality to each person with whom they interact. This "divide and confuse" strategy often sets family members, therapists, and even the PO against one another regarding the proper response to the offender's behavior, keeping the "heat" off of the offender.

It is not surprising, really, that an offender will appear quite different to a therapist trying to build a supportive relationship, as opposed to a case manager trying to help them negotiate their way through day-to-day life, and to the PO, who is most responsible for public safety and who can quickly take away the offender's freedom. Needless to say, each of these individuals responds to the offender somewhat differently, and each may believe that they have the best idea on how to deal with them. Unfortunately, these varying opinions, and not coincidentally, a measure of professional pride, can lead to arguments about the best course of action.

Although splitting is usually regarded as an act of the offender, one that is at best manipulative and at worst sociopathic, this definition is too simplistic. Splitting is a process, not an act. <u>Professionals, including POs, are also participants in splitting, and quite frankly, sometimes the actions of these professionals *create* the splitting process</u>. Whenever there is a possibility of splitting, the offender's case should be respectfully discussed among the treatment team, sometimes with expert outside consultation, to flesh out any necessary changes to the supervision plan. Without such consultation, an incredible amount of time and effort can be spent arguing about the status of one offender.

The PO can, of course, unilaterally make a decision based on concerns of public safety and place the offender into custody where they will be re-evaluated in jail. However, if all members of the defacto team responsible for the offender remain at odds, the "victory" by the PO in re-incarcerating the offender will be short-lived. You will be working with the same people on other cases, and you will most likely continue to work "at odds together" regarding this offender. Thus, whenever a team gets intensely at odds regarding a single offender, suggest the possibility of splitting, and see if you can, by comparing observations, see if the offender's interactions with various people have created the adversarial situation in which you find yourselves.

Finally, borderline offenders are, not surprisingly, quite reactive to other people's emotional reactions. The attitude of the PO should be similar to a perfect uncle or aunt, someone who wishes the offender well, yet undeviatingly enforces the rules. By maintaining a type of "warm emotional distance," you won't get emotionally worked up over things, and the offender will find less to react to as well.

Figure 31.4 Example of Splitting

Crystal has returned to her abusive husband on five occasions, and has violated several restraining orders that she took out on him. Her children are in foster care because she did not protect them from his sexual behavior towards them. She is on probation for a fourth degree assault against her husband.

She shifts from rage at him, to complaints about how the police were too brutal during his last arrest; to panic stricken calls to her therapist begging for help; and no-shows to the prosecutor's office for meetings regarding her upcoming testimony in his trial.

- One investigating officer regards her as her husband's partner in crime, saying, "If you let someone abuse your kids, you are as culpable as the abuser."
- A second officer feels sorry for her. She reminds the officer of her own daughter, someone who tries so hard to do things right and fails over and over again.
- The prosecutor regards her as a manipulative game player, who is using the system to try to get crime victim's compensation.
- Psychiatrist thinks her erratic behavior is due to bipolar disorder and is medicating her.
- Her counselor sees her behavior as a manifestation of her own trauma as a child, and has accused the police of being insensitive to abuse victims.
- Her substance abuse counselor sees her as co-dependent.
- Her children love her passionately, and have blown out of several foster homes. Crystal has told them that they are in foster care because "the judge said so."

Figure 31.5 Review: Dealing with Splitting

- Stay focused on whether or not there is really an emergent issue.
- Don't be reactive to the manipulative complaints or side issues the offender brings up.
- If they are a frequent caller or are involved in a case that brings in players from many different systems and agencies, you have to pool resources to arrive at a common viewpoint and plan concerning the offender.
- Maintain a "warm emotional distance," like a solid uncle or aunt, in essence say, "I wish you well, here are the rules, and I won't lose sleep over things if you don't comply but I do wish you well."
- Be aware that the borderline character is typified by "black-and-white" thinking, impulsive reactions to one's own emotions, idealization/hatred of other people, including the PO, and splitting. Their dysfunctional actions are NOT necessarily or exclusively self-destruction – they may frequently or exclusively lash out in violence towards others, most typically for due to inter-personal reasons. Therefore, they are most dangerous to intimates, and beyond family members, the PO often becomes the closest person in such an offender's life, putting them, too, a particular risk.

CHAPTER 32

Bad Intentions—Recognizing the Strategies of Opportunistic and Manipulative Offenders

In order to satisfy their need for instant gratification, many offenders attempt to manipulate nearly everyone with whom they come into contact, including family members, strangers on the street, and yes, even their PO. Some offenders use manipulation as a means of furthering their criminal actions, while others view people in general as opportunities to gain something they want. A few others live for hate and destruction, and delight most in duping people so that they don't even know how "dirty they were done." Some manipulative offenders lie so that no one can pin them down, using a "divide and disappear" strategy so that the more powerful beings in their life argue about them, instead of focusing directly on what these manipulative offenders are really doing.

Manipulative Strategies

People can enact manipulative strategies from a variety of emotions and intentions, such as those born of revenge, malice, desperation, laziness, guilt, or as the result of drug and alcohol use.[8] You must be vigilant in detecting manipulative behaviors, and require proper verification of any information given by the offender, including verification of treatment, employment, or residence. In particular, POs should be wary of offenders who appear to be overly compliant, especially those offenders who have committed serious offenses, such as sex crimes or offenses involving the use of weapons or violence. Quite often, some of the most dangerous offenders on your caseload will be the ones who report each month on time, attend to any special conditions of their supervision plan, and in general appear to be compliant low-risk offenders. This seemingly compliant behavior may in fact be nothing more than an attempt to manipulate and control *your* behavior. Remember, your offenders realize how busy and overworked you are. Their motives are hardly altruistic. What the offender is likely trying to accomplish is to manipulate you, his PO, into *never* making a field visit to their residence. After all, why would an already hectic PO bother to make a field visit to the residence of a compliant offender!

Figure 32.1 Author's Experience with an Overly Complaint Offender

One of the authors used to supervise a young offender who was heavily involved with gang related activity. He had been charged, but ultimately acquitted, of several homicides. This particular offender was one of the most polite and compliant young men you would ever wish to meet. He reported as directed, provided clean drug samples, said "yes sir," and "thank you" during his interviews. However, his extensive history of violence, drug related criminal activity, and the alleged multiple homicides, sent up any number of red flags. Don't allow familiarity and politeness to supersede your sense of caution and safety when supervising apparently compliant offenders.

POs must exercise caution when making a field visit to the residence of a compliant offender. Manipulative behaviors are not employed only to keep you, the PO, *away* from the offender's home. They may seek to draw you further into the residence, or lower your guard with offerings of a comfortable chair, or perhaps a cup of coffee. Often their dishonesty is based on "lies of omission." For example, he perceives your caution at entering his house, and says:

- "You can come in. The lock doesn't work anyway."
- "My roommate's here. She's cool."
- "I guess you are a little uncomfortable going into a person's apartment seeing as I had trouble with my last PO. You don't have to worry. That was personal. It had nothing to do with you."

None of these statements establishes, in the slightest, that he doesn't mean to assault you. Another sign of coercion is a reassuring promise when none was asked for.

Offenders sometimes use stories to overload you with information to keep your attention away from what they are doing, either in your presence, or generally speaking, out in the community. They charm you so that you actually look forward to that offender's office visit, but remain unaware of what is really going on.

Manipulative offenders will also ask their PO for personal information, such as marital status, children, in which part of town the PO resides, and so forth. These questions seem to be innocent enough, just the normal back and forth of a pleasant conversation. What the manipulative offender is doing, however, is gathering information, something that they can use later in the relationship, or perhaps to fuel their current fantasies. POs should refrain from answering any personal questions an offender may ask, and redirect the conversation back toward your professional duties.

Figure 32.2 Guarding Personal Information

POs can also reduce the amount of personal information available to offenders by adhering to the office safety precautions outlined in Chapter 9 related to the display of personal photographs and other personal information.

Manipulative offenders are also quite adept at behavioral observations, such as noting the body language of others. They are particularly interested in potential victims, those who are easily intimidated or frightened—including other offenders. If you are supervising a particularly manipulative offender, you may wish to reduce the time that they spend in the waiting area of the Probation Office. Although you don't often think about the subject, the waiting area in your office is often filled with society's more vulnerable and gullible individuals, who present easy targets to the manipulative offender. And if you recall from an earlier chapter, mentally ill offenders are some of the most victimized members of society.

These offenders are also interested in those who put up any kind of a front, including an attempt to appear tough. All the manipulative offender has to do is challenge the "front," and the "fronting" PO begins reacting like a yo-yo on a string, trying to keep up appearances, to an offender who has already read them inside and out.

Manipulative offenders are also likely to blame others for both their failures and their behaviors. Nothing is ever their fault: they were simply in the wrong place at the wrong time; they didn't know their friend had a gun in the car; it is the POs fault for their incarceration or their violation hearing. The fact that the offender is liable to blame others for their problems is one reason why verification and documentation of the offender's stated compliance with treatment, employment, drug screens, and residency status are vital. The onus of verification should be placed on the offender, and they must be required to produce letters of participation in, or completion of treatment. At the very least, offenders must sign release of information forms, so that the PO can verify they are actually going to treatment as required. If an offender fails to sign a release of information, or presents repeated excuses as to why they have not yet signed one, chances are they are lying about their participation. Employment verification can be documented with paystubs or official proof of employment, such as a 1099 form.

Another means of manipulation is that of flirtation and sexuality, which can manifest in any gender configuration between the offender and the PO, including same sex. All POs must address any flirtatious behaviors or sexual innuendo with the offender immediately. Firm limits must be set as to the professional nature of the relationship, and what constitutes acceptable conversation. If this issue is not addressed instantly, the offender will view it as implied acceptance, which may lead to further advances or even attempted blackmail. It may also lead others, both offenders and co-workers to assume that something is going on between the offender and PO. This is yet another reason that POs should not be isolated while interviewing offenders, regardless of gender, either in the office setting or during a field visit to the offender's residence.

Manipulative offenders also view their relationships as transactions, with an eye toward gaining an advantage or placing the other individual in their debt. The manipulative offender will sometimes deliberately make things difficult, only to then suddenly "give in," or become compliant. The likely purpose for their new-found compliance is to engender a sense of gratitude within the unwary PO, or at least a lessening of frustration, toward the offender. Along with a sense of gratitude however, can come a lessening of supervision or investigation.

Figure 32.3 The Tactic of Making It Difficult

It used to be a truism that sex offenders were "sectored," that their kink was fixed so that they could only "get off" on one thing. For example, if a person was a pedophile towards small girls, they would not be interested in teenagers or boys, or if they were fixated on exhibitionism, they would not be interested in forcible rape. Research has shown that this is not true. To be sure, many sex offenders have victim profiles, sexualized or violent acts with which they are obsessed. However, many are also opportunistic and far more adaptable and/or indiscriminate than used to be assumed.

Therefore, imagine a long-drawn out interrogation regarding a man who steals underwear from the driers at an apartment complex, who has, once again, been caught. He plausibly denies the crimes this time, then, caught out, *implausibly* denies, and finally, after a long time, "gives it up." What a sense of relief! Case closed. So you never think to ask about the rapes or the molestations, or the window peeping that have occurred one township over. Like a magician, he gets you focused on "one thing" only.

CHAPTER 33

Tactical and Safety Considerations Related to the Supervision of the Psychopathic Offender

---

Figure 33.1 Authors' Note

There is considerable overlap in this chapter with the safety recommendations made throughout this book, particularly in the former chapter on manipulative behavior. In Section XI, we will discuss what to do when facing someone presenting with Hot, Predatory, or Aggressive-Manipulative Rage, all modes that the psychopath can manifest when they become dangerously aggressive. Here, the authors are highlighting the most salient point's specific to psychopathic individuals. We believe that this information is so important to officer safety that it must be presented as a stand-alone chapter for easy reference.

You may also encounter another term, "anti-social personality disorder." This term is really just another name for an aggressive criminal. What makes the psychopath unique is that they are "aggressive narcissists." They only care about themselves and they will use what ever means they like, without guilt or remorse and with delight at the destruction they cause, to satisfy their desires.

The terms psychopath and sociopath are interchangeable and evoke very strong reactions. Estimates are that 1-3 percent of any culture's population, and perhaps 40 percent of the prison population in the United States is psychopathic. A small percentage of offenders commit most of the crimes in any society, and although there is a sociological component to crime, the psychopath, to a remarkable degree, seems independent of such factors.

Over the years the entertainment media as well as sensationalized news accounts of horrendously violent killers and rapists have introduced an image of the malevolent criminal mastermind or the sadistic predator into the public's consciousness. Without a doubt, violent psychopaths do exist, but they are often rather mundane in appearance and affect, blending in with their surroundings without attracting any undue attention.

Figure 33.2 Examples of Psychopaths in the Movies

Instead of thinking of some movie monster such as Hannibal Lector, a much more useful image would be Johnny Depp's character in *Pirates of the Caribbean*. In his role as Captain Jack Sparrow, Depp plays an aggressive narcissist; he is attractive and likeable, but also utterly selfish and quite willing to violate social norms. A second image would be the Matt Damon character in *The Talented Mr. Ripley*, an inoffensive chameleon-like man, who has no desire to kill anyone, but when circumstances "require" it, he does so without hesitation.

Although psychopathic offenders can be charming and ingratiating, they can also be violent, provocative, dishonest, arrogant, and quite willing to break the law. Some are remarkably talented, even brilliantly creative. However, the only thing they really care about is themselves. Everything we have just discussed in regards to manipulative strategies in the last chapter is relevant to a discussion of psychopathic offenders. However, the psychopathic offender presents problems beyond what you will experience with the "ordinary" criminal personality, however manipulative the latter may be.

Just as a cougar is known to attack whenever a vulnerable animal turns its back and exposes its neck, psychopathic offenders feed off vulnerability. Because of their manipulative charm, they can easily get under the defenses of others. They will gravitate to the most vulnerable people on your team. They study everyone with whom they come into contact, making note of any apparent weaknesses and developing new strategies of manipulation and control. For example, "Hmm, when Officer Gibbs tilts her head and smiles while I'm talking, I find myself relaxing a little. I can use this the next time I'm trying to get close to a child." Not only do they lack a sense of remorse at the harm inflicted upon their victims, they often take uncommon delight in it.

Don't assume, by the way, that we are merely talking about the offender you are supervising. This may be the lawyer who is defending the offender, or the prosecutor who should be doing his/her job. This can also be the victim whom you believe you are protecting, who is, in fact, setting up you or someone else.

Due to their grandiose narcissism, such offenders don't view themselves as being under supervision for the purpose of rehabilitation and they tend to treat the entire criminal justice system with disdain. In fact, some of modern history's most notorious psychopaths, such as Richard Speck, the murderer of eight young nurses, have insisted on defending themselves in court as a result of their vainglorious attitude that they are smarter than everyone else.

Because such offenders are easily bored, they deliberately agitate people whenever possible: in the waiting room for example, through gossip, initiation of conflict, or provocative actions. Some psychopaths are violent predators, but most are not. Many are fundamentally parasitic and they revel in the instigation of emotional drama or conflict through the use of lies, rumors, and/or intimidation.

Without a doubt, the most dangerous are the sexually violent psychopaths, who use their guile to groom others for exploitation, prior to enacting sexual assaults. Although common sense would dictate against a PO ever fostering a personal relationship with an offender under their supervision, a psychopathic offender may even attempt to groom and seduce their PO, just for the thrill of destroying their career, or for the purposes of blackmail or privilege. One irony is that it is the most dangerous offenders who are most likely to succeed in fostering such a relationship with their PO.

As with many offenders, psychopaths are impulsive in their actions and their sense of invincibility often leads them to ignore consequences. Such offenders owe their allegiance to no one, although they may form quasi-sentimental attachments that last until a stronger interest or desire pushes them away. This loyalty is on the level of, "Who do you think you are, patting my dog without my permission!"

Their impulsivity can also result in sudden and unexpected displays of violent behavior if they are frustrated in their desires. Many psychopaths are violent as a means of obtaining that which they desire: "just business," so to speak. For others, the act of violence itself is gratifying: their propensity for physical and emotional violence, coupled with their charming manipulativeness and the fact that there are **NO** therapeutic interventions that can "cure" the psychopathic personality, means that POs must remain observant and wary when interacting with these offenders.

Although the truly psychopathic offender is a bit of a rarity among the overall offender population, POs will benefit from becoming familiar with the behaviors and characteristics of such offenders. The authors strongly recommend Robert Hare's illuminating work, *Without Conscience: The disturbing world of the psychopath* for a detailed discussion of this subgroup of offenders.[9]

Once you realize that an offender is primarily psychopathic, your goal must be the protection of the community, not rehabilitation. The old adage of "trail 'em, nail 'em, and jail 'em" would seem to apply toward the supervision of these offenders. POs must enforce the orders of the Court unfailingly, monitor such offenders closely, and violate their probation or parole quickly for violations. And, although this approach seems to fly in the face of the material presented thus far, in this instance incarceration is likely to be the best, if not the only means of increasing public safety. When supervising and interacting with the true psychopathic offender, POs need to remain conscious of the fact that these individuals are quite skilled in reading other people: how strong they are, their susceptibility to manipulation, and most significantly, what danger they represent to themselves. Therefore, your personal and professional integrity is paramount as you have a lot to lose if you succumb to the psychopathic offender's attempts to manipulate and control you, including your reputation, your career, and your personal well-being.

Figure 33.3 Substance Abusers May Present as Psychopaths

Substance abusers often act like psychopaths while using. Addicts in remission who truly are engaged in treatment usually begin to abandon manipulative and strategic behaviors. Psychopaths, on the other hand, don't. They may use different strategies when they are sober, but they will never abandon a tactical, manipulative approach.

Tactical and Safety Considerations

The following is a list of tactical and safety considerations for POs:

1. **You will be attacked through your "best" and your "worst" points.** The notion that the psychopathic offender will attack your weak points seems quite logical, and they certainly do. If you are insecure about your personal appearance; for example, the psychopath will either make you feel more insecure, or in a more sophisticated tactic, reassure you that he or she, at least, finds you quite attractive. What is harder to notice is when you are attacked through your best points. For example, if you appear to be physically fit, they will try to consult with you about your exercise regimen, or ask where and when you workout. If you love children, they will find a way to ask your advice on an alleged phone call from their ex-wife about putting their child on medications. They might really have a child who needs medication. But they are asking you in order to gain some traction—not to get your help. For such an individual, anything can be leverage. Remember, they don't even have to lie. The truth is an even better tool!

2. **Notice when others start making excuses for the offender.** When conned or manipulated, people often find a way to rationalize what the psychopath is doing, or has done. For example, after a near assault at the mental health clinic where he goes for his domestic violence group, a counselor says, "You have to understand. He was brought up that way. When you threatened him with a violation, it was like a flashback to the way his father treated him." Don't allow others, either members of the offender's family or treatment professionals, to sway your opinion or prevent you from attending to your professional duties.

3. **Track any manipulative strategies, document them well, and alert all other members of your team to the manipulative strategies an offender is using.** Consult and consult again. Don't discount the observations of other officers. They are often very important, especially those of correctional officers who interact most directly with then offender in question. Consult yet again.

4. **You may be intimidated.** The most obvious manifestation of intimidation is fear. There is always a reason for fear. If you are frightened of an offender, consult with your fellow officers or supervisors immediately. What is more difficult to recognize is an unconscious attempt to avoid being frightened by colluding with, or giving in, to the demands of the psychopath! Ironically, the intimidated officer may sometimes claim that they have a special rapport or working relationship with the offender; when in fact, all they are doing is giving the predatory offender what he or she wants.

5. **Be aware of grooming behaviors.** The "grooming cycle" is a pattern of behavior designed to alleviate the intended victim's fears and apprehensions, all the while targeting them for attack. The offender will make their target feel a little off-balance, making them anxious, scared, or flattered. Then they lessen the pressure while making a request that the PO would have granted anyway. The offender begins to "train" the PO to experience a sense of relief when granting a request.

Figure 33.4 An Example of Grooming

The offender stands too close to you (slightly, not enough to require you to issue a command that they back up). Then, simultaneous to moving back to a more comfortable distance, he asks for a glass of water. His goal is to cause you to associate granting a request with a release of tension. If successful, the offender will make requests that get closer and closer to a moral or ethical line. Once he can get you to do something *over* the line; however, slightly, you are now compromised, an object of blackmail or worse. Hard eye-contact, shifting to friendliness, is another common grooming tactic.

6. **Guard all personal information.** As discussed previously, personal information can be used in a variety of ways. The psychopath can use such information to determine points of leverage against you. They can talk publicly about you, apparently displaying intimate knowledge of your affairs. In the worst case, such information can be used to track you down outside of your professional life, or make you fear for the safety of your friends and family.

7. **Don't get beyond the horizon line.** <u>Don't meet psychopaths alone!</u> Don't close your office door when interviewing them, and have back-up present when you conduct field visits. You are vulnerable to false accusations. You are vulnerable to manipulation when no one is present to witness and monitor the interaction with the offender. You may not even perceive manipulation is happening. Remember you are vulnerable to physical attack at any time the psychopathic offender believes that it is to their advantage, if their rage is triggered, or simply because it would be enjoyable!

8. **How to detect calculated splitting.** As stated earlier, the psychopathic offender uses gossip, rumors, misdirection, and blatant lying to set all the stakeholders involved in their supervision and treatment against each other. Regular communication and consultation with the various members of the treatment team is the best way to detect and confront splitting.

SECTION VI

Communication With Offenders That Have Severe Mental Illness or Other Conditions That Cause Severe Disability

CHAPTER 34

Overview

This section offers detailed descriptions of the most significant behaviors that mentally ill offenders may display, regardless of diagnosis. Along with each description will be suggestions for the best way to communicate with such offenders. Please note, however, that a lot of the strategies in various sections overlap. Some are generally applicable, while others are specific to only one type of behavior or symptom. Just because you might be reading about paranoia for example, doesn't mean that your paranoid offender is not also disorganized, delusional, or manic. What you are trying to develop is a range of communication tactics that cover as many situations as possible.

When people hear the term "mental illness" they think of severely impaired individuals, who may display disordered or unusual behaviors. This is a common misunderstanding. Many behaviors that are a manifestation of a mental or emotional disturbance are not particularly dramatic. Furthermore, most encounters that you will have with your mentally ill offenders are not emergencies. Nonetheless, the basic principles of communication presented here will serve you just as well with those who are manifesting a mild level of disorder, as well as those who are on the extreme end of the spectrum.

As the establishment of safety and the de-escalation of aggression are the primary purposes of this book, we focus on general patterns of offender behavior, regardless of the cause. In this vein, we can generally distinguish two levels of concern: mental illness and character disorders. By **mental illness**, we mean any mental condition that severely disturbs the offender's ability to *function* in ordinary society. **Character disorder** (also called "personality disorder") means any habitual way of relating to others that *causes significant difficulties*, sometimes for the offender and/or almost always for other people with whom they are interacting. Chapters 30 through 33 describe the paranoid, borderline and psychopathic personalities, the three types of character disordered people POs are most likely to encounter.

Mental illness, in this vein, does not only refer to such disorders as schizophrenia, bipolar disorder or depression. Character disorder does not only refer to such conditions as borderline, anti-social, histrionic or paranoid personality disorders. For example, intoxication can be considered a time limited, substance induced mental disorder or character disorder, depending on its level of severity. Beyond any medical condition, people, otherwise normal, can display acute, "out of character" behaviors, due to problems or stressors in their lives. Thus, for the sake of this discussion, substance abuse, distinct neurological disorders, as well as atypical episodes brought on by stress or other factors, all function as either a mental illness or a character disorder, depending on the offender's behavior. The cause may be relevant if making appropriate referrals for treatment; the PO, however, should most emphatically focus on the behaviors, whatever the cause.

The Undamaged Self[10]

You are walking outside on an icy winter day. You slip suddenly and spin toward the pavement. You thrust out an arm that breaks your fall. It also breaks your right wrist. Your life, for a few weeks or months, is different. Even the simplest tasks are difficult and may require assistance. Still, even though you are inconvenienced, and the injury probably changes your mood quite a bit, you are still "you," the same person as before your injury. In due time, your injuries will heal, the accident forgotten, as you continue through life. Such is not the case with mental illness.

Severe mental illness can cause mental and emotional disturbances far more profound than the temporary inconveniences brought on by physical injury. One's ability to think is distorted, and with delusions, reality is skewed. Perceptions may be bizarre, even hallucinatory. Emotions swing from high to low, or shift into realms at odds with one's immediate circumstances. <u>Mental illness is an assault on one's worldview, but there is a still a person behind the symptoms.</u> The offenders under your supervision aren't simply bundles of raw emotions or distorted cognitions. There exists an essential part of each of them untouched by their mental illness. We can choose to speak to the illness, or speak to the *person* who is ill. That core part of his or her psyche is the person we are trying to reach, not only for human reasons, but tactical reasons as well.

CHAPTER 35

Struggling in a Fog—
Dealing the With Symptoms of Disorganization

Figure 35.1 Author's Note

See Chapter 64 for a detailed discussion of de-escalation of disorganized offenders in a state of chaotic rage. See Chapter 69 for information dealing with agitated developmentally disabled offenders.

Understanding Disorganization

Disorganization is a general term used to describe what it is like when offenders can't adequately organize their thinking, perceptions, behaviors and/or emotions so that they can function well in the real world. This can include developmentally delayed offenders, profoundly psychotic offenders, those suffering from any kind of dementia or delirium, as well as those who are severely intoxicated (a chemically induced version of the same phenomenon).

Due to their cognitive limitations, developmentally disabled offenders are not skilled at problem-solving situations. Furthermore, they often lack the maturity to manage complex or frustrating situations, and the criminal justice process is nothing if not frustrating, confusing, intimidating, and frightening.

Psychotic offenders also become disorganized when they really deteriorate. Oddly enough, their delusions may have served them as an organizing principle. For example, if you believe yourself to be surrounded by enemies, or are on a mission to save the world, you have to concentrate, because of your mission, as delusional as it may be. When one becomes disorganized even one's delusions break down into chaotic thoughts, which are often manifested in incoherent speech.

> ### Figure 35.2 The Disorganized Offender
>
> You will know you are dealing with a disorganized offender because they are nearly incoherent, or it is otherwise impossible to communicate with them. They may seem to shift from one emotion to another, for no logical reason, and it is very hard, if not impossible, to hold their attention. Disorganization is an "over-arching" category. A disorganized person can be latent and/or concrete, have mood swings, paranoia, anxiety, extreme agitation, confusion, delusions, and hallucinations, and information processing problems, to name only a few. We discuss elsewhere in the book, specific strategies for these other syndromes. This chapter is concerned with the overall phenomenon of disorganization due to mental illness.

Small Bits at a Time

To better communicate with disorganized offenders, POs should divide tasks and instructions into small bits. Make sure that you are very specific concerning what you expect them to do. There is no point in being irritable. That just makes things more difficult and confusing for the disorganized offender because they usually don't know why you are upset.

POs may find it necessary to write down critical information and instructions for the disorganized offender, such as office appointments, Court hearings, therapy sessions, and the like. Additionally, POs must maintain close communication with other members of the offender's treatment team, as it is unreasonable to expect disorganized individuals to understand and comply with complex supervision stipulations without added support and direction.

Be realistic about what they can do. POs should not expect severely disorganized offenders to do something that is beyond their individual skill level, or their current mental status. Of course, the offender should still be held to a high standard, just don't make it an impossible one.

Creating Room for Success

Although supervising disorganized offenders can be difficult and often frustrating, offenders should be rewarded for positive behaviors, not just punished for negative ones. While positive reinforcement is usually rewarding to all offenders, it can mean a great deal to mentally ill and disorganized offenders. Indeed, this may be the only positive feedback they have ever received, and it will often help them adjust to community supervision in a positive manner.

Over Stimulation

Loud noises, the presence of many people (particularly if more than one is talking), too much background noise or even bright fluorescent lights, won't only be distracting, but also may further agitate the disorganized person. Consistent with both control and safety concerns, move the individual to a less stimulating environment whenever it is possible. It is particularly important with disorganized offenders that only one person speaks to them at a time.

Keep It Simple

The disorganized offender pays far more attention to non-verbal communication. Therefore, keep the emotion out of your voice, and limit your physical gestures. Self-control is particularly important when de-escalating disorganized offenders. Your sentences should be short and each should only have one "packet" of information.

Let Me Repeat Myself

When we are not understood, our usual impulse is to elaborate. We use different words, expressive hand and facial gestures, and the emotional tone of our communication intensifies. With disorganized offenders, simply repeat the same statement or question word-for-word. When their disorganization is profound, you may need to repeat information and statements several times. The aim is not to browbeat them. You should not increase your volume, shouting at them to get through. Repetition is a touchstone of stability. If you change your vocal tone, or get irritated, you will absolutely defeat the purpose of the repetition. Rolling your eyes, making side-long glances of amusement at your back-up, sighing, raising your voice, pointing, standing close to them to get their attention, snapping your fingers, or suddenly clapping, to name only a few, undermine safety, whether you are repeating the same words or not.

By repeating yourself several times, with a clear measured tone of voice, you can have the same effect on the disorganized offender as you would were you to shine a light on a footpath in the fog. In this latter example, you have shown the lost person where to put their feet. By repeating yourself and telling the offender exactly what you want them to do, you provide a verbal lifeline that they can focus on rather than the chaos that is otherwise overwhelming them.

Magical Thinking

"Magical thinking" is telling stories which you then believe. It is most common among small children, senile and demented adults, and developmentally delayed individuals. Offenders displaying magical thinking don't show the same fixed quality of delusional offenders (Chapter 39), where a fundamental truth is suddenly revealed and then locked into place their mind. Rather, the disorganized offender verbalizes his fantasies, repeats them, and then believes them to be reality.

As far as POs are concerned, you will usually observe magical thinking in a developmentally disabled offender, and is often presented as be fable-making, the kinds of stories told by very young people, either young in age or young in mind. Once you have established that a claim or statement is not true, there is little to be gained by arguing with the offender about magical thinking. Sometimes just let it go. Other times, you can say, even with a little tiredness in your voice, "I've heard that story before. You don't have to tell me again." Then, simply move on to the next topic at hand and shift the offender's focus toward the actual issues of concern regarding their treatment and supervision plan.

Figure 35.3 A Note on False Confessions by Developmentally Disabled Individuals

Important: Research on false admissions to crimes reveals that a large number of such confessions are made by developmentally disabled individuals. The developmentally disabled offender may do something similar with their PO, when feeling emotionally pressured or if they are trying to impress or please you. You will get the most reliable information from developmentally disabled offenders when they are calm and feel safe.

Figure 35.4 Dealing With a Disorganized Offender

You will know you are dealing with a disorganized offender when he/she is:

1. Nearly incoherent, or otherwise impossible to communicate with;
2. Shifting from one emotion to another with no logical reason;
3. Distracted and you cannot hold their attention;
4. Acting in a bizarre or chaotic manner.

When dealing with a disorganized offender you should:

- Divide tasks into small bits.
- Give simple, specific instructions.
- Be realistic about what the person can and can't do.
- Repeat your instructions rather than elaborate on them and don't change your vocal tone.
- Don't argue with magical thinking—redirect them to discussing what, if anything is emergent.
- Allow only one person to speak to the disorganized offender.
- Whenever possible, minimize environmental distractions—the TV in the background, other people talking, and bright lights, etc.

CHAPTER 36

Latency—Dropping Stones
Down a "Well"

Latency is a behavior that is often a manifestation of disorganization, but because of both its significance and its confusing nature, we have chosen to discuss it as an entity of its own. Latency is a behavior in which offenders respond to communication in a much delayed manner. You ask a question, and they talk to themselves quietly as they puzzle out what you might be saying. Perhaps instead, they don't even make eye-contact, and engage in odd movements. Some latent offenders may simply stare away, a vacuous look on their faces.

Figure 36.1 How to Recognize Latency

You will recognize latency when the offender to whom you are speaking not only delays his or her answers for a long time, but also when they do reply, their communication is somewhat odd and disjointed. You will notice that they do not really responding to the questions asked. This is different from being silent or defying you. You get the sense that they are not "there," that it is about something going on inside of them, and not about you at all.

Imagine your words to be like a stones dropping into a well. If things go as expected, you hear a splash as each stone hits the water. Now, imagine the latent mind like an old well with bricks sticking out, and a tangle of tree roots halfway down. Each stone hits the roots and bounces off a brick one after the other. This time, you don't hear a splash. You hear nothing. So you start throwing more stones, one after another. You now have any number of stones bouncing around, colliding into each other, adding to your frustration and their confusion, without the first stone ever reaching the bottom of the well. All that is happened with the latent person is that they get more confused and overwhelmed. In other words, adding more words doesn't enhance communication with latent people.

Figure 36.2 Example of Latency

The PO comes upon an offender on his caseload, in front of the offender's residence:

- **PO.** "Why are you tying yourself to the railing?" (*30 seconds pass with the latent man standing and staring at the ground, frozen.*)
- **PO.** "Why are you tying yourself to the railing?"
- **Offender.** (*The mentally ill man slowly raises his head, and his eyes vacant, slowly He says,*) "Uh, rail roaded." (*He then resumes his tying himself to the railing with thin string.*)
- **PO.** "I can call for help so you can go to the hospital. I know there is someone there that is able to help you."
- **Offender.** (*The mentally ill offender stops tying himself, his hands still holding the string in mid-knot. His lips move as if he is talking to himself. He raises his eyes, lowers them, and raises them again. He says*), "Don't take me steal me." (*He then resumes his activity without eye contact.*)

Note the PO's exemplary patience. This contact is not a failure. The officer has ascertained that the individual is so profoundly ill that he is unable to communicate even his identity. That the officer is calm probably keeps the offender from becoming fearful or combative in response.

Coping with Latency: Keep Things Simple

Although communicating with a latent offender can be frustrating, and often time consuming, the PO should remain calm. Indeed, any frustration or anger displayed by the PO will only further confuse them. Keep your sentences and instructions short yet direct, and minimize the use of qualifiers, such as "you might" "maybe" "kind of," etc., that you ordinarily put in your sentences. Officers should also try to minimize the use of hand gestures or changing facial expressions. This does not mean you should speak robotically, but simplicity is best.

It is totally useless to try to "get through to them" by yelling. All this does is drive them further into the latent state, as they get more frightened, overwhelmed or confused by the irate PO yelling incomprehensible things at them.

Latent offenders usually don't need things explained in further detail; they just don't "get it" the first time. Say the same thing again and again. This is like somehow throwing the same stone down the well over again, reinforcing the original. Rather than adding a new stone, you have added weight to the one already there. Now that stone can get through the roots and bricks and hit bottom.

Figure 36.3 How to Speak to a Latent Offender

You will find the following points helpful when speaking to a latent offender:

- Keep your sentences short.
- Don't change your vocal tone.
- Repeat the instructions using the same words and the same tone of voice.
- Pause between sentences, giving the offender time to process what you have said.
- Try to get the offender to repeat back your instructions (No guarantees on this item!)

CHAPTER 37

Withdrawal from Intoxicating Substances

Figure 37.1 IMPORTANT NOTE: The Question of Dual Diagnosis

Given all the attention paid to the subject, the reader may question why we have not devoted a large section specifically to the behaviors of "dual-diagnosis" offenders (those with both substance abuse and mental health issues) as a separate concern. There is no doubt whatsoever, that dual diagnosis can profoundly affect every aspect of an offender's life, including their success or failure in a community corrections setting. Substance abuse makes it much harder to heal from or even manage mental illness, and mental illness makes it much harder to recover from substance abuse.

This book, however, is concerned with the issues of safety and de-escalation from extreme states. Imagine all the descriptions of behavior necessary to distinguish between, for example, a solvent inhaling offender with bipolar disorder, a marijuana smoking offender with social phobia, and a schizophrenic who injects a mixture of cocaine and heroin. To be sure, each and all of these concerns are relevant when it comes to treatment and, as far as the PO is concerned, finding resources to best help the offender. The only thing that we are focusing on however, is behavior. Whatever substances they may have ingested, whatever illness or syndrome they may be suffering from, we are concerned with the behaviors that they are displaying. This is the only data relevant for crisis intervention. <u>In a crisis, deal with the behavior, not the cause.</u>

Many mentally ill offenders actively use or are addicted to drugs and/or alcohol. These offenders are "dual diagnosed;" that is, they have been diagnosed as having a mental health disorder as well as substance abuse issues. Obviously, the abuse of drugs and/or alcohol can have a negative effect on mentally ill offenders, which not only complicates their recovery, but also can be life threatening if the offender experiences a severe reaction brought on by mixing drugs and/or alcohol with their prescribed medications. Others develop conditions (amphetamine psychosis, for one example) that function exactly like mental illness, although the primary cause of their illness is different.

Although offenders are advised by their doctors, their therapists, and of course, their POs to abstain from drugs and alcohol, especially in combination with their prescribed mental health medications, many fail in this regard. Complicating matters is the fact that some offenders may have been abusing drugs and/or alcohol for many years before they were even diagnosed with a mental health disorder. Breaking the cycle of addiction for long-term drug users, while attempting to get them to address their underlying mental health issues, can be a Sisyphean task,[11] where you work like that mythic figure, pushing the offender up the slope of addiction treatment only to have him or her fall down the slope of decompensation into mental illness, and then when you push them back up *that* slope so that their mental illness is under some control, they relapse again on drugs.

Unfortunately, certain offenders enjoy the effects of combining illicit substances with their prescribed medications, such as opiate abusers enhancing their "high" by taking the prescription medication Klonopin. Other offenders may be too addled by drug and alcohol use to remember to take prescribed medications, while others simply prefer the drug-induced state of consciousness to that of being properly medicated. In any event, POs are encouraged to not only obtain a working knowledge of the various psychotropic medications which their offender's may be prescribed, but also to familiarize themselves with the wide array of illicit substances and prescription medications used (and abused) by many offenders. Being familiar with the symptoms of drug use, either independently or in conjunction with prescription medications, will better prepare the PO to de-escalate an offender who is going through withdrawal.

Withdrawal is a Medical Emergency

First and foremost, alcohol and drug withdrawal is a medical emergency. There is no specific withdrawal anger or rage. Use whatever tactics necessary to de-escalate and control them, based on their behavior. The PO should summon medical attention immediately, and then focus on keeping the offender calm while waiting for medical assistance.

Offenders in withdrawal are often in pain or feeling quite ill. They are also frightened or irritable, and very much focused, in a completely selfish way, on getting their needs met. This may include a high level of resistance to seeking medical attention, or assurances by the offender that they are well enough to be left alone. Of course, the offender often merely wants the PO to leave their residence or terminate the office interview, so they can go out and acquire more drugs. The signs of withdrawal can include:

- **Unstable coordination.** Try to get offender to sit or lie down for their safety.
- **Restlessness and agitation.** Try to reduce any stimulating input.
- **Unpredictable and sudden actions.** Keep your movements calm and slow so that you don't elicit a startle reflex on their part, which can easily turn into an attack.
- **Slurred or incoherent speech.** Speak to them in a calm, quiet voice and make an extra effort to understand what they are saying. Provide short explanations.
- **Abnormally rigid muscles.** This type of offender will present with tense muscles.
- **Being argumentative and demanding.** Try to redirect them or de-escalate depending on the mode of anger or rage they exhibit.

Figure 37.2 Calming Offenders in Withdrawal

Be calm and firm. Redirect them when they get very demanding. Reassure them that help is on the way. You are simply trying to delay things until the ambulance and/or back-up arrives. To reiterate, this is a medical emergency. A person in withdrawal may die without help.

There is no specific withdrawal rage. They will display terrified, chaotic, hot, cold, or predatory rage (Section XI). Use the tactics that best fit the mode of rage they are experiencing.

CHAPTER 38

Psychosis: Delusions and Hallucinations

Whatever the diagnosis (i.e., schizophrenia, bipolar disorder, trauma based, depression, drug induced), the syndrome of psychosis is typified by delusions and/or hallucinations. A **delusion** is first and foremost a disturbance in cognition. It is a belief that does not fit reality. A **hallucination** is an unreal perception through any of the senses.

What is a delusion?

A delusion is usually referred to as a belief that does not conform to reality. Actually, it's a lot more than that. People from different cultures have different beliefs. Shared cultural beliefs, however, are not delusional, even if you can't conceive how others could see the world as they do. Sometimes, there is nothing remarkable about the delusional belief, except that it is not true. For example, everyone knows the FBI follows people. The question in this case would be, "Is the FBI following this particular offender?" Lots of people have eccentric beliefs: unconventional religious rites, non-traditional dietary and health habits, a belief in aliens, crop circles, or telepathy, etc. Some of these are possibly *your* beliefs: they are eccentric to others, but not to you. Unusual ideas and beliefs are not necessarily delusional.

A delusion is a fixed belief that is not reality based. It may not be strange or weird. It is definitely not true, either in total, or it is distorted. A fixed belief is one that it is like being a member of a one-person cult. All the confusing thoughts the offender may have had, all their worries, prayers, fantasies, or ideas suddenly coalesce into **BELIEF**. Such beliefs are unshakable, inarguable, and unaltered by conflicting evidence.

Types of Delusions

The following is a list of the different types of delusions:

- **Grandiose.** An offender with this type of delusion believes that they have been appointed to a special mission, that they have extraordinary or unusual powers, or are godlike, remarkable beings.
- **Religious.** Often linked with grandiose delusions, an offender may become preoccupied with religion, focusing all their attention on their beliefs, which may be self-made or associated with mainstream doctrines. To reiterate a previous point, it is not the religious belief itself that makes it delusional, because religion is based on faith, not knowledge. It is the locked-in quality of the belief. To be sure, this is a subject of debate. A cult belief functions as a mass delusion. Different from a religion, one is locked in by the cult. In a religious delusion, one is locked into the belief by one's own mind.

- **Jealous.** The offender may believe, against all evidence, that their partner is unfaithful to them. Jealous delusions surpass the almost always irrational nature of ordinary jealousy. The jealous delusional offender concocts infidelity out of the slightest glance, a change in clothing, or a five-minute delay in returning home, etc. Perpetrators of domestic violence, particularly those with a paranoid or borderline character structure (Chapters 30 & 31), often manifest this type of delusional psychosis in periods of stress.

- **Delusional stalking (erotomania).** The offender may believe that another person is in love with them, is married to them, or has been somehow designated as theirs, whether they know it or not. Special requirements for communicating with those who display erotomaniac stalking behaviors will be discussed below.

- **Persecutory (paranoia).** A paranoid offender may believe that people, institutions, or other powers have hostile intentions toward them or have committing evil actions against them, that others are sending energy toward them, thinking about them, talking about them, or looking at them with malevolent intent. In addition to general strategies for managing any psychotic offender (Chapter 39), there are specific strategies for communicating with a paranoid offender (Chapter 30).

What are hallucinations?

An offender may hallucinate, but realize that it is a disturbance of perception rather than reality. Hallucinations are perceptions through any of the five senses that don't conform to reality. Hallucinations are often, but not always, accompanied by delusions. It is possible to perceive a hallucination, but be neither delusional nor psychotic. For example, people suffering from several days of jet-lag may complain of hearing voices. However, they are quite aware that the voices are caused by sleep-deprivation, and pay them no more heed than people do when they have a song "stuck" in their head.

Types of Hallucinations

The following is a list of the different types of hallucinations:

- **Auditory.** There are two levels of hallucinations perceived through hearing. The first level is *auditory distortion.* One mishears what is said, something that is frequently part of persecutory delusions. For example, a paranoid offender is sitting near someone in a restaurant who says, "Do you want the chicken or the ribs?" They hear, "Let's get this chicken in the ribs." The second level is true *auditory hallucinations.* Close your eyes when someone speaks to you. Do you still hear their voice? Of course you do. When offenders have an auditory hallucination the voices are equally real. This is not mere imagination. PET scans reveal that the neurons of the brain of the offender experiencing auditory hallucinations are "firing" just as those of a healthy person do when they actually hear something. The psychotic offender actually *hears* the voices. That is why you can't simply say, "The voice isn't real;" that makes as much sense to them as someone saying your foot isn't real. <u>Paranoid offenders, in particular, often display a "listening attitude.</u> They enter a situation that evokes their paranoia, and expect to be victimized, accused, talked about, and/or assaulted. Then, they either mishear people based on what they expect to hear, or in more severe cases, actually hear hallucinatory voices uttering just what they expected or feared (Arieti, 1974).

- **Visual.** Offenders may experience ***visual distortions***. The distorted visual image appears to move, melt, emerge toward them, or even speak. Think of a Salvador Dali painting in which the objects melt and flow. The second level is true ***visual hallucinations***, in which objects or beings appear that no one else can see.

- **Olfactory.** This is sometimes a result or symptom of brain injury, as the part of the brain that detects odor(s) is at the front of the head, a frequent target of injury. If a previously non-psychotic offender complains of hallucinatory smells, immediately get them checked medically. This is often an emergent situation that, if not addressed, can result in permanent brain damage. Other offenders, without head injuries and purely psychotic, can get focused on their own body smells, and believe, for example, that they are rotting away. Other times, they believe they can smell poison gas seeping through the walls.

- **Tactile.** These are sensations felt within the body. The sensation of bugs crawling on the skin is a frequent side effect of such drugs as methamphetamine or cocaine. Tactile hallucinations can also be a side effect of the offender's psychiatric medication. A medical doctor should always check this symptom. Anybody experiencing tactile hallucinations should be regarded as a high risk of assault, first of all because they are very likely on stimulant drugs and secondly, because the sensation is maddening – think of the worst rash or prickly heat you've ever experienced multiplied times twenty.

The Torment of Hallucinations

Hallucinations torment their victims in a variety of ways:

- For unknown reasons, hallucinated voices are almost always cruel. Offenders can be ordered to do awful or degrading things, or they may simply hear awful sounds and ugly demeaning words. Visual hallucinations can be as haunting as ghosts. Olfactory hallucinations are often foul, and tactile hallucinations are almost always very unpleasant sensations.

- Offenders try to tell others what they perceive, but their experience is denied over and over again. They can be teased or laughed at. Ironically, the people they tell often torment them in ways similar to the torment of the hallucinations.

- Psychotic offenders find that their worldview is called into question every day. They don't know what is real and what is not. Imagine reaching to pick up your coffee, and not knowing if the liquid will disappear from the cup, or if the handle will suddenly twine around your finger like a little snake. Imagine this is true of every object in your life. In such circumstances, the offender finds it difficult to trust anything at all.

CHAPTER 39

Communication With Offenders Experiencing Delusions and Hallucinations

Disengage

It can be very draining to talk with a delusional offender. Like a cultist trying to convert you to their group, the offender may try to convince you that what they believe is real. They may insist that you accept their beliefs, or even more problematic, insist that you *do* believe, but simply won't admit it. They become focused on debating your resistance, or furious that you deny what is, to them, absolutely true.

There is often no good reason to continue such a discussion. Delusions are not like some sort of backed-up fluid that you vent and drain away. The more the delusional offender talks about it, the more preoccupied he or she becomes, and more agitated as well. While delusional offenders may feel locked in their inner world and desperate to communicate what they are experiencing, discussion and argument seem to cement the delusions even further.

Figure 39.1 Rule #1: Disengage

There are many occasions when nothing at all can be accomplished by talking about delusions or hallucinations. When there is no emergency, and no need for investigation or information gathering, disengage.

Islands of Sanity

Imagine being dropped overboard into the ocean. It is cold and rough among the waves, and there are all sorts of sea-life that demand your attention, everything from sharks to jellyfish. There seems to be no way to escape, and it is so overwhelming that you can't take your mind off of it.

Even in the ocean, however, there are small patches of land: islands. If you can only get to them, you can put your feet on solid ground. For psychotic offenders, too, there are "islands of sanity," areas of their lives where they are not delusional. They may be convinced, for example, that someone is poisoning their food and only canned goods are safe to eat, or that someone is beaming messages directly into their brain. But when you bring up the subject of football, and the two of you begin talking about how the Steelers' demolished yet another opponent, the offender takes his mind off his delusions, and for a brief moment, has a moment of respite. If you steer conversations (beyond, of course, the requirements of the

Court) toward these islands of sanity, they may begin to see their PO as the most stable person in their life, someone with whom they can have moments of clarity and peace.

Figure 39.2 Rule #2: Move Toward an Island of Sanity

Pay attention to subjects where the offender is not delusional, so-called "islands of sanity," and whenever possible, direct your conversation there, rather than allowing it to focus on delusional subjects. Make links, when you can, with other subjects that are also not tainted by delusions. Think of yourself as expanding the size of the "land-mass," making an area where it's predictable and safe. If the offender gets stuck within his or her delusions, you may find that changing the subject requires real finesse. Nonetheless, do so whenever you can, because talking about delusions makes it worse.

NOTE: These "islands of sanity" are not necessarily "nice" subjects. One of the authors worked with a very dangerous man for nine months and the only subjects about that he was not floridly psychotic were bar fights and motorcycles. It was safer talking about the sound of a cue ball impacting on someone's skull than what he had for dinner or what his childhood was like.

Threat Assessment: When *should* you talk about the delusions or hallucinations?

Some of most dangerous mentally ill offenders are those whom you see over and over again. They frequently decompensate, or go off their medications; therefore, it is necessary to do a brief threat assessment every time you see them.

Imagine a delusional offender who is sure that she is the Archangel Michael. If you recall this biblical story, Michael, the righteous sword of the Lord, casts Satan out of Heaven. Further imagine that this woman believes she perceives Satan's work in the behavior of people around her. Based on her past history, you must intervene when she gets preoccupied with her delusions, because some time ago, seeing evidence of Satan's corruption among her neighbors, she tried to acquire a sword at a pawn shop. Had she not praised the dealer for his help in cutting Satan out of the hearts of the children, the police would not have been called, and the family down the street could have been maimed or killed.

Therefore, whenever this woman begins to talk about God, angels, Satan, or anything similar, it is a good idea to ask questions about that which she is preoccupied. Some questions you could ask her follow:
- Mrs. Hampton, are you telling me that you think you have seen Satan? Where?
- Why do you think that this is Satan's work?
- Do you think you should do anything about this?
- What do you think you should do?

If Mrs. Hampton's answers are bland and not aggressive, at the right moment change the subject to an "island of sanity." If her answers seem to manifest dangerous ideation, then immediate action may be required. For example, if she were to say, "Don't call me Mrs. Slut Whore-of-Babylon-Hampton! I'm Michael, the Lord's most beloved angel. Satan will have no place on this earth when I take my righteous sword in my strong right arm!" You will need to take action immediately.

Dangerous answers are an alarm call to get help, and the PO should alert the other members of the treatment team, conduct a search of her residence for weapons, or perhaps take her into custody for obvious safety reasons, and stabilize her in jail. She may have to have her medications adjusted, or need to stay in a treatment facility for an extended period of time. Whatever the appropriate response, the PO must act when she is acting or thinking dangerously. And consider this, an offender who believes herself to be the mightiest angel in Heaven and on a mission from God is likely to object when you try to take her into secure custody. Be very alert to danger!

Figure 39.3 Rule #3: Talk About the Delusions to Assess Risk

Talk about the delusions as a means of threat assessment. Ask direct questions, particularly in regard to the person's intention to hurt him/ herself or others. When contacting such an individual bring up the issue of concern yourself, if they don't do so on their own, just to see if they have become seriously delusional again. For example, "The last time we talked, you told me about the Angel Michael and Satan. Are you worried about the Devil today?" Remember, the distinction between this rule and the previous two is that in this case, you are assessing risk, not just indulging in a conversation about offender's preoccupations.

Don't Agree: At Least Most of the Time

It might seem to be easiest to take the line of least resistance—simply agree with the delusions, or pretend that you, too, perceive the hallucinations rather than get caught in arguments with a mentally ill offender about reality. However, there are a number of problems in doing so. Some of these problems are listed below:

- Agreement with delusions and/or hallucinations will entrench them even more deeply into the offender's belief system.
- Agreement can also lead to the PO being *incorporated* into the delusions and hallucinations. Sometimes this can be merely wearying, as the offender wants to talk incessantly about their delusions with the only person who seems to share their point of view. This can also become dangerous if the offender decides that you are in collusion with their perceived enemies
- Just because someone is mentally ill doesn't mean they are stupid or naïve. They may realize that you are simply pretending, and regard you as either scamming them or making fun of them.

In almost all circumstances, do NOT agree with delusions or hallucinations.

Figure 39.4 An Exception to the Rule

Sometimes the mentally ill offender will incorporate their PO into their delusions in a positive way. For example, an offender believes he has a secret team of advisors who tell him what to do. Recently, he announced that his PO was on the team, and he had therefore decided to listen to what she said and follow her advice. Don't try to "prime the pump" by claiming a positive role in their delusions, or simply accept it if the offender so "appoints" you. Rather, consider this development from all sides. It may be worth consulting with the treatment team or a mental health professional. You have to assess if there is any risk that the delusion might "mutate" in a dangerous way. If, in your considered judgment it does make tactical sense, the most you should do is accept this information silently. Do not say it yourself. In the example above, you might reply, "Well, all I know is that if the doctors think you should take your medications, then I think that's a very good idea." In other words, go with the flow.

Figure 39.5 Rule #4: Don't Agree With the Delusions

In almost all circumstances, don't agree with the delusions. At most, if you have a consensus that it is worth the risk, passively accept their perception in the interest of their complying with something that will keep everyone safer.

Don't Disagree: At Least Most of the Time

The problem with arguing with delusional or hallucinating people is that you are telling them that their perceptions are lying to them. If they had any trust in you before, it is unlikely that telling them that the world as they see it is not real will improve that rapport.

Sometimes, however, a delusional offender may ask, or even plead with you, for disagreement because they don't want to believe what their delusions seem to tell them. At other times, a hallucinating offender can make a tenuous distinction between real perceptions and hallucinations and will ask if you think something hallucinated is real. In these cases, *when you have been invited*, you may state that not only do you not perceive or believe the hallucination or delusion, but you also don't think it is real.

Figure 39.6 Rule #5: Don't Disagree—At Least Most of the Time

Don't engage in arguments about whether the psychotic offender's perceptions are real. However, if they <u>ask</u> you for a "reality check," then you can state that you don't believe that the delusional belief is correct or the hallucination is real. In this case, you are helping the offender understand that what he or she perceives is not the "rule" of the world.

Important Exceptions to the "Do not Disagree" Rule: Delusional Stalking

Stalking delusions are dangerous because they involve another person as the victim.[12] In addition, the offender is often possessed of an absolutely entitled sense of their right to approach or harass the victim, either in person, or as is becoming more common, through the use of electronic media such as text messages, email, or social networking websites. Such unwelcomed advances may be criminal in nature (especially if the offender is already under supervision for a crime against the same victim), and the offender must be confronted about their behavior immediately.

For offenders convicted of stalking, harassment, domestic violence, sexual assault, or similar offenses, their supervision plan will likely include a "no victim contact" stipulation, giving the PO a solid legal basis for any necessary violation proceedings, including the arrest and detention of the offender for continued contact with the victim. Public safety, i.e., the safety of the victim, is the PO's paramount concern, and officers must act quickly in response to calls from the victim reporting harassing or threatening behavior.

In lieu of any evidence that the offender is indeed contacting the victim, or their delusions are centered on an unknown or fanciful victim (a movie or TV star for example) POs must calmly, but directly, inform the offender that the subject of their delusions is not destined for, in love with, or otherwise involved with them. Calmly and directly tell the offender they have no right to the victim they stalk. Tell the delusional stalker that stalking is a crime and tell them they will be arrested (other types of stalkers know it is a crime and a type of emotional terrorism, and do it anyway, but the delusional stalker may honestly believe that what they are doing is right).

If the offender threatens or hints at committing an act of violence against the subject of their delusions, the PO may wish to conduct a search of the offender's residence to locate any weapons or other contraband, as well as evidence that they may be keeping the victim under surveillance. At the very least, the PO should contact the other members of the treatment team to alert them of the offender's delusional thoughts and behaviors. In the event that the PO becomes the subject of an offender's delusions, the same precautions must be taken; however, the supervision of the offender should be transferred to another officer, with a strict no contact stipulation imposed upon the offender.

Figure 39.7 Rule #6: Exception—Disagree with the Delusion of Erotomania
Calmly and directly tell the delusional offender they have no right to the victim they stalk. Define to them that what they are doing is stalking, and if you are not able to arrest them, do whatever you can to ensure the safety of the victim, including consultation with experts in threat assessment of such cases, the possibility of a forensic mental health evaluation, and the establishment of a safety plan with the victim.

Differentiation: Distinguish Between Your World and Theirs

Delusional beliefs are nearly inescapable. When an offender experiencing psychotic symptoms attempts to talk about their delusions, they are often brushed off, minimized, or even ridiculed. Of course, POs should never act so callously or dismissively with an offender, although as we just learned, you can't simply agree, or disagree, with them either. How, then, can POs respond in a respectful way to their offender's delusional thinking, while also trying to get the offender to recognize the distinction between your world and theirs?

Differentiate yourself from them. To differentiate is to perceive or express a difference. The authors mean that you should acknowledge an offender's perceptions and beliefs, while also informing them that, although you don't share their perceptions, you are not arguing that theirs are invalid, unrealistic, or fantastical. You are, however, attempting to have the offender also concede that other viewpoints do exist. Here are some examples:

1. Alice, I see the table and chairs, the pictures on the wall, and the books on the floor, just like you do. But you see something that I don't. I don't see a vat of boiling oil in the corner of the room. No, I'm not saying you don't see it. I believe you do. I'm just saying that it is something you see that I don't. I don't know why, but that's the way it is.

2. Sal, I only hear two voices in this room, yours and mine. I don't hear a woman's voice at all. What do you hear her say?

3. Jamey, I know about the Democrats and the Republicans. I've never heard of the Illuminated Ones. I'm not arguing with you here. I'm just saying that I've never heard of them, so I'm not the person to talk about them.

Remember, the point here is not to convince the offender that their delusions are not real, or even that they are wrong. Basically, differentiation helps you keep the lines of communication open. Think of two people from different cultures, trying to explain what it is like to live in their respective worlds, or even two beings from different planets. If the mentally ill offender finds him/herself shut-down or discounted when he tries to talk about perceptions or beliefs, it is very unlikely that he/she will be open about any other area of concern to the PO. In some circumstances, you can act in concert with their belief without endorsing it. For example, "I can't see the laser beams, but I know lasers don't pass through solid objects. Maybe you will feel safer sitting in that ambulance over there."[13]

Figure 39.8 Rule #7: Differentiate

Give the offender the "right" to their own perceptions and beliefs. Inform them that while you don't perceive what they do, you are not arguing with them about what *they* see or believe. In some cases, take their delusions into account without agreeing with them. Example: "I don't see any razor blades on the tree branches, but if I did, I wouldn't walk around in the park after dark where I couldn't see what I might run into. I'd stay home when the sun went down."

Steam Valve When the Pressure is Too Great

Some offenders, either psychotic or manic (Chapter 40) are so full of things to say, think, or feel that they seem like they are going to explode from the pressure. Their speech can become pressured as well. Words burst out of them in a cascade. Sometimes they make sense, but they totally dominate the "air time" in the room, talking over other people. Even if there is a task to be done, they can't focus and they make it nearly impossible for you to focus as well. Other times, they make no sense whatsoever. Their words may sound like poetry as they link words by sound, not by meaning. They may jump from idea to idea, in what are called "loose associations," or "tangential thinking."

Obviously however, you can't partake in a one-sided conversation where the offender does all of the talking. The PO must regain control of the interview. Sometimes the PO simply has to say, "You have talked enough for awhile. We need to move on to other matters." For some offenders this works quite well; it is honest, it is direct, and it sets a limit.

At other times, one needs to let out a little pressure like opening a valve in a steam pipe. Then you take over saying one portion of what you have to say:

1. Put out a hand, palm down, fingers curved at waist level to interrupt them. If they do not perceive it, put up both hands, using a little drama in your facial expression to get their attention and interrupt.
2. Let them speak for a little while about their preoccupations, and in the process, they have let out a little pressure, just like you would with a steam valve.
3. Sum up what they said in a sentence or two. Put a little energy in your voice to prove that you are really "with" them. Then, ask or say something, getting either some compliance or a bit of information. "That is serious. Politics right now are terrible! You HAVE to tell me more about the left-wing conspiracy, but before you do, did you attend your treatment session last night?"
4. In return, let them return to their cascade of ideas, allowing a little more pressure to be released.
5. Once again, firmly interrupt, and ask the next question or get agreement on the next item on your list.

In essence, you sum up what they said to prove you were listening, and *then* ask your question or make your statement. "Steam-valving" is for the purpose of letting the offender say enough of what is pressuring him internally so that he does not fight you for the conversational floor.

Figure 39.9 Example of the Steam-Valve Technique

Offender. I was looking outside my window at the birdfeeder, and it was covered with gold finches. The lemony yellow just burned my eyes so badly I closed the curtains. My eyes were burned by the fiery birds.

PO. *(Interrupting firmly)* "Charles, I want to hear more about those birds. I haven't seen any goldfinches this year. But first, did you call your psychiatrist for an appointment?

Offender. Yes, I did, behind the closed drapes, where the birds couldn't burn my eyes out. I called and talked to a very nice nurse. They have a sound that is piercing to the brain, and a single glance can burn your eyes to a crisp—the birds, not the nurses.

PO. I can see you are worried about your eyes. That's why you have the sunglasses, huh? I want you to tell me how the sunglasses are working, but first, what day is your appointment?

Offender. It's on a Thursday, but I don't know when, or what time. I'm burning among the birds, you see, with their lemony scalding flame.

As you can see, the PO was able to get the information that the offender actually did make an appointment, but he doesn't know when. At this point, the PO can call to confirm the time. As you can see, it is pretty likely that this individual needs to have his medication levels adjusted!

This steam valve technique is useful with offenders whose speech is a cascade of words, ideas—often tangential or delusional. You listen, and then, tactfully but firmly, interrupt. Ask a question or interject a statement, get a response, and then let them return to their cascade of words. Listen a bit, and then interrupt again. Remember, you must show in your response/interruption that you have been listening to what they say.

Figure 39.10 Rule #8: Steam-valve

This is useful with offenders whose speech is a cascade of words and ideas that are either all over the place (zigzag) or delusional. Listen and then interrupt. Sum up what they said, and tell them you want to hear more, but before they do, you have a question (or instruction) for them. Then let them return to their cascade of words. Listen a bit more, then interrupt again. Continue with multiple sequences of release of pressure, interruptions and questions until you get the information you need.

Physical Space, Physical Contact, and the Use of the Eyes with Psychotic Offenders

Concerns about eye contact and physical contact are incredibly important in regard to offenders with psychosis. Even more than in ordinary circumstances, be acutely aware when you are inadvertently "pressuring" the psychotic offender by standing or sitting too close to them. Consider this *your* responsibility. Don't expect them to necessarily tell you. The first sign that you are too close, if you are not paying attention, may be an attack, as the psychotic offender believes they must protect themselves from your "invasion."

Other psychotic offenders are not aware of personal space and stand or sit too close to you. Firmly, without aggression or heat, tell them to move back. "Monty, I really want to hear what you are saying. But you are standing too close to me. Take four big steps back and tell me more."

For many psychotic offenders, direct, sustained eye contact seems to pierce them to the brain. It's as if you can read their thoughts. Other mentally ill offenders can misinterpret direct eye contact as aggressive, threatening, or seductive. Therefore, if they are uncomfortable with being looked at directly (you will know it!); occasionally "touch base" by making brief eye contact, then ease your eyes away and then back again. Of course, never take your eyes off of the offender so that you are unaware of any precursors to assault. Furthermore, if the psychotic offender becomes agitated or aggressive, here, you must make direct eye contact to establish control.

Figure 39.11 Rule #9: Body Spacing, Body Contact, and Eye Contact

Be aware of physical spacing—don't stand too close, and don't accept the offender standing too close to you. Most psychotic offenders are made anxious by direct eye contact, experiencing it as either a threat or a challenge. Limit eye contact when it is not emergent so that you have to establish control through command presence, a situation where direct eye contact is a necessity.

CHAPTER 40

Welcome to the Rollercoaster:
Tactics for Dealing With Symptoms of Mania

Mania is a state of high energy. Manic offenders need little sleep, and can be excited, grandiose, agitated, or irritable. They often have flights of fancy, which can be either creative or completely irrational. Their speech is often pressured. Not only is it rapid, but there is a sense that they have more to say than they can get out.

They are usually extremely confident, even to the degree of believing themselves to be invulnerable. Manic offenders are often selfish. They feel wonderful, and their own needs and desires are the only things that matter. Their judgment can be extremely poor and impulsive, and they engage in behaviors that can put them or others at risk.

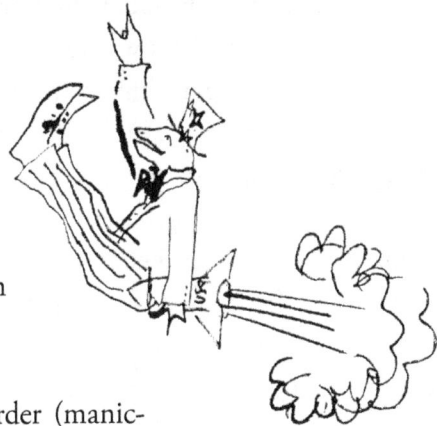

The manic state is associated most commonly with bipolar disorder (manic-depression), in which periods of mania are one-half of a cycle in which the other is periods of depression. Some drugs can also cause manic episodes (particularly stimulant drugs such as amphetamine or cocaine), and not infrequently, mania can also be a side effect of psychiatric medications.

Figure 40.1 Beyond Mania is Chaos

Offenders with different brain malfunctions can have periods of agitation that may look very much like mania, but this kind of delirium is usually more extreme than the classic manic state. Such offenders are usually quite confused and disorganized. On the other hand, manic offenders can get so agitated, called "manic excitement" that they shift into a delirium state. All such individuals are de-escalated using the strategies described in Chapter 64 on Chaotic Rage.

Manic offenders are particularly vulnerable because they are most susceptible to making harmful decisions when they feel wonderful. Imagine the best spring day of your life. The sky is blue, birds are singing, and a gentle breeze keeps things just cool enough to be comfortable. You wake up and literally jump out of bed, happy to be alive. You have so much energy that it feels like there is champagne in your veins. You know you will make some new friends today, so you are going to go to the park, the club, the bar, whatever, and just enjoy life. Imagine that feeling day-after-day, multiplied by ten or twentyfold. Can you see how easy it would be to begin to make unwise choices, how your confidence could lead you to, for example, hijack that freight train because you always wanted to be an engineer?[14]

When you feel this good, it seems like a good idea to feel *even better*. Thus, manic offenders very often want to party. Drugs and alcohol are very tempting, spending money to buy anything and everything you want leads to credit cards run to the max, and often the energy turns sexual and the manic person gets involved with people who may be inappropriate for them or even dangerous. On the flip side, manic offenders, stimulant drug users or not, sometimes try to calm themselves with other drugs: barbiturates, heroin, and alcohol. Alcohol can have a "paradoxical effect" on some manic offenders, further exciting rather than sedating them.[15]

Manic offenders often talk in rapid cascades of words, a waterfall of ideas leaping from one area to another. Sometimes you can follow their thoughts, although they are speaking very rapidly, but at other times, they leap and zigzag, making connections that seem to have little or no meaning. In extreme manic states, offenders can become psychotic, displaying, in addition to their mania some or all of the symptoms of grandiose, persecutory, paranoid, and religious delusions that any other psychotic offender might.

Some manic offenders become very irritable. They can have hair-trigger tempers, and may also be provocative. Rather than merely being reactive, some will aggressively tease and taunt other people. It may seem to be in good fun, at first, but it goes too far—way too far. Others may simply try to pick a fight. Because manic offenders can easily become angry or even violent, the authors recommend strongly that POs familiarize themselves with the latter sections in this book concerning the de-escalation of anger and rage.

Brittle Grandiosity

Manic offenders can act as if they don't have a care in the world. They spin ideas, one after another, and expect both agreement and admiration. They seem utterly self-confident. However, truly self-confident individuals are resilient; unfair criticisms seem to bounce off them. They can respond either with a gracious laugh or a dignified response. Think of manic grandiosity, however, as a fragile structure, like a tower made of spun sugar. It glitters, it glows, and it is huge! But tap the wrong strut or beam and the entire tower falls down in shards.

- If you criticize offenders who are manic, they can experience your criticism as a personal attack, and from giddy happiness, they suddenly turn on you in rage.
- If you tease them about their somewhat irrational ideas, try to joke around with them, or laugh at something funny that they said, they easily misinterpret these, too, as an attack, thinking you are making fun of them.

In other words, consider the manic flight of words to be a kind of hysteria. Even when they appear happy it is as if they are on a giddy flight, hanging onto a helium balloon. It certainly is thrilling—until they look down! Miscalculated teasing or criticism is experienced as if you are poking at the balloon with a needle.

Figure 40.2 WARNING: They may be acting like comedians, but they are not trying to be funny!

One of the writers recalls a little guy who had lined up over five thousand "matchbox" cars on every projecting surface of the inside of his house. None were glued, but they were perfectly balanced, even on the molding on the walls! Because he had overdosed, we took him to the hospital. He was given charcoal, and as he sat on a gurney, belching black fluid down his chin into a pan, he was talking non-stop, chirping like a little bird, asking why, if this medicine was so bad, they had given it to a man like him? It was both a reasonable question and under the particular circumstances funny. One of the nurses began to laugh, and he frisbeed the metal basin he was holding right at her head, and still spewing black vomit, grabbed her by the throat, screaming, "This isn't funny. Nothing's funny!"

Watch Out! Mania Can Be Infectious

Although manic offenders can present themselves as brilliant conversationalists, witty, sexy, provocative, entertaining, POs must be wary of being seduced by the their overt friendliness or entertaining demeanor. Don't allow an offender's apparent personality ("He's such a nice guy, a lot of fun!") to cloud your professional judgment and responsibilities.

If you accept, or go along with, the manic offender's viewpoints without contradiction and appropriate limit setting, they will assume you are in agreement with them. They will assume that their actions and behaviors, no matter how non-compliant, are acceptable. However, when you subsequently violate them for an escalation of those behaviors, they can turn on you suddenly in betrayed anger.

Probation and Parole Officers must firmly establish an appropriate professional relationship with each manic offender under their care, with clear-cut limits on each relationship. POs must focus on their duties and maintain their integrity. Don't get swept up in an offender's behavior, no matter how apparently innocuous or entertaining it might appear. Manic offenders can be very manipulative, while appearing to be friendly and engaging; they are only doing so in an effort to control the relationship. Remember, the manic offender may be very provocative—think of the relationship of the Road Runner and the Coyote—trying to set you up for an over-reaction or making you look like a fool. As stated earlier, they often sexualize interactions; therefore, you must be very cautious that they don't perceive sexual interest on your part based on you letting pass some innuendo or mild flirtatious comment.

There is an old expression: "He's a drag," referring to someone who slows the party down. That is not a bad idea with the manic person. Remember, as a PO you are not expected or required to befriend any offender (other than from within the confines of the professional relationship), and you can't worry about being liked, or even respected, by those offenders you supervise. Therefore do the following:

1. Stay centered.

2. Don't get swept away or swept up in their energy.

3. Focus on slowing things down. Speak slowly, and take things step-by-step.

The Medication Struggle: It Is NOT Like Diabetes

As stated earlier, mania is a unique state in which one feels wonderful, healthy, confident, and effective, when one is actually not doing well at all. If the mania is due to abuse of drugs, offenders must stop using if they are to heal. If their mania is a side effect of their medication, then they must see a doctor.

When the problem is a symptom of the offender's bipolar disorder, medication can usually control the symptoms. However, some bipolar offenders believe, in some ways correctly, that they will feel worse when they take the medications. Yes, perhaps they will be calm, more organized, sleep better, and not get into trouble. They may avoid crushing periods of depression as well. But life will lose a wonderful glow, and the hours of each day will be more like lead than

gold. Unlike almost any other condition, profoundly manic offenders feel best when they are most ill. Offenders with bipolar disorder will resist taking their medication, unless their lives on medication are rich and interesting.

When encouraging a bipolar offender to take medications, many professionals and family members say, "It's a condition like diabetes. You need to take it every day. It's not like medicine for a sore throat that you take until you are cured, and then never have to take again." This is true, but there is a vast difference between diabetes and bipolar disorder. If a diabetic does not take their insulin, they quickly become seriously ill and they feel awful too. If an offender with bipolar disorder discontinues their medication, they often feel much better. Therefore, in addition to cautions to take their medications, POs should focus their discussion on how the e offenders' lives are better *while on medication*. Ordinary medicated life should be tangibly better to them than the un-medicated carnival of the manic state. Otherwise, it is highly unlikely that the offender will be compliant with their medication regimen.

Figure 40.3 Review: Dealing with an Offender in a Manic State

You will recognize the manic offender because they will display super high energy. They will often be talking very fast and their ideas will "zigzag" from one to another. They often act like comedians, with a rapid-fire delivery. Their behavior may also be either sexualized or hair-trigger aggressive. In either case, they will very likely be provocative:

- Remain calm and centered.
- Be conscious of their "brittle" state of mind, in spite of how confidently they behave. Grandiose does not mean strong!
- Don't bluntly criticize their actions.
- Don't tease or joke around. If you use any humor, it is for the purpose of slowing them down, not having fun.
- Don't join in what sounds like fun. It is not.
- They may try to provoke you (think of the Road Runner and Coyote, or Bugs Bunny and Elmer Fudd).
- They can be very volatile, exploding into rage with the slightest provocation. Be relaxed but ready for the worst.
- If the manic offender is also psychotic, that will probably take precedence. In these situations, you basically have a hallucinating or delusional person who also happens to be moving and talking very fast.
- Try to enforce compliance with their doctor's orders, particularly concerning medication.

CHAPTER 41

Communication With Offenders
with Dementia (The Elderly)

Effectively dealing with elderly offenders in the context of community supervision, particularly if they are also mentally disabled, is one of the most challenging situations an officer might face. Officers will almost always outweigh and outmuscle them, and even if the elderly offender has retained substantial strength (tendon strength, hence grip, is the last to go), they may be physically fragile.

Figure 41.1 Concerning Physical Force and the Elderly Offender

If physical force is required to safely bring an elderly offender under control, then it is required. However, because of the particular vulnerabilities of elderly people, your defensive tactics instructors should consult with medical specialists, particularly paramedics and emergency medical technicians, regarding the type of physical guidance and restraint that offers the least risk of injury. This should be integrated into your training scenarios.

So what do you do with an elderly aggressive offender? If you apply a come-along hold, for example, they easily can get a broken wrist or arm (one of the authors, and not the PO, accidentally did this to a slender wristed woman while applying a level of force barely enough, he thought, to get her attention! The result was a broken bone!). If you find it necessary to tackle the elderly offender or man-handle him/her to the ground, imagine the outcry that a broken pelvis or thigh might engender, injuries like this have killed elderly individuals!

Are there any verbal interventions that might possibly keep the situation under control at a lower level of force with an elderly, demented offender? Remember, older adults are not a monolithic category. They are people, just like us, simply older. Every character type, every mode of aggression, every mental syndrome, and every de-escalation strategy applies to the elderly as well as those of other age groups. Despite their age, elderly people do assault others, particularly those involved in their care. Their rage can emerge from dementia, medical conditions, pain, adverse drug reactions, mental illness, pure meanness or hate, or any number of stressors.

Many elderly offenders may be prescribed a number of medications, from a number of doctors. Not all the medical practitioners may be aware of one another, and the elderly offender, rather than being demented or mentally ill, may be suffering from a complication from drug interactions, or, due to age and confusion, taking the prescribed medications improperly. Don't rule out the possibility of a medical emergency due to such medication problems. They are quite common.

Figure 41.2 Human and Tactical Concerns With Elderly, Aggressive Offenders

Be aware that elderly offenders may be resistant to help. This may be due to disorganization and confusion brought on by dementia, by a combination of severe depression and fear, or by pride ("At least I still have the strength to refuse someone."). The following will be helpful in handling elderly offenders:

- Speak respectfully, befitting the age and seniority of the person. Too many people speak in a patronizing demeaning tone to elderly people, and even if cognitively impaired, they know they are being talked to as if they are children.

- Use their honorific and last name unless specifically invited to use their first name. If you wish to achieve a more informal relationship, ask "Would you prefer to be called Mrs. X or by your first name?" Let them *offer* the first name.

- When it is not an immediately emergent situation, take a little bit more time. Attempt to "nibble around the edges," talking about life, about family. Sometimes the volatile rage that elderly people display comes from a deep depression; they are isolated, confused and no one seems to care if they live or die. Be aware, however, that many elderly offenders have lost everyone in their lives, due to a lifelong history of criminality.

- Be prepared to get enormously frustrated at their leaden stubbornness, that "they simply won't do what is good for them." What appears as inertia may be a profound expression of fear. Remember that the most proximate change that many old people are concerned with is death, and therefore, any situation provoking anxiety evokes the fear of death. **You may think they are defiant; they may simply be scared out of their wits.**

- Don't talk around or about the person to others as if they are not present.

- Don't barrage them with choices, decisions, or too much information.

- Paranoia, (Chapter 23) whatever the cause, is one of the frequent triggers of rage in elderly people. Particularly those with dementia or adverse drug reactions. As the person becomes suspicious, you can often change the subject, so that the object of their suspicion recedes from their awareness.

- The rage and violence that emerges with elderly people is frequently chaotic. Please refer to Chapter 35 on details regarding communication with disorganized people and Chapter 66 on de-escalation of people in chaotic states.

- Be aware that the offender's behavior may very possibly be brought on by improper use of their prescribed medications, or interactions between different prescribed and over-the-counter medications.

SECTION VII

Suicide

CHAPTER 42

Why Is Suicide a Concern of a
Probation/Parole Officer?

Among their other responsibilities, POs also act as counselors to their offenders. However, most POs aren't certified therapists and one could legitimately assert that counseling a suicidal offender should be the responsibility of a mental health professional. Nevertheless, POs should be able to recognize the signs of distress and frustration that often lead to suicide attempts, and should also know what to say or do while trying to get them assistance.

The suicidal offender is not the only individual for whom you should be concerned. Suicide is an act of aggression. You could say that the difference between suicide and homicide is in what direction the weapon is pointing. This is most clearly illustrated in the phenomenon of "suicide by cop," the deliberate action of trying to force a law enforcement officer to kill oneself. Therefore, your ability to recognize and address signs of aggression and suicidal thoughts is essential to a PO's safety. The PO may have to take immediate action by either taking the offender into custody for their own safety, or make a referral to a mental health professional for further intervention.

Why would you even suspect that an offender is suicidal?

For those who are not suicidal, the act itself may be incomprehensible. Such people find it difficult to believe that life's problems could be such that suicide is even a consideration. For the suicidal offender however, suicide is a problem-solving answer to the seemingly unending pain, trauma, and frustrations of life. They feel trapped, unable to imagine any other possible solution to their problems, unable to conceive of an end to their torment, However, problem-solving activity that it may be, suicide is also an act of violence that if successful results in the death of a human being. This is an important consideration because of the offender's expression of anger and desperation, and the fact that there is often a weapon involved. Therefore, POs should use extreme caution when interacting with a suicidal offender, especially during a field visit at the offender's residence. In fact, POs should conduct a search of the offender's residence for weapons following any verbalizations of suicidal thoughts, especially if the offender specifically states that they would use a weapon to commit the act.

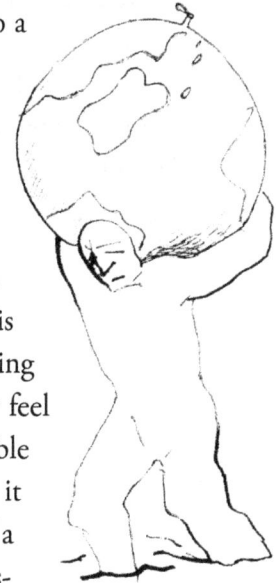

Warning Signs

Many books and training manuals on suicide focus on demographics, presenting lists enumerating the suicide rates among various ethnic groups, age, educational and economic status, traumatic life events which often trigger suicide attempts, and so forth. Although such general information can suggest some viable warning signs, <u>you need to notice what is significant about the individual offender in front of you, and not merely to which category he or she conforms.</u> Following is a list of things that you should pay attention to in assessing suicidal tendencies:

- Significant negative changes in the offender's life, such as divorce, the death of a loved one or significant other, problems at school or the worksite, and disappointments such as being dropped from a team or club in the case of youth, or the loss of employment in the case of an adult. Of course, a major factor is often the threat of re-incarceration.

- Other warning signs may include a radical change in clothing or appearance, particularly styles that sets one apart from the society of which they were previously a member, hostility towards peers, workmates, family, or social services staff, social withdrawal and isolation, the giving away of prized possessions, writings or drawings with morbid or despairing themes, a depressed demeanor, and allusions to a lack of a future or to the "pointlessness of it all," or reassuring statements when you know nothing has changed for the better, such as: "You don't have to worry about me anymore. I'll be taking care of things. It's not an issue, anymore," etc.

- Sometimes, without knowing why, you may have a sense of foreboding, or at other times, think something "ridiculous," like, "I don't think that guy will live to see thirty," or "I wonder if this is the last time I will see this person." Such thoughts are often—let us emphasize, <u>very</u> often—an intuitive sense that something is very wrong. Approaching someone out of concern when your "evidence" is so vague requires some tact, but approach you must. This "intangible signs" are signals that everything is not okay.

CHAPTER 43

The Basics of Intervention With an
Offender Who May Be Suicidal

To begin, you must ask yourself if you are the proper person to ask this offender any questions at all. Don't believe that because you are "good with people," that this boy, girl, man or woman will open up to you, even if they are on your caseload. Does this offender respect you? Have you acted in ways in the past that would lead them to feel otherwise? Have you been unsuccessful in establishing a relationship of trust with this offender, despite making a valiant attempt towards that end? If you feel that you are not the person to speak with them about suicide, your task is to refer them to an appropriate mental health professional, and to relate your concerns and observations to them. However, if time and circumstance dictate that you are the person to speak with them, what then must you do? See list below for helpful information on what to do when speaking with a possibly suicidal offender: (Note: some of these strategies may seem contradictory. As you read them; however, you will be able to imagine or recall the type of person you should approach in that specific way).

1. **Where should you speak?** Try to speak where you will have no interruptions. At the same time, you don't want a place that is so private that you and the offender are isolated.

2. **Demeanor.** Too much direct eye-contact, close physical proximity, or an overly-gentle, "concerned" voice may shut them down. Speak easily but not overly confidently. If you present yourself as too "together," they may experience this as an implicit judgment on them, their lack of ease contrasting so dramatically with your confident demeanor. Sit at an angle, with only an occasional glance toward the offender. Your occasional eye contact will then have significance, rather than being experienced as a constant, intrusive examination.

3. **Meander.** With a wary offender you may wish to "wander around," so to speak, talking about this and that. As long as they are talking, they are not killing themselves. This gives you time and also helps to build trust.

4. **Ask direct questions.** When you have a real concern that an offender is considering or planning suicide, you must be more direct. Don't tiptoe around the subject, as vague statements leave the person an "out." Instead of asking an offender, "are you thinking of hurting yourself," ask "are you thinking of killing yourself?" Such direct questions often come as a relief because it indicates that there is someone who is strong enough to listen to what is really going on inside them. If the offender is not suicidal, they will let you know. If they are outraged by your questions, explain why you are concerned. They should be able to give you a clear explanation why you don't need to be concerned. One final point, asking them if they have thoughts of suicide won't put the idea in their head if it was not already there.

5. **Speak in a calm matter-of-fact tone of voice.** If you sound nervous, you will appear unreliable. If you are joking or off-hand, the offender will feel that you are not taking them seriously. If you

are overly concerned, overly warm or sensitive, you will sound like a hovering counselor, that soft-voice, earth-tone wearing, gentle soul who can't be trusted to stand up and fight, but seeks refuge only in being "nice." A calm, matter-of-fact tone shows that you are not panicked by their situation, and that you can handle anything they say.

6. **Act as if you have all the time in the world.** If you act like there is little time, the offender you are talking with will believe you, and they will rush to a decision or conclusion. When you take time, you give time, and the suicidal offender begins to believe that there is enough time to figure out a better solution than suicide.

7. **Don't give advice too soon.** Until you become more familiar with the situation, don't hand out advice. Even then, keep it to a minimum. For example, if you immediately say, "Think of your family," the individual might think, "Yeah, they'll be sorry. Their tears dropping on my grave are the best payback I can think of!" The assessment process is a means to get them to reveal themselves, so they feel less isolated, and furthermore, so you know the right thing to say.

8. **Never dare them to do it.** That kind of stupidity only works in the movies. The archetypal stupid sentence is, "Cutting? If you were serious, you would cut your wrists lengthwise, not crosswise." The idea here is to "scare the person straight." It is obvious the aggressive intervener thinks that they are attention seeking and not serious, and they try to shock them with the reality of what they are doing. In all cases we can recall, such "interventions" are born out of frustration, irritation, burn-out, or plain dislike of the often repeatedly suicidal person. It is a statement for us, not them. One of the authors met a man who took such advice regarding multiple lengthwise cuts. His crippled arm looks like corduroy, due to seven elbow-to-wrist razor slashes to the bone.

9. **Don't debate.** Some offenders use suicidal behavior as a way of attaining some personal power in a world over which they have little control. Debates about the meaning of life, religion, or the immorality of suicide will break rapport, particularly if you are "winning."

10. **The most powerful intervention with suicidal individuals is that you are talking.** The suicidal offender, almost invariably, feels completely isolated, cut off from life and from people. A sustained, respectful conversation conveys on an almost primal level that they are still worth something, because you, who are worth something, find them worthwhile by speaking to them. Communication itself heals.

CHAPTER 44

Essential Questions

The Basic Questions

The following are the standard questions for assessing suicide risk. As you can see, there is a progression in which greater specificity indicates greater danger. You are not in the role of a therapist, but even if you were, the basic questions would be the same. You are assessing if the offender is safe, and determining the need to contact a mental health professional or the police. As always, your tone should be calm, straightforward, and non-threatening. Don't use the following questions as a mere checklist. Instead, use them in the natural flow of the conversation while understanding that the offender may wander off on all sorts of tangents before being ready to answer the next question.

The Four Questions

Question one. "Are you planning to kill yourself?" If they answer no, follow up with questions and statements why you believe they might (You received a call from their boyfriend who stated that the offender was going to "end it all," perhaps.). If they can't counter your suspicions satisfactorily, then you may need to call emergency response personnel to assure their safety despite their denials.

If the offender replies something along the lines of, "I don't want to kill myself, but sometimes I pray that I won't get up in the morning," this could be termed passive or soft suicidal ideation. Don't minimize this, as the offender's pain is very real, although their lack of an immediate plan usually allows you sufficient time to refer these offenders for a mental health evaluation or further consultation with other members of their treatment team. Should the offender refuse to answer, but you have reason to believe they may be suicidal, a referral for a more detailed mental health assessment may be necessary.

If the offender answers "yes" that is a clear sign of their thought processes and intent. Follow up this answer with more detailed questioning, or take immediate action to ensure the offender's safety, perhaps even taking them into custody for further evaluation and stabilization.

Question two. "How would you do it?" Obviously, this question is asked in response to the offender answering "yes" to question one. If their response is "I don't know," then you should have time to address the issue by negotiating an agreement to seek or accept treatment after further supportive discussion. If the offender says that they "could do it all sorts of ways," and offers a long list of possibilities, or simply says, "I'm not telling you that," this is manipulation. This doesn't mean they won't make an attempt, but their response usually stems more from an "I'll show you!" attitude. At this point, you must make it clear to them that such suicidal threats are taken seriously and take them into custody or have them evaluated by a mental health professional rather than dancing around, so to speak, trying to coerce from them how serious they really are. If the offender specifies a particular method (poison, overdose, hanging) or weapon (firearms or edged weapons), the level of risk has just increased exponentially.

Sometimes, the suicidal offender will offer a plan and a back-up plan, for example, "I want to jump off a bridge, but I think I don't have the guts. So, if I can't, I'll just overdose." This is usually not a manipulative strategy because it denotes careful planning. You may wish to conduct a field visit to their residence or living quarters to search for drugs.

Question three. Often suicidal offenders may have decided on a method, but it is one that they have not yet acquired or have access to. Be sure to ask follow-up questions to ascertain if they have access to the method they have named. Examples of follow-up questions follow below:
- "Do you have any pills?"
- "What kind?"
- "Where are they?"
- "Have you done any study on what would happen if you took them all?"

Question four. "When will you do it?" This question helps you gauge immediacy, and to determine if the offender has established the plan to make others suffer, and if there is anyone else who is "timed" to suffer, e.g., "on my mom's birthday." The more "positive" answers you get to these questions, the greater the risk of a lethal outcome.

Follow-up Questions

In most cases, particularly when interviewing an offender regarding suicidal risk, you will have fully accomplished all that you need to do. You know that the offender is or is not suicidal, and how close to the act they are. In many cases, however, you may have to keep talking for the following possible reasons:
- They trust you and want to talk more.
- They are on a phone and you are trying to keep them talking to you.
- It is a barricade situation, and the offender is talking on the other side of a door.

As offenders continue to talk, they often pull back from the intent to kill themselves on his/her own, or they will be more amenable to de-escalation because they feel that at last, someone is willing to listen. Simple communication brings people away from suicide, even without a solution to the problems that drives them toward it. Below are some follow-up questions that may prove helpful in your investigation:
1. "Have you tried to kill yourself before?"
2. "Have you ever tried to kill yourself another way?" Desperate people become very concrete and literal, only thinking of their chosen method. They may have made several attempts before, by other means.
3. Have you ever *felt* like killing yourself before?
4. What stopped you? Who stopped you? Be sure not to make them feel like they "failed" when they were not successful in a previous attempt. When they recall someone or something that

stopped them, this may help them regain a sense of responsibility for the people who care for them, or some other factor that kept them alive in the past.

5. "Has anybody in your family or someone you cared about ever tried to kill themselves?" Such people have "shown the way."

6. "Have you been drinking? Using any drugs?" *(Don't push this one if you have a sense that the person will be more worried about getting violated for use or possession than finding a solution to the situation.)*

7. "What's happened that things are so bad that suicide makes sense?" OR What happened TO-DAY that you decided to kill yourself?

8. "What else have you tried to do to get yourself out of this situation?" (Be careful, a sensitive or angry person could respond by thinking or saying, "Oh, so now you think I'm stupid!" or 'Now I have to explain myself again! I don't **KNOW** why having a girlfriend and straight A's in all my classes isn't enough!!!!!!!").

9. Other areas to talk about include if the offender has suffered any recent losses, is ill, or has little or no social/family support.

CHAPTER 45

The Art of Communication
With Suicidal Offenders

Dialogue is the lifeline. Suicidal offenders feel profoundly alone. They believe that nothing can end their pain, but death. They are often depressed or very bitter and angry. These emotions isolate them. When one is isolated, one does not even feel half-alive, because to be human is to be in relationship with others. <u>When you are able to establish a dialogue with the suicidal offender, your power, beyond anything you say, is that you are speaking.</u> By definition, the offender is no longer alone. Someone is hearing them out. Someone grasps how terrible life is for them. As time passes, the very fact of talking with you makes them feel alive again, and this gives hope, even when their situation has otherwise not changed.

Don't wear your heart on your sleeve. Quite often the stories that suicidal offenders tell are poignant and painful. However, this can also be a very sophisticated type of manipulation, and offenders who dramatize their problems, only to later minimize them or discount those who tried to help, can enrage or frustrate us. The authors are not encouraging cynicism here, but as POs you can't allow yourselves to become so emotionally involved that you feel betrayed, or simply burned out, if the offender rejects your efforts to help

Don't make guarantees of how wonderful life will be. When the suicidal offender makes demands of you, don't give a guarantee of results, just honestly explain the difficulties that lie ahead. For example, "No, I'm not guaranteeing counseling will help. You will have to work hard in therapy; it won't be easy. In fact, it might be the hardest thing you've ever done, but it's something you haven't tried." Honestly outweighs empty encouragement.

Identify the intended victim(s), beyond themselves. Try to ascertain who the suicide is intended to hurt. You will also get a better sense if the offender is also homicidal, intent on taking others along. You can tell if others are intended to suffer by asking "Who will find your body, or who will identify you?" Some offenders are shocked at the question, so preoccupied with their own pain that they didn't even think that a loved one would find them upon returning home from work. Others describe that same scene with happiness, hoping that a specific family member will discover their body.

Don't try to bolster their "self esteem." You may know that they have a talent, that they are attractive, or have a wonderful family. If you point this out to them—"You have so many reasons to live!"—you will most likely break rapport entirely. It is very likely that they know these things themselves. They look in the mirror and they see the beautiful face, but inside, they feel corrupt and foul. They look at their mom and dad, whom they painfully and deeply love, and think, "They would be so happy without me." They have a talent, and they know it, but even as they play the piano or paint or score thirty points in a game, they merely feel an aching misery.

Figure 45.1 Deepening Rapport With the Suicidal Offender

Once you have achieved a deeper level of rapport, it is quite sound to talk about what the person loves: their vocation, hopes, and dreams, their family, or their talents. The goal here is to participate in reminding the offender of the value of their life. However, they have to realize this, themselves as they talk about these things. It is not effective to tell them what is special about them. If that were all it took, they would not be suicidal in the first place.

Talk about their family. A natural follow-up of the last question is to begin speaking about their family, and the implications of their suicide upon them. You must be careful here. The suicidal offender may become enraged with you, perceiving this as a manipulative trick to make them feel guilty. However, once you get a sense that the suicidal offender does care for his or her family, particularly children, such talk may be very powerful. For example, one PO, talking to a suicidal offender on a cell phone who was holding a gun to his temple, asked him what he would say to his daughter were she the one on the phone with the gun. The offender began to tell the PO how much he loved his daughter, and started speaking as if she was on the line, telling her why it was important that she lived. When the intervener stated that it was very likely that his daughter would say the same things to him, the suicidal offender put down the gun, gave his location and surrendered.

Suicide is selfish. If you get a sense that the suicidal offender does love their children, partner, and/or friends, but are so preoccupied by their own pain that they don't realize the implications of what their suicide, one can ask, "What happens to your pain if you do kill yourself." Quite frequently, the suicidal offender says that their pain will be over. The reply to that, in a regretful tone, is, "That's not really true. You just wrap your pain up in a package and hand it to your loved ones to carry." This can sometimes shock them into considering the implications of their actions. **Caution:** This type of intervention only comes after some long talking. Many suicidal offenders are so preoccupied with their own painful situation that they become too selfish to care about their family. Rather than a healthy shock, they will resent you for reminding them of what they are trying to extinguish.

Suicidal threats without following through are not a betrayal of you. You will deal with offenders who dramatize their problems, only later to minimize or discount those who gather to help them, particularly with those who make repeated attempts or threats. This can enrage or frustrate you. It is ironic that contempt, irritation, or frustration is exactly what they expect from people, and that is what their behavior elicits. One of the occupational hazards of working with people who suffer is that not all those in pain are endearing; some are frankly quite unlikeable. Others don't even have the ability or resources to accept help when it is offered. It is the hallmark of a professional that you don't become burned out simply because some offenders either play games, or are playing on an entirely different field than you assumed.

How to respond to internal questions that sidetrack us. "I don't know if I would want to live in such a miserable situation." It's not about you! The fact that they are talking with you means they still have some hope for another answer. "Why is it important that they live?" OR "I know I should care, but I don't." In cases like these, make death itself your enemy. Your attitude should be that you will do your best to speak for life. You are a voice from the land of the living to one trying to cross over into the land of the dead. *"Not on my watch!"* If they wanted to die, they should not have come into contact with you.

The Taxonomy of Suicide

This tool can be used to help gauge the seriousness of the offender's suicidal intent, and what type of suicide it might be. Given that suicide is a form of murder, let us categorize the act in roughly the same manner as a homicide. See below:

- **Aggravated first degree suicide.** This would include killing oneself in a heinous or torturous way, because the person believes he deserves to suffer. Another example would be a suicide calculated so that a loved one will find the body. A third would be a murder-suicide.
- **Premeditated first degree suicide.** This would include any planned suicide.
- **Second degree suicide.** This includes impulsive actions that are usually due to extreme emotion or intoxication.
- **Assaultive self-harm with intent to commit mayhem (first degree assault).** The offender does not mean necessarily to die, but they do something horrible to themselves, often with the intent to show others, "See how much I'm suffering!" or "See how much you make me suffer." The distinction between the previous item and this one is a hard call; you may not even be confidently able to make distinguish which it is. However, if you are aware that the offender didn't consciously intend to die, you would work with him/her in a different way. The professionals to whom you might refer such an individual would also find this useful information, if you happened to acquire it.

Figure 45.2 Example of Intent to Commit Mayhem (No intent to die)

A young man returned home to find his father on the couch having sex with the young man's new girlfriend. (He was unaware that his girlfriend shared affection for crack cocaine, his father's drug of choice. They immediately recognized each other as kindred spirits when they met). The young man pulled out a fish boning knife and yelling at the two of them, stabbed himself right in the abdomen. Miraculously, the flexible blade threaded its way between his internal organs and all he needed was a few stitches. He said to me, "I didn't want to die. I didn't even think of that. It's just that my dad has always done stuff like this to me. Every time I trust him, this is the result. I guess I didn't know whether to stab him for doing it, or stab myself for being so stupid as to trust him again."

- **Assaultive self-harm.** This includes suicidal gestures, such as cutting oneself and other self-mutilating actions (See Chapter 46 & 47).
- **Self-sacrifice.** Rare though it may be, this would include actions that have the intention of helping others, like throwing oneself on a grenade to save ones comrades.

Figure 45.3 Example Self-Sacrifice

A young girl, aged twelve, disclosed sexual abuse by her father. Her mother slapped her in the face for "talking dirty." She suffered this for years, but when her father began turning his attention to her younger sister, she thought, in the irrational magical way of a child, that if she did something as awful as suicide, maybe someone would help her sister. Her mother had made it clear to her that telling did not help. Thankfully, her attempt to kill herself failed, and a very good hospital social worker asked her the right questions, thereby getting help for both girls.

- **Self-execution.** This includes suicide that is primarily directed by a sense of guilt. Such an individual believes that they deserve to die for some unforgivable transgression. We are confining this category to those who have actually done something terrible, not someone who, due to a sense of pathological guilt brought on by mental illness, decides that they do not deserve to live.
- **Survivor's guilt.** This particular form of "self-execution" is usually the outcome of a traumatic event. It is particularly common among frontline war veterans. The intense bonds between soldiers are among the most profound relationships that humans can experience. Facing death, only the trust and dependence upon one's comrades may keep one alive. A powerful sense of being "of one flesh" develops, where the man on the right is one's right arm and the man on the other side is one's left arm. When comrades are killed, one can simultaneously feel like a part of oneself has been killed, but at the same time, one feels terribly guilty to still be alive, as if one abandoned them. One feels like one does not have the right to the joys of life, that the other person or people were better than you, or perhaps worst of all, that life-and-death is a random throw of the dice, which suggests there is no meaning to one's comrades' sacrifices.
- **Mercy self-killing.** This category includes so-called "assisted suicide" or other suicides in which the offender is seriously ill and wishes to "die with dignity."
- **"I'm taking my body out of here."** This is an attempt at final control over one's own fate; something that can range as an act of heroism against intolerable violation or oppression to the act of a psychopath in prison whose only way of thwarting the people who hold him against his will is to kill himself.

CHAPTER 46

Self-Mutilation

One of the most confusing actions that an offender can take, at least to those outside the situation, is self-mutilation. When it is potentially life-threatening, or is an enactment of something that looks like a suicidal attempt, but somehow has survival "built in," it is referred to as "para-suicidal behavior." (See Chapter 47) This primarily includes cutting ones wrists or other actions that could, taken to an extreme, have resulted in death. Among self-mutilating behaviors that the authors have encountered are:

- Rubbing an eraser on the wrist until all the skin is peeled away and one has a weeping lesion in the flesh.
- Repetitively stubbing out a burning cigarette on one's face and genitals.
- Stabbing oneself repeatedly by dropping a knife between the fingers, any error resulting in a wound in the web between them.
- Running a needle in and out of the flesh of one's belly.
- Hacking over one's wrists on the corner of a table, and then, after being stitched up, tearing out the stitches with one's teeth and attempting to spray blood on nearby correctional officers.
- Repetitive incidents of slicing open the abdominal wall all the way to the fascia that holds the organs. (A former nurse did this to herself.)

The hallmark of all of these actions is that the offender does not intend to die. There are a number of reasons why an offender would commit such acts:

- **Self-hatred.** The offender punishes himself or herself through self-torture and/or disfiguration.
- **Attention seeking.** Attention-seeking cases are usually, but not always, typified by more superficial wounds. Such offenders "require" others to pay attention to them, particularly family members or loved ones, who become afraid that they will be responsible for their death if they don't act. In the case cited above of the young man who threaded a needle in-and-out of the folds of his belly, he was an unpopular and socially awkward boy who sought attention. And, by means of this action he received some; in fact, at least once a day as other students would dare him to do it again.
- **Primitive medicine.** Similar to the historical European and American medical practice of bloodletting to "cure" a variety of physical and mental health illnesses, these offenders are metaphorically "draining out" the poisons in their bodies by bleeding themselves.
- **A struggle to feel something.** Some offenders in the throes of deep depression or trauma literally feel numb. Absent any apparent emotions, they use these torturous acts help them feel alive.
- **Stress reduction.** Physical wounding results in the release of endorphins. These are neuro-chemicals produced by the body that have a pain relieving effect similar to opiates such as morphine

and heroin. A common term for this is "runner's high," that folks experience after a particularly vigorous workout. Offenders can become habituated to this endorphin release, and activities that stimulate it can become addictive. Some turn to acts of self mutilation instead of exercise to feel the same effects.

Figure 46.1 Example of Stress Reduction by Self-wounding

A young woman told one of the authors that, after years of verbal and emotional abuse by her father, "I felt like I was walking on egg shells all the time. Then, when my mom and I finally left, it was like I couldn't stand any emotions at all. Even when I was happy, I would still feel like I was going to explode." She described one day cutting herself on the forearm with an Exacto knife, and to her shock, felt a sense of warmth and peace. Not psychological warmth alone, but a warm floating sensation as well. Several weeks later she tried it again, and it became an addiction.

- **Rehearsal.** Some offenders want to commit suicide, or profess to do so, but their underlying fears make them hesitant, resulting in numerous "failed" attempts at suicide.

Figure 46.2 The Line of Self-mutilation has "Moved"

We must be aware that the line of self-mutilation has "moved." We see individuals with multiple piercings, including one's tongue or sexual organs, who have voluntarily branded themselves, and others who some even have implants of metal placed under the skin, to end up with "devil's horns." Most of these people talk about endorphin release. Many claim that they are making their own bodies into works of art. As strange or repulsive as we may find some of these body modifications, this is not an emergency, unless the person puts themselves at medical risk.

In an ambiguous situation, you need to ascertain if this is a suicide attempt, and also try to determine how seriously they are wounded. If it is just some grotesque piercing that would be their prerogative, unless you believe that they are severely mentally ill. In the latter case, just to be safe, bring them in to be evaluated by a professional.

In short, action is necessary if you have either a psychiatric emergency (a genuine suicide attempt) or a medical emergency, either intentional or accidental. Imagine an offender who had NO intention of suicide, but decided on a do-it-him/herself splitting of their tongue in emulation of a snake (one author has seen such an unlovely sight. It took a lot of days and a fair amount of dental floss.). However, when you arrive for a field-check, you find that the bleeding is not stopping and they are toxic with some sort of infection.

CHAPTER 47

Crying Wolf: Identifying and Helping
Para-suicidal Offenders

Yreplace_You have surely supervised offenders who seem to be in, or seem to create, a constant state of crisis. Everything is an issue, and the most minor problems or setbacks are likely to cause an inappropriate amount of emotional stress and drama. One of the primary outcomes for these offenders is repeated suicide attempts, threats of suicide, or self-mutilating behaviors.

Do NOT try to manage this type of behavior on your own. Instead, you need to refer the offender to the proper treatment facility or therapy sessions related to suicidal and para-suicidal offenders. At the very least, a PO must consult the other members of an offender's current treatment team to discuss any concerns for the offender or disturbing behaviors. Although the scope of this text does not allow for a discussion of detailed planning for such offenders, let us discuss both the problems they engender and offer an example that gives general principals of case management.

Many of the problems engendered by such behavior are unsolvable. In Western society, we view this as a manifestation of mental illness, and generally speaking, believe ourselves required to try to help the offender. This requires our law enforcement and emergency medical personnel to strive to intervene, repeatedly, in the actions of those who either reject our help, or repeat the actions as if all our interventions are irrelevant. Let us consider the damage they cause:

- **Compassion burnout.** "Burnout" can be caused by the unrelenting stress and non-stop pace of today's criminal justice system. POs may feel disillusioned and overburdened by the seemingly insurmountable problems of the offenders whom they supervise, and often find it difficult to summon the energy needed to care for their offenders and supervise them properly. Quite simply, we get sick of such offenders. We see them only as manipulative and self-involved. Beyond whatever justification one might find for that point of view, it unfortunately expands. Many officers begin to view all mentally ill and suicidal offenders through the distorted lens that burnout creates. This becomes a safety issue. When we begin to view others with contempt, they can easily respond with their own negative emotions. Thereafter, interactions between POs and the mentally ill become increasingly volatile. Remember, too, that a mentally ill, perhaps suicidal person might have a negative interaction with one contemptuous officer, and decide to take it out on another, at a later date.
- **Damage to society.** Suicidal threats, alone, can take up an enormous amount of man-hours, not only for POs and other law enforcement, but also for the emergency medical system. With our economy severely stressed and our medical system currently in unknown financial waters,

the hundreds of thousands of dollars that may be needed every year to manage the behavior of a single para-suicidal offender, however beyond their control, makes such acts, from one perspective, acts of violence against our society. The bottom line is that hard-working citizens pay for any public service. When you have such an offender on your caseload, a committee needs to be set up to figure out the best way to deal with the situation. Ideally, this committee should include representatives from law enforcement, parole/probation, emergency medical response, hospital ER, the mental health system, and the prosecutor's office.

a) If the offender has made repeated suicidal threats without action, they should be prosecuted. Among the charges that can be levied are false reporting, abuse of the 9-1-1 system, and interfering with medical care. While in detention, it is the responsibility of the PO and the offender's mental health treatment team to maintain contact with them, and begin working with them so that they get a sense of reward when NOT using suicidal threats to get attention.

b) If they have actually enacted suicidal gestures, even wrist scratching or taking a few pills, no one will prosecute them. The risks of a more serious suicidal attempt will be viewed as too high. However, a comprehensive plan can be set up so that the individual gets more emotional rewards and attention by NOT engaging in para-suicidal gestures.

Figure 47 Do you have difficulty having compassion for such borderline offenders?

Do you remember some of the homes you have visited with small children, some of whom cling to you, hoping that you will take them out of their horrible circumstances and how you thought that if someone, even you, did not get that child out of that house **right now**, their life would be blighted forever? Do you remember, however, that there were, allegedly no grounds to call for a Child Protective Services Evaluation? Yeah, those offenders! Some of the most troublesome, manipulative, repetitively para-suicidal offenders on your caseload now are *those children*, now grown up.

SECTION VIII

Recognizing Patterns
of Aggression

CHAPTER 48

The Cycle of Aggression

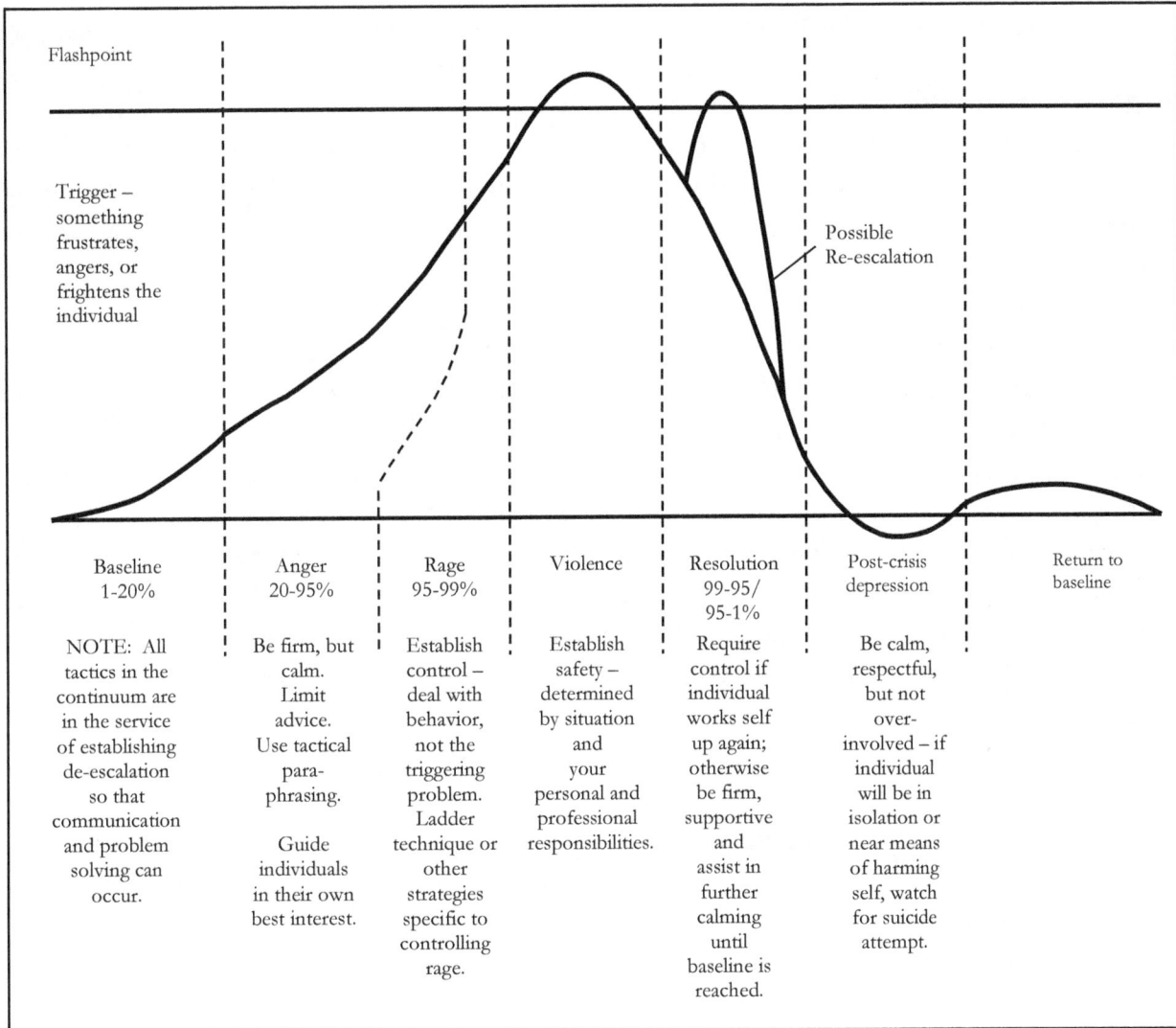

Flashpoint

Trigger – something frustrates, angers, or frightens the individual

Possible Re-escalation

Baseline 1-20%	Anger 20-95%	Rage 95-99%	Violence	Resolution 99-95/ 95-1%	Post-crisis depression	Return to baseline
NOTE: All tactics in the continuum are in the service of establishing de-escalation so that communication and problem solving can occur.	Be firm, but calm. Limit advice. Use tactical para-phrasing. Guide individuals in their own best interest.	Establish control – deal with behavior, not the triggering problem. Ladder technique or other strategies specific to controlling rage.	Establish safety – determined by situation and your personal and professional responsibilities.	Require control if individual works self up again; otherwise be firm, supportive and assist in further calming until baseline is reached.	Be calm, respectful, but not over-involved – if individual will be in isolation or near means of harming self, watch for suicide attempt.	

An outburst of aggression occurs in a cycle that starts with relative calm and ends with relative calm. The aggressive cycle often appears to start with an apparent "triggering event" though, in fact, the crisis may have been culminating for some time. The reader may recognize the term trigger, being familiar with it in terms of relapse in regard to substance abuse. The same concept applies with acts of violence. Just as many addicts have certain triggers that elicit the urge to use drugs; aggressive offenders have triggers that cue them to become violent.

Baseline: From 0 – 20

When we are calm, we are at **baseline,** which is represented as "0 – 20" on the accompanying chart. At baseline, we use the parts of the brain most responsible for our better human characteristics: thinking, creativity, and forming social relationships. The reason that the rating scale goes up to "20" is that we wish to underscore that one can have a little heat and energy, and still be fully rational. When communicating with people at baseline, we usually use some kind of *dialogue,* a reciprocal exchange (even if one person is doing most of the talking) in a mutual effort to get closer to the truth.

Anger: From 20 – 95

A triggering event elicits a change in both thinking and feeling. This event can be something that threatens the offender's sense of safety, frustration at not being able to obtain what they desired, or simply a cue that they are now justified using a skill (aggression) with which they are confident. Once aggression is triggered, the offender becomes irritable, then angry.

If baseline is presented as being "0 – 20" on the scale of aggression, with actual violence being "100," anger represents the numbers 20 through 95. Regardless of the numeric value of their anger, the offender is trying to communicate with you. However, because we perceive their attempts to communicate to be obnoxious, domineering, frightening, or just plain irrational, we often don't construe their actions as communication. The offender, on the other hand, experiences an increasing sense of frustration or desperation, and not infrequently, a sense of helplessness at their inability to make themselves heard, further fueling their anger. Unfortunately, for many offenders with anger issues and poor coping skills, the bromide, "if the only tool you have is a hammer, then every problem looks like a nail," applies. There are several reasons such offenders grow angrier as the perceived or actual conflict continues:

- Certain offenders simply can't accept anyone disagreeing with them, especially when they believe they are right.
- When you don't seem to grasp what they are saying, you are perceived as being disinterested, too obtuse to understand, or your lack of comprehension implicitly accuses *them* of stupidity or unreasonableness.
- When you don't agree or comply with them you are frustrating the offender in achieving something they desire.
- Many offenders have a misconstrued and hypersensitive sense of "respect," especially in the social context of our nation's inner-cities. The offender often sees resistance, disagreement, or perceived slights as being disrespectful, causing them to lash out in anger or violence in an effort to regain their "street cred."

As offenders become more agitated, the areas of their brain that mediate basic emotions take over. At this point, equity, negotiation, or compromise becomes less and less attractive. In their frustration, angry offenders shift, increasingly, to attempting to dominate you, trying to *make* you see things their way or to comply with them. Their domineering behavior is, as much as anything else, an attempt to "get through" to you.

Think of arguments you have had when, frustrated, you said such things as: "No, that's not what I'm saying! Do I have to explain it again?" or "Let me put it another way!" or "You just don't get it! What do I have to say to make you understand?" We become progressively more intense, often raising our voices (as if that will help the other person understand) because we want the other person to grasp what we are saying. This type of escalation is counter-productive, despite our intentions, because we tend to make less sense when we are angry.

For some offenders, anger is accompanied by physical arousal, which functions as a feedback loop, driving them toward further arousal. When their heart rate rises 10 percent to 15 percent above baseline due to emotional excitement the offender no longer cares about the truth. They care only about being "right" and proving others "wrong." The disagreement has become a win or lose situation. Such an offender interrupts more frequently, cutting others off and picking out the flaws in the other person's argument.

To de-escalate and control an angry offender, the PO should attempt to *"line up"* with them. When you line up with the offender, you prove that you are not only focused on, but also understand what they are saying, thereby proving that their concerns are important. This in itself is powerfully disarming, not only calming them down, but also helping the PO to work together to actually solve the problem.

Rage: From 95 – 99

As you can see on the chart, rage is represented as 95 to 99 on the aggression scale. How can you tell the difference between anger and rage? When someone is angry, you too, may become angry. You might also become concerned, upset, hurt, confused, and/or frustrated. Usually, however, you will not be afraid. Why not? Although angry people may *later* become violent if they are further agitated, that is not their aim. Instead, their intention is to communicate with you, albeit dramatically, loudly, or forcefully. At worst, they are trying to dominate or intimidate you into doing what they want. As abhorrent as this may be, it is still communication.

When offenders are enraged, however, they are, in effect, trying to "switch themselves on" to becoming violent. Many people slowly work themselves into a state of rage as a prelude to violence. Of course, others can lash out violently with seemingly no prior warning, verbal or otherwise. Usually however, even non-communicative offenders will signal their anger or intentions through their body language and other non-verbal forms of communication. POs should be aware of these warning signs of impending aggression, as manifested on the intuitive level in Chapter 13 & 14 and based on observable behaviors, as discussed in Chapter 50.

Most of the time, anger does not result in violence. One reason for this is the various self-inhibitors that work to control our behaviors and prevent us from acting out our baser instincts. But within a state of rage, the offender is *trying* to overcome those inhibiters, so that they can do what they actually desire: act violently. Some of the prime inhibitors are listed below:

1. **A fear of consequences**. The fear of counterattack, legal consequences, social disapproval, financial costs, and a host of other possible negative outcomes serve to inhibit one's resorting to violence to settle a dispute.

2. **Morality**. Although some political and social ideologies may define another group as less than human and therefore fair game for violence, most individuals possess a core set of moral or religious principles that prevent them from harming others.

3. **Self-image**. A man may see himself, for example, as the kind of person who does not hit women, make a public display of aggression, or lose control of himself. A woman may see herself as caring, nurturing, and empathetic to the plight of the less fortunate. A positive self-image, and fears of tarnishing that image, will often preclude an individual from committing a violent act.

4. **The relationship**. A feeling of responsibility toward the other person, e.g. friendship, love, family relations, etc., will hold an individual from violence.

5. **Learned helplessness**. Some offenders, survivors of abuse for example, have tried to defend themselves in the past and have failed repeatedly. They may believe that fighting back is a futile effort, only leading to further pain and abuse. Their rage, however, is there—inside. There are phrases like, "a cornered rat," or "the worm turns," which describe a person who has suppressed their rage, sometimes for years, before acting out in violence and rage.

Rage therefore, is a set of behaviors, including both physical actions and verbalizations that serve to do away with one's self-inhibitors, so that nothing holds them back from violence. Offenders in a rage state are no longer trying to communicate; they are working themselves up to an attack.

What is the difference, then between rage and violence? Anger is a rocket ship all fueled up with some fumes coming out, and the countdown initiated. Rage is right before lift-off. The rocket has not yet moved, but there are flames and steam billowing out, making a terrible roar, so loud the ground shakes. It is a roiling moment of explosive, tenuous equilibrium. Fuel could still be cut to the rocket engines so that it sits silent on the launching pad, but there are only a few moments to act, because the rocket is about to lift off. Lift-off is the equivalent of the initiation of **violence**.

What we *should* experience in the face of rage is fear. This is not a bad thing. Fear tells us that we are in danger and that we must do something NOW! We will most likely be able to handle the situation, but we had better devote every power we have to survival. Fear switches us on, so that our internal emergency response systems are activated. Fear demands attention, but it should not paralyze us into non-action, mentally or physically, in the face of anger and rage. Fear is merely an emotion. A sense of powerlessness, on the other hand, is a *conclusion* that some people reach when they are afraid. This limits their ability to control the situation, or to defend themselves.

Once the PO notices the onset of anger within an offender they would be well-served to begin preparing mentally for a potential violent act and begin identifying an escape route, or if necessary, to ready themselves for actual physical confrontation, all while attempting to de-escalate the offender.

To work with the enraged offender, you must establish *control*, especially if their behavior presents an immediate threat to you, themselves, or others. De-escalation and control tactics, whether they are verbal or physical, are geared to establish the conditions that make the aggressive offender no longer dangerous.

Figure 48 The Difference Between Anger and Rage

Imagine someone hands you a huge plastic container. Through its translucent sides, you can see a dark, hairy shape, a Goliath Bird-Eater, the world's biggest spider. It rustles around the container shifting in your hands like it's filled with mercury. Is it creepy? Sure it is. Is there any reason to be afraid? Not really. As long as the lid is on the container firmly, you are absolutely safe. This is the equivalent of anger. Internally you say, "I'd better keep the lid on this thing."

Now, imagine your "friend" takes the container back, and to your surprise and horror, takes off the lid. The spider emerges onto the floor right next to your leg. It raises its front legs in threat-display and opens and closes its ¾ inch fangs. There is something poisonous, hairy, and mean in the room, and it is not enclosed in any container! The spider is out of the box. This, metaphorically, is rage.

However, the fear that now arises within you doesn't mean that you are helpless. You can step on the spider or jump up on a table. If you are ticked off enough, you can grab your "friend" by the neck and make him sit on it! A belief that you are helplessness near the spider is an interpretation, not a fact. Fear is simply the warning cry—the drums at the brink of battle—that demands that you *must* act right now.

To deal with the enraged person, you must establish *control*, especially if their behavior presents an immediate threat to you, to themselves, or to others. Control tactics—be they verbal or physical—are geared to establish the conditions that make the aggressive person no longer dangerous. In essence, using our metaphor above, we say, "Put the spider back in the box. Now!"

Violence: 100 on the Scale

Violence does not begin when someone is hit or injured. Violence is perpetrated simply through the fear of imminent danger and attack. Some of the legal terms for this are terroristic threats, harassment, harassment by communication, stalking, and menacing. In short, a violent act occurs whenever there is good reason to believe that you or someone else is about to be hurt. In the face of such a situation, your guiding principle is to establish safety, and you must use the effective means of protecting yourself and those around you. Very often, the best thing to do is to escape and get help. This is especially true for POs conducting fieldwork alone.

Although actual physical self-defense tactics are well beyond the scope of this book, POs should refer to Chapter 10 as well as keeping themselves in peak physical condition. POs should also avail themselves of any offered self-defense training, including the use of firearms, through your individual agencies. As with any skill, self-defense techniques must be practiced regularly to ensure their viability in the event of an actual confrontation.

CHAPTER 49

Why would an offender
become aggressive?

Aggression is not an alien or unnatural emotion. Without a capacity for aggression, humanity would never have survived. Yet, much aggression seems far apart from the basic activities of hunting or self-defense. Much of it is irrational, self-destructive, vicious, or cruel. Why would someone be swept by rage when it causes so much harm? Why would they be prepared to throw away a future, even a life, driven by emotions that they themselves might be horrified to have expressed even a few moments later? Why would they choose to take on police or their PO, even in situations that they have little possibility of winning? POs can better control an aggressive offender when they understand what has driven the offender to anger. Below are some of the factors that can drive an offender to become aggressive.

Feels confused or disorganized. Anger and rage can develop because the offender is confused or disorganized. They cannot understand what is going on around them, or "inside" them, due to cognitive distortions or a chaotic situation (too much information for them to figure out). Among those who experience this confusion are those who are mentally ill, autistic, developmentally disabled, intoxicated, and those experiencing overwhelming emotions.

Feels enclosed, trapped and/or beset with problems. Some offenders feel helpless, enclosed, trapped, or beset with a myriad of seemingly unsolvable problems. This is often similar in effect to confusion or disorganization, but it is accompanied by a particular anguish. The offender usually perceives one person or entity as the agent of their situation, and they fight desperately to get free from his or her influence or oppression. Mental health professionals and even some POs can elicit these feelings in certain offenders when they analyze and interpret the offender's every action in an intrusive manner.

Has a fear of an attack. The fear of attack elicited by an actual or perceived invasion of personal space is often a precursor to aggression. Each of us has a sense of personal space, a "bubble" within which an outsider is only permitted if invited (See Chapter 14). A violation of this personal space can elicit aggressive reactions and behaviors. Understand that in stressful or volatile situations, you will be perceived as an attacker if you encroach upon another's personal space, no matter your intentions.

Feels wronged or feels a loss of power. An offender may resort to aggression if they feel they are being wronged, or feel as if they are losing their sense of autonomy and power, something that must happen to many mentally ill offenders, either for their own safety, or to keep them from disturbing or interfering with other people. Some mentally ill offenders experience a sense of personal violation when they are being limited in their actions or forced to conform to rules, despite the fact that such restrictions are in their own best interests. This is especially true of paranoid offenders who may believe that they are being oppressed by systems or powers beyond their control. As their PO, you may be designated, in such an offender's mind, as the representative of the controlling entity.

Is hallucinating or having delusions. Hallucinations and delusions can also play a significant role in the likelihood of aggression with mentally ill offenders. The offender may feel compelled to act as the voices demand or in trying to make the hallucinations stop by any means, become violent. On other occasions, the voices, visions, smells, and/or sensations are simply distracting and irritating.

Has used organic stressors of some type. The use of drugs and alcohol, along with other organic stressors can also make an offender more likely to become aggressive. The drug and alcohol component to aggression is relatively self-explanatory, and one does not need an overactive imagination to realize just how desperate drug addicted and alcoholic offenders can become when in the throes of their addiction. By other organic stressors the authors are referring to a lack of sleep, a lack of regular exercise, and/or an insufficient or non-nutritious diet. Such deprivations can cause changes in perception, mood, and cognition, which can lead to an increase in irritability and/or hypersensitivity.

Feels shamed or humiliated. One of the most powerful driving forces of aggression is a sense that one has been shamed or humiliated. Shame is not a mild sense of social embarrassment; it is a sense of being exposed and victimized by others with no hope of relief. Shame and humiliation are driving forces for revenge-based aggression if they remember, correctly or incorrectly, something the PO did that offended them in the past. They may brood about past grievances, their anger slowly escalating until they explode into rage or violence. This is a particular problem for POs, where offenders may bear a grudge against a previous PO, and they try to take it out on their current PO.

Is acting out of protective rage. Offenders may act aggressively out of a sense of protective rage. This type of rage is not confined only to parents, but also as expressed by an offender who is trying to protect another individual from being victimized. The closer one feels to the victim, the more one's identity is "merged" with that of the victim and the more aggressive the person will be in their defense.

Figure 49 Example of Protective Rage

For example, one of the authors supervised an offender suffering from brain trauma who once beat another guy severely with a metal pipe because that individual was taunting a person in a wheelchair. The offender did not know the person in the wheelchair, but he just did not think that picking on such a person was acceptable behavior.

Act out of a sense of entitlement. Some offenders may resort to aggression due to a sense of entitlement. For many offenders entitlement is intertwined with desire, and therefore they will use any means necessary to obtain that which they desire.

Violence for enjoyment. Others simply take pleasure in intimidating others and acting violently. For them, there is a joy in making others submit and a delight in causing pain. If you attempt to deny this ugly truth, you will convince yourself, in error, that you are safe or in control of the situation, and remain in the presence of the dangerous offender too long.

Finally, anything that elicits profound emotion can cause an offender to become volatile or aggressive. Emotional stressors include a recent loss through the death of someone close, dysfunctional family dynamics, romantic and other interpersonal relationships, job loss, divorce, infidelity, or feelings of insecurity. Certainly, the criminal justice system elicits strong emotions, and each and every interaction with the PO brings those emotions back to the fore, heightening the chances for an aggressive interaction between the PO and the offender.

CHAPTER 50

What does escalation look like?

As an offender escalates in their aggressive behavior(s), they are priming their bodies to posture, to intimidate, to fight, and/or to flee. They can display a variety of different behaviors.

Escalation Behaviors

Physical and emotional withdrawal. Some offenders will avoid eye contact, stop speaking, or respond only with short phrases or monosyllabic answers. Of course, some offenders are more naturally withdrawn and reserved; this does not mean that they are readying themselves for an aggressive outburst. Instead, here we are discussing a heretofore friendly and engaging offender who lapses into sullen hostility or refuses to engage in conversation.

Figure 50.1 Physical and Emotional Withdrawal

If you notice an offender behaving in this manner you should approach them and engage them in order to elicit a response. For example, you may ask "Hey Tim, during each of your prior office visits you said hello and asked me how my day was going. But today, you just looked at the floor. Something's bothering you today." Note that you did not ask, "What's going on?" Direct questions will merely give the offender an opportunity to ignore you or reply with simple answers such as "Nothing" or "I don't know." By treating their behavior as meaningful as well as demonstrating that you are in sync with them, you are more likely to get a truthful response, such as "I just had a really bad argument at home, and don't want to talk about it" or, of more immediate concern, "You know what's going on! You know what you did!" Such a response is the quickest way of ascertaining if the offender is a threat to anyone in your agency, or in the community.

Nervous, anxious, or frightened demeanor. Such offenders usually lash out in defense. They are not looking for a fight; they are trying to protect themselves.

Overwhelmed or disorganized behavior. Offenders who speak in repetitive loops, muttering incoherently to themselves or pacing, are displaying symptoms or either a chaotic mental state or perhaps intoxication. Offenders in this state can be unpredictable, and they may react to a PO's attempts to communicate with sudden, unexpected aggression.

Hostility. Any offender displaying open expressions of dislike or hatred should immediately put the PO on guard, as a plainly hostile demeanor can escalate into violence quite easily.

Seduction. Seduction is not reserved for just sexual expressions or desires. In communication from offender to PO, seduction can be viewed as masked aggression. The offender is trying to get the PO to collude with them, perhaps in an attempt to convince the PO to not file a violation report, or perhaps in an attempt to place the PO in an uncompromising position. An example would be: "C'mon, it's just a novelty item. That's not really a pipe. You aren't going to violate me over a toy, are you?"

Mood swings (Chapter 27). These involve rapid shifts in mood and emotional affect, from boisterous to morose, then shifting to belligerence. Such offenders present a particular risk due to their unpredictability and their inability to control their own emotions.

Hypersensitivity. Hypersensitivity is most common in paranoid offenders (Chapter 30), but others can also be hypersensitive. Paranoid offenders in particular, may complain of being stared at, watched, or controlled, and feel perpetually under threat of attack. When there is no apparent enemy, they will find one, or even create one. The hypersensitive offender can react aggressively to even the most inoffensive and harmless attempts at communication, more so if they believe they are going to be censured for violations of their supervision plan.

Authority complex. Many offenders have difficulty with accepting authority. When their PO tries to set limits or say "no," these offenders become very frustrated and/or outraged, refusing to comply with rules. Rules and limitations are, in their view, oppressive or humiliating. The ability of the PO to place them in jail or take them back before the court for violations is of little concern to this type of offender. Their attitude is simply an expression of their hatred for authority.

Electric tension. This is the feeling you get before a thunderstorm hits. We can't underscore highly enough that you must ALWAYS trust this feeling, this intuitive sense that you are approaching a dangerous situation (Chapter 14).

Changes in Cognition.

Cognitive distortions. Cognitive distortions are thinking patterns where the offender makes broad, negative assumptions. For example, an offender misses a single meeting at his substance abuse treatment facility and assumes he will be sent back to prison. Therefore, when he sees his PO, he is already convinced of the injustice he believes will be perpetrated upon him.

Interpersonal cognitive distortions. This occurs when the offender infers the worst of what the PO is saying. For example, "Tia, you have to start complying fully with the court, or I will have no choice but to violate your probation." And her response is, "YOU ARE VIOLATING ME???!!!!!" By misinterpreting what they are hearing these offenders can become instantly more guarded and/or aggressive.

Becoming less amenable to reconciliation or negotiation. The offender focuses increasingly on dominating the conversation or situation, on winning the argument, or on taking out their frustrations on the object of their anger, rather than trying to find a peaceful resolution. The offender focuses on being "right," and not on the facts. Because only their own ideas and desires have any importance to them, they refuse to consider other perspectives.

Deterioration of concentration and memory. This causes difficulty in the offender's ability to communicate, to solve problems, or to recall problem-solving skills. As their information processing skills deteriorate, their judgment consequently becomes worse and worse. They can't evaluate what is really in their own self-interest.

Figure 50.2 Example

A PO was arresting a male suspect for a violation. The offender blamed his wife for talking with the PO several days before, which he believed led the officer to pick up on the violation. On the way to the police car, furious, he told the officer, "If you take me to jail, she's going to throw away my dope. I paid good money for that." This resulted in a second charge of possession of methamphetamine.

Changes in Patterns of Verbal Interactions

Silence. Potentially aggressive offenders may lapse into a morose, sullen silence, often accompanied by signs of physical agitation such as hunched shoulders, knitted brows, and glaring at the floor or at other people.

Sarcasm. Sarcasm can be considered to be hostility shaded in humor or passive-aggressive phrases. Offenders may jeer at you, or sneer scornfully, demeaning your position, or even the entire criminal justice system. Many offenders don't view POs as true members of the law enforcement establishment. (That is until they are placed in jail for violations and the PO is one of the few people with the ability and the authority to release them.) Sarcasm should also be interpreted as thinly veiled threats, and these must be taken seriously, lest the offender believe that he or she can continue to treat their PO with disrespect without fear of consequence.

Figure 50.3 Implied Threats

During the calendar year of 2009, there were several police officers killed in the line of duty in the hometowns of both authors, in Pittsburgh and Seattle. Not long after the incident in Pittsburgh, an offender who was not happy that his probation was being violated told his PO, "No wonder people like you get shot all the time." This was seen as an implied threat to the PO's safety, and the offender was taken into custody immediately and lodged in the jail to await his appearance before the court. Of course, POs can't jail every offender who is sarcastic and non-compliant; however, such implied threats of violence can't be left unaddressed.

Deliberate provocation. Offenders will do or say things to upset or irritate their PO deliberately. Provocation is a challenge, an attempt to elicit a response from the PO that will justify them in becoming increasingly hostile, if not violent.

Playing word games. Offenders will deliberately twist or misinterpret what PO says, trying to confuse them or make you question your own memories of previous encounters. Some offenders always misremember or "forget" directives, and then try to blame the PO for their position. This is why proper note taking and documentation is vital.

Abusive or obscene language. The use of abusive or obscene language should put the PO on guard immediately, especially if the language is threatening or portends a violent act. In these cases the offender uses language to shock or stun the recipient, causing the PO to focus on what the offender is saying, and not on what they are doing (such as moving ever closer, or surreptitiously reaching for a weapon).

Figure 50.4 Concerning the Use of Abusive or Obscene Language

Note, however, that some offenders, and quite frankly, POs, use obscenities as adjectives and punctuation. An offender may swear to illustrate their own emotions and ideas, with no intention of using their words as a form of attack. Although your senses may be heightened by their use of vulgarities, the PO should respond in a calm manner, perhaps asking the offender to refrain from such talk. However, the PO must be able to distinguish between true aggression and simple speech patterns, or they may end up escalating what is a very benign interview, even though foul language is being used.

Repeated demands or complaints. Some offenders will make repeated demands of the PO to do the most simple tasks for them, such as making appointments, providing letters of compliance for the welfare department or housing authority, asking the PO to provide an excuse for the offender having missed a treatment session, and so forth. When the PO rightly refuses to attend to every little detail, an offender may attempt to "turn them in" by telling the PO's supervisor that the officer was uncooperative and inattentive to their needs. By making constant demands of their PO, the offender is looking for a pretext to legitimize their sense of grievance, creating an issue they consider to be worth fighting about.

Clipped or pressured speech. Some offenders couch their aggression by appearing to be overly polite. They often use very formal or stilted language, presenting themselves as being in control when they are actually seething with aggression or a sense of injustice. This is often the hallmark speech of someone with paranoid traits (Chapter 30).

Implicit threats. As with threatening sarcastic remarks, any implied threats made by an offender must never go unanswered or ignored. An offender who boasts of past acts of violence, or who warns their PO that they might not be able to stop themselves from reacting the same way in the future, must be confronted quickly and directly. In the office setting, the PO will have ready backup from fellow officers. In the event that the PO is threatened while conducting field work, he or she should retreat immediately if possible and return to the offender's residence at a later time with sufficient backup to conduct a search for any weapons or contraband.

Changes in Physical Organization and Disorganization

Facial Expressions. Facial expressions can vary a lot, depending on the mode of aggression. Facial expressions will be discussed in more detail in Section XI. The following list is not hard-and-fast, but there is real likelihood when the following facial expressions are displayed the person means what follows:

- **Clenched teeth.** An attempt to contain or control intense emotions.
- **Bared teeth.** A threat display. You may have noticed certain people smiling who are really baring their teeth.
- **Frowning.** Is often associated with anger.
- **Staring eyes.** (Particularly if there is tension in the cheeks and all around the eyes. Can be an attempt at intimidation or manipulation or targeting the other as prey.
- **Biting or compressing the lips.** Is associated with barely controllable intense emotions.
- **Quivering lips.** Is associated with fear or unhappiness.
- **Tightening the lips.** Is associated with an attempt to control or contain intense emotion.
- **Pulsating veins in the neck**. Is associated with building anger and rage.
- **Dilated pupils.** Is associated with drug intoxication.
- **Avoiding all eye contact**. When coupled with other expressions of aggression, this can be associated with planning an attack, hiding intentions of an attack, or, paradoxically, an attempt to disengage so that they won't be forced to fight.
- **Voiding.** When angered, some people have an urge to void themselves, clearing their bodies for the fight. Nausea and vomiting can occur with reduced blood flow to the gut. Other people feel a need to urinate or an onset of diarrhea. These behaviors occur when an individual is in a state of intense fear or otherwise full of adrenalin.

Breathing. Offenders who are gearing themselves up for an attack often take deep breaths, which can be slow or fast, depending on how quickly their anger is building.

- Those going into defensive aggression, fearing they will be harmed, usually breathe in a shallow, rapid, and irregular pattern, almost like panting or gasping. Some hyperventilate, breathing so fast that they go into a panic state. They may become violent out of a terror induced panic.
- Offenders who *want* the confrontation (the belligerent), and are looking forward to it often breathe very deeply, from the abdomen through the chest.
- Psychopathic offenders and others who are "professionals" at violence often maintain a smooth easy breathing pattern throughout.

Changes in Actions

As an offender becomes increasingly tense and agitated they may try to discharge the tension by pacing, often typified by rapid jerky movements. However, more predatory offenders tend to relax when they are preparing for an attack, because they are comfortable with violence.

Deliberate rejection in word and deed. Some offenders simply pay no heed to their court ordered stipulations and ignore any and all attempts made by the PO to enforce compliance. Their behavior makes their intentions, and their feelings toward authority, abundantly clear, and nothing a PO does will change their non-compliant behavior and/or criminal activity.

Posturing. As an offender moves up the scale of aggression they will begin to posture, inflating their chests and spreading their arms to make themselves look bigger, invading their victim's personal space, pacing, smacking their fist in their hand, breathing faster, etc. They may move in quick jerky starts and stops, moving toward their victim and then back again repeatedly, as if working themselves up to attack. These actions are an effort to intimidate, prior to adopting a fighting pose.

Positioning. Offenders looking for a fight or confrontation square off directly in front of their target, while those looking for a victim tend to move to the corner of the person, trying to obtain an angle on them so that they can attack more easily.

Fighting pose. A combative stance, as opposed to posturing, is often a crouch, with the chin tucked in and the hands raised. In some instances the offender may brandish a fist or a weapon. Be aware, however, that those most skilled at violence can often attack from a position of complete relaxation. One subset of aggressors, the predatory (Chapter 69), tends to relax when they are preparing for an attack. They are at home with violence, like a tiger or a snake. These individuals sometimes smile while making eye contact with you.

Figure 50.5 Experience: Appearances Are Deceptive

Those best at being dangerous often don't act dangerous! One of the authors was acquainted with a man with a reputation in some circles as the best street fighter in a section of Tokyo. He was middle-aged, short, pudgy, and out of shape. He couldn't box or wrestle. However, every morning, for one hour, he would stand in front of a mirror, and practice smiling, relaxing or gazing with a puppy-dog-like apology, perfecting utter harmlessness. Right beside the mirror was a small leather bag at head height. That was how he practiced his nearly perfect sucker punch (which was always followed by a head stomping).

Trespassing and power testing. An aggressive offender will intrude on your personal space, "accidentally" bumping into you. The offender may also test their victim's power to defend themselves by picking up, mishandling, or even breaking the other's possessions.

Visual sexual assault. Male offenders, in particular, will use their eyes to trespass on women, running their gaze over their bodies in what can only be considered a "visual rape." This is one reason why POs should always have the offender lead the way to the interview room or office. Female officers, especially, should never allow a male offender to follow them back to their office.

Displacement activities. Offenders may hit, kick, or throw objects in an effort to discharge tension, as a threat display, or as a "warm up" to an attack.

Scapegoating. This is displacement activity directed to another person. For example, an offender, angry with his PO, turns to another person in the waiting room and snarls, "What are you looking at." They want to say it to their PO, but they warm up on the bystander. This action is also an assessment tool, as they are tracking what you, the PO does in response to their verbal abuse. Other offenders will do this, often more subtly towards a family member in the PO's presence.

Making a dramatic scene. The offender "acts crazy," either to get closer to you than you would let someone who was purposefully targeting you, or to get you so preoccupied with calming them down, you lose sight of larger tactical concerns.

The Edge of Attack

Skin tone. An angry offender has a flushed face: the pale skinned turn red, and the dark skinned turn even darker. In essence, blood at the surface of the skin is a threat display, as if to say, "See how angry I am!" If they blanch—light skinned people turn bone-white, and dark skinned people get a grayish tone—this indicates RAGE. The threat is no longer potential. It is NOW.

Pacing. Increased pacing, while muttering to oneself, is arousing, bringing oneself closer and closer to the edge or attack. Along with this, some offenders engage in more and more displacement activity.

Internalize all signs of rage. Other offenders will internalize all signs of incipient assault, and thus, when the assault does occur, it seems to appear instantaneously. Right before an attack, however, the offender often stops breathing for a moment. This is often accompanied by a "quiet," the "calm before the storm," as if you aren't there. In the latter case, the offender sometimes has a "thousand-yard stare," where he or she seems to look beyond or through you. Some offenders, particularly, the psychotic aggressors, get eerie smiles on their faces, that hold no mirth. In this case, they are usually listening to voices, or psychotic thoughts within.

Going berserk. As the attack is incipient, these offenders can "lose it:" shaking, yelling, and acting berserk.

Explosion and the Aftermath

The crisis will be some form of assault, either verbal or physical. As discussed throughout this text you must do whatever you must do to ensure your own safety and that of those around you, up to and including the use of force to control the offender and the situation.

After the explosive episode, the aggressive offender moves to the *resolution* phase in which they gradually, sometimes *very* gradually, return to baseline. Their body relaxes, cognitions improve, and their actions are less stilted and threatening. After resolution, there is often a *post-crisis depression*, which is due partly to the physical depletion one experiences after the rush of adrenaline that accompanies any threatening situation, and which is partly psychological. The offender may be remorseful, apologetic, resentful, or merely withdrawn. This issue of communicating with an offender post incident will be discussed in greater detail in Chapter 72.

SECTION IX

The De-escalation of
Angry Offenders

CHAPTER 51

Preemptive De-escalation

In many instances the PO can use the tactic of preemptive de-escalation to calm an offender who seems to be brooding or obsessed with something, anything from a legitimate grievance to a delusion. An early intervention can enable the PO to avert a crisis before it happens. This technique may be more useful with an offender with whom the PO is familiar as he/she will be familiar with characteristic changes in the offender's demeanor, although the PO should certainly be able to recognize any offender's escalating irritability and frustration during an interview.

Sometimes an offender, mentally ill or not, comes in a little heated, but still rational. He or she is able to be polite to the person at the front desk and they are able to wait for their appointment. Nonetheless, they are upset. It is best the PO ask what they want or need. If you have a solution to the problem, explain it clearly to them, give them an idea how long it will take and what they should do in the interim. Always try to explain the process. Many offenders in this condition will de-escalate on their own if provided with the proper information and a time where they can expect either a resolution or further follow-up. This is particularly valid with service-level complaints.

If you notice that the offender is truly irritated, however, you should not necessarily attempt to address their irritation immediately. In many circumstances, try and draw them into a conversation about a benign subject such as the weather, the local sports team, or another area of interest to the offender. Such seemingly harmless topics can be used as an assessment tool. If they resist your trying to help them refocus, this tells you immediately that the situation is becoming serious, and your primary goal becomes one of preventing an escalation of the offender's anger and frustration.

Begin by stating impartially that you believe something is upsetting them, and that they don't appear to be themselves today. Don't pose your concern as a question, such as "What's wrong with you today?" or "Why do you seem so upset? Is there some sort of a problem?" By asking a question, you give the offender an opportunity to simply "close the door" and deny that there is a problem. Instead, use phrases like, "You are really down today. Something is going on." or "You looked really stressed out when your father dropped you off today." These phrases give the offender an opening to present their problem to you without feeling they are being interrogated.

After the offender has opened up to you and has begun discussing the issue, use open ended questions regarding possible solutions that require them to respond, such as "I see why you are so upset, but how do you think you can take care of it?" or "What do you think can be done to resolve this?" Open-ended questions are intended to bring the offender into the conversation by making them consider their options and offer their own solutions. This also gives the PO an opening to suggest other potential solutions to their problem, or to discuss the possible ramifications of the offender's suggestions.

Please note however, that questions should only be addressed to an offender who is mildly upset or agitated, not to one who is truly angry or enraged. The questions are used to "slow down" the offender to make them think. An enraged offender is beyond processing your questions, let alone being ready to think about alternative solutions. Likewise, if you notice that your questions are making the offender angrier, stop asking them, because questions demand an answer, and an angry or enraged offender will view your continued questioning as an interrogation or a failure to understand their problem.

POs should also offer positive feedback and reinforcement for any suggestions or actions taken by the offender to resolve their own issues in a constructive manner. This will encourage the offender to seek productive solutions in the future. POs should always promote the idea that offenders, especially mentally ill offenders, are able to solve their disputes in a civilized manner, as responsible adults. After all, they won't be under your supervision forever (although it may seem like it), and they can't rely on their PO to help them with all of life's setbacks.

POs can assist their offenders in developing positive outcomes by reminding them of any negative consequences that may have resulted from previous crises or problems when the offender resorted to anger or violence. Encourage them to use the coping strategies and skills they have learned to deal with difficult situations: everything from walking away, exercising, writing ideas in a journal, whatever has worked for them in the past.

Sometimes the situation can be resolved simply by allowing the offender to tell their story in order to get "it" off their chest. There is no need to problem solve and no need to interrupt. In such cases, listening with attention and respect is all that is needed.

A word of caution is necessary here though. POs must differentiate between an offender "getting something off their chest" and venting. Venting can be viewed as a form of verbal aggression, albeit toward another individual or entity who is likely not present. The danger in allowing an offender to vent for any length of time is that venting in and of itself becomes arousing to the offender. In such a case the PO will have to step in and de-escalate the offender, perhaps directing the conversation on to another topic, before the offender has worked themselves into a state of rage. This subject will be covered in more detail in subsequent chapters in this section.

CHAPTER 52

Physical Organization in the Face of Aggression

In Section II of this text, the authors discussed the issues and concerns regarding staff safety, both in the office setting and in the field as essential components in the development of a safety mindset. We offered safety protocols and procedures ranging from the arrangement of office furniture, risk assessment, and mindfulness while conducting field work. In Chapter 14, we discussed the study of body spacing as a means of honing intuitive skills. In this segment, the authors will discuss the subject of body language, body spacing, and positioning on a tactical level.

Tactical concerns such as whether to sit or stand when interacting with the offender, the time and location of the interview, the issues being discussed, and the history of the individual offender all have a direct impact on a PO's ability to defend him/herself. These questions should be considered before each interview with each offender, no matter their previous history of compliance and cooperation. As a PO remember, how you stand, how you breathe, eye contact, and your gestures are all essential factors in calming aggressive offenders. You can say all the right things, but if you look like you are afraid, irritated, or angry, your verbal interventions and commands will have little to no effect, and the situation will only get worse. Furthermore, you will not be able to successfully and safely de-escalate an offender if you are *overwhelmed* by the fear of violence. That fear only gives the aggressive offender power. On the other hand, knowing that you can handle the violence the offender might offer gives you the power to negotiate a safe resolution.

Please note that the authors don't wish to give the impression that POs should be in a constant state of combat readiness, assuming a defensive stance during each interview with an offender, and going through a day tense and hyper-alert to the slightest threat. Instead, we wish to impart the importance of body positioning as a component of personal safety and self-defense.

How to Organize your Body

Use Circular Breathing. Breath slowly, with the entire torso, not high in the chest. When you breathe rapidly with your chest, you tend to hyperventilate, which "tells" the brain that you are in trouble because you need more oxygen now! Deep, forceful chest breathing, on the other hand, excites the more primal areas of the brain: not flight, but fight. Circular breathing (Chapter 18) is ideal to maintain oneself in crisis situations.

For those who are not able to use circular breathing effectively, a more simple method is to inhale on a four count, hold your breath on a four count, and exhale on a four count. [16] Controlled breathing, of any kind, is effective in helping you keep cool and focused. Without it, feelings of nervousness or agitation will appear in your behavior, and may make the situation worse. On the other hand, when you are centered, people tend to feel calmer in your presence.

Figure 52.1 Concerning Breathing Patterns

Think of officers in your agency who walk into volatile situations and everyone simply calms down. Think, also, of officers who escalate the situation the moment they arrive. Were one to track their respective breathing patterns, you would probably be able to predict what was going to happen observing two or three breaths.

Standing or sitting. Based on concerns for your own safety, you always have to judge if you should be standing up or sitting down as you converse. In the office setting, you will most likely be seated, and your office furniture should be arranged to facilitate your safety. However, remaining seated when someone is menacing you is unwise. During field interviews, you will be standing, either in the street or just inside the offender's residence. At these times, you should be aware of potential avenues of escape, and not allow yourself to be maneuvered into a position where your exit route is blocked. POs should not encumber themselves by holding unnecessary items, such as a cup of coffee, car keys, or paperwork while interviewing offenders in the field either.

Move slowly and smoothly. Agitated offenders startle easily, and any sudden movements or gestures on your part may be interpreted as an attack, or simply surprise the offender into a physical reaction. By breathing slowly and moving smoothly, you intend that the offender mirrors your actions and attitude. Not surprisingly, overt frustration, anger, or hostility toward the offender will cause them to become more fearful and/or aggressive, increasing the likelihood of a physical altercation. Don't make any sudden moves, unless the fight has started.

Establish eye contact. In most cases, try and establish some type of eye contact. As with the other aspects of body language discussed above, you must be both non-threatening and non-threatened. Glaring at the offender with hostility or darting your gaze around nervously will just serve to make the offender more ill at ease, and may actually cause them to attack preemptively.

- Some psychotic offenders find eye contact to be very invasive. Particularly when they are calm, or only slightly agitated, angle your body in such a way so that they don't feel confronted or forced to make eye contact with you. Even with these offenders, however, you must make eye contact to establish control if they escalate into real aggression.
- Some offenders may be so frightening that you feel apprehensive about making eye contact with them. Others are so chaotic, manipulative, or disorganized that you find yourself unable to focus on what to do or say when your eyes meet. If situations like these, look between their eyes, at the bridge of the nose or the center of the forehead. You will find yourself far

calmer, and the offender, *if aggressive*, will not be able to tell the difference. You will just appear very strong.

- There is a disinterested "no-eye-contact" that can be used with *aggressive-manipulative* people (Chapter 68).

Regardless of the exact nature of the situation or the offender's mental state, never look totally away from the aggressive offender. If you turn your attention away from the offender for even an instant you have given them an opportunity to attack undetected. An attack takes but a split second, especially in close quarters, despite your body positioning and spacing. The offender must be aware that *you* are aware.

Stand at an angle. This is sometimes called a "blade stance," because you stand with one foot in front of the other, the back foot at a 45-degree angle with some space between, thus angling your body. Don't line your feet up, heel to heel ("T-Stance"). There should be at least a two fists space between where your heels fall on the "east-west" axis. This stance does not have to be overtly threatening, or give the appearance that you are fearful. Indeed, this stance can be calming, as the offender can tolerate your proximity better than if you were standing squarely in front of them, a more confrontational posture. Of course, this stance also allows you to react more easily to an attack.

You can and should also sit with a "blade stance" in many situations. You sit on the edge of your chair, with your lead foot flat on the floor, and your other placed on the ball of the foot. You look interested and attentive, but in fact, you can easily get up without the use of your hands, or need to lean forward to get back on your feet.

Don't stand too close to the offender. POs can't lose sight of the fact that offenders also have a sense of personal space, and some offenders, especially those with a mental illness, may have an *extreme* view of personal spacing issues. Some of these offenders will see any intrusion into their zone as an attack, and may respond with violence. For everyone's safety, POs have to carefully consider how close they get to an aggressive or disorganized offender. They will become more agitated, uncomfortable, or uneasy the closer you get. Step back so that the offender doesn't feel pressured or intimidated, and by all means do not get so absorbed in communicating with them that you are not aware of their distress at your proximity.

Don't allow the offender to stand too close to you. Just as POs must be aware of proper spacing between themselves and the offender, they also have to warn the offender when he/she approaches too closely. In essence, the PO needs to maintain proper spacing between themselves and the offender. If an offender keeps trespassing into personal space, tell them calmly that you are happy to talk about their problems, but they should step back: they are standing too close. You should not display any signs of fear or unease. By responding calmly and firmly, you are letting the offender know that you are alert and aware of danger, as well as able to take care of yourself.

Figure 52.2 Intercultural Spacing and Eye-contact: One Author's Experience

As you surely know, various cultures have different "rules" regarding physical proximity and distance. To make matters more complicated, people within any culture are more diverse than you could possibly imagine.

I lived in Japan for well over a decade. It is a truism that people from East Asia don't like direct eye contact as much as people from America. However, I have had some Japanese people stare so deeply in my eyes that I felt like they were counting the wrinkles in my brain

On another occasion, I was teaching a safety class to a group of security guards, all Hispanic. I was demonstrating the proper physical spacing to accompany verbal de-escalation, and one of the men stood up and said, "Bro, you white guys, you kill me. If you acted like that in the 'hood, no one would want to talk to you. We stand like this." And with that, he walked up, a little off to the side, shook my hand and put the other arm around my waist, in friendly embrace. Everyone in the room was laughing, and I asked, "So, it's midnight, and you are on your rounds here on campus, and that's how you go up to the guy in the 'hoodie," with one hand in his pocket, peeking in the window at the girl's dorm? After the laughter subsided, the man pointed at a quiet fellow sitting in the back and said, "Yeah, I know, I know. And another thing, Jose, over there, he doesn't like anyone standing close to him." (laughter again, then he said to Jose) "We still like you, man. That's just how you are."

So do not assume that someone is close to you because they are from "x" culture. Someone *from* x culture may be getting close to you with the intention of harming you, just like someone from your own. To be sure, you should take cultural conventions into account. At the same time, such individuals are now living in "your" culture (wherever our reader resides) and therefore, in setting your own limits regarding space, you are teaching them how better to survive in their new home. Therefore, if someone is too close for your comfort, whatever culture they are from, tell them, tactfully, to move back (so that you can continue your conversation with more ease, and conceivably, safety). Each situation is different. But bottom line, you shouldn't loom over them nor should they EVER loom over you or in a professional context, shake your hand and hug you with the other arm.

Keep your hand quiet. When communicating with an aggressive offender, POs should minimize hand gestures and other movements that could be misinterpreted as an attack. When adopting a comfortable stance, clasp one wrist with the other hand. Don't clasp one hand in the other because you may begin wringing them unconsciously if you get nervous, making you look scared and perhaps evoking the aggression you are trying to avoid.

By clasping your wrist, you broaden yourself slightly. You will feel solid rather than nervous. Furthermore, you can easily bring your hands upwards to fend off or block a strike if you have to, without looking like you are ready to do so. There is no apparent fight in your stance, just strength.

Use your hands as a calming fence. Fences lend a feeling of security.[17] Some of us lean on a fence to talk to our neighbor, but we also have a sense of privacy and protection. Similarly, when you place both of your hands, in front of you, palms out, you establish a boundary between you and the offender. The arms should angle from the body at about thirty degrees, and the hands should be relaxed and curved slightly. If the offender comes close enough that their body or hands touch yours, with your arms in this position, there is no doubt that they are intruding on your personal space. Upon making physical contact with you, most offenders will back off. If they don't, this means that they are either no longer aware of personal boundaries, or worse, they are about to attack. You can also use your upraised hands to push away or fend off the offender if necessary. Your hands should be relaxed, and not clenched in a rigid, fighting posture. Your hands and arms should express that you are closed off to physical contact, but open to listening.

Another option is to hold your hands at about chest height, palms up, with the back of one hand in the palm of the other. In this case, you can "talk" a little with your hands, moving them in unison. You are moving naturally, but at the same time minimizing your gestures. If you move your hands too much, you will further confuse those in chaotic states, or betray your own anxiety. The advantage of this posture, however, is that your hands are higher, even more ready to ward off an attack.

Figure 52.3 Don't Use Only One Hand

Paradoxically, holding up *one* hand, although weaker from a combative perspective, is more likely to provoke the offender. Rather than a fence, a single hand becomes the leading point of a triangle, your shoulders being the other two points. Offenders may experience this as if your hand is up to shut their mouth.

Don't touch the irritated person hoping to calm them down. There are very few occasions where touching angry offenders will make the situation better. Such situations do exist with distraught children, perhaps, but not with adults, and *particularly* not with aggressive offenders. The only times you will touch a potentially aggressive offender should be to handcuff them, control them, or protect yourself.

Try to get the offender to sit down. Pacing and stomping around is stimulating, and when you are standing, you are more ready to fight. On the other hand, we associate sitting with peaceful communication. Whenever tactically possible, try and remain seated, and instruct the offender to remain seated also. Should the offender repeatedly rise out of their chair, the situation is obviously escalating. If the offender stands, you should stand as well, because otherwise you are at an immediate disadvantage.

If they try to disengage, let them. Assaults frequently occur when the offender tries to disengage, but the PO insists on working things out *right now*. This is almost always a mistake, especially if the offender is leaving to calm down. However, if the offender is too enraged, or has overtly threatened to commit an act of violence *after* they leave, then public safety becomes the PO's more immediate concern, and the offender must be detained until the issue is resolved satisfactorily.

Arresting the offender is not always necessary, nor is it always the solution, but they should not be allowed to leave the office when they are in such a highly agitated state. Under such circumstances the PO must attempt to de-escalate the offender to a more rational emotional state before allowing them to leave the office. Sometimes this will simply entail allowing the offender to "cool off" in the PO's office, or perhaps contacting a family member, or a member of the offender's treatment team to come to the office in an attempt to defuse the situation.

CHAPTER 53

Tone and Quality of Your Voice
for De-escalation

Use a firm, low pitch. In most situations, try to pitch your voice a little lower than is usual for you, only slightly lower than normal, not necessarily a baritone; it should also be firm and strong. An angry person will focus on your tone rather than the content of your words. Don't betray any negative or angry emotions. A bored tone with either impatience or condescension is guaranteed to evoke more anger, not less. A calm, low-pitched voice communicates to the offender that you are in control of yourself and the situation.

When you pitch your voice lower, you feel a little vibration in your chest. When we are upset or frightened, we may feel out of control of everything, including our own body. Under stress our voices tend to go up in pitch. When you feel the vibrato of your voice in your chest, you get immediate feedback that you have taken control back of your own body, restoring your sense of power. The following will be helpful for controlling your voice:

Slow down. Generally, you should speak a little slower than the offender you are de-escalating. However, don't speak with an exaggerated slow motion quality, or in such a way that they think you are trying to hypnotize them. By slowing down, you are trying to get them to resonate with your slower energy, and also to keep yourself from being swept up in their aggression.

Don't be overly "sweet" or condescending. When communicating with an angry offender, especially an adult offender, don't use a condescending or patronizing tone. Talking to adult offenders, even those with a mental illness as if they were children, will cause the offender to become even more angry and agitated, possibly in an effort to prove to you that they are not a child (See Chapter 70 for an exception to this rule).

If necessary give clear firm verbal commands. You will sometimes find that a lower pitched voice won't grab and hold the offender's attention. For offenders who are very disorganized or angry, the use of a low-pitched voice won't be as effective, because it won't penetrate through the fog of their hysteria or agitation. When necessary, such as when a weapon is present, POs must give the offender clear, firm, and loud commands to cease and desist. Don't yell shrilly or with a pleading tone. Be firm and authoritative, letting the offender know that you are in command, while at the same time offering them an opportunity to negotiate a safe resolution to the crisis.

When necessary use of a dramatic voice Sometimes the best tactic is to use a dramatic voice, loud and somewhat enthusiastic, using charisma to grab attention.

Figure 53.1 Examples of the Use of a Dramatic Voice

A mentally ill woman is upset because she thinks people in a courthouse lobby are laughing at her. You say, "Claire, I SEE you are upset! I'D be upset too if I thought those people were laughing at me! Now COME ON over here!" Indicate with your body where you want her to go, moving as if you are absolutely certain she will comply. "C'mon. I want you to tell me EXACTLY what happened! EVERY word! Let's go over here where no one can bother us!"

Show her that not only are you giving her your complete attention, but the drama means that she is important, the center of the action. By moving her somewhere else to talk, you remove her from the scene that is upsetting her.

When to use the "battle cry." There are almost no situations where you should be yelling at the offender. There is one exception however. When the offender is moving toward you to attack, or is otherwise presenting immediate danger to another you should roar like a lion to startle and freeze the offender's motion momentarily with commands like "STAY BACK" or "STEP AWAY," so you can evade, counter, or escape. The way you do this is as follows:

- Open your eyes WIDE!
- "Slam" your stomach BACKWARD to try and connect your navel and your spinal column.
- Tighten your throat. (This will be a little painful to some people, leaving a raw throat for the next day, but it's worth it if it saves you or someone else from harm).
- **ROAR** a command.

Figure 53.2 The Choice of Words for a Battle Cry

When an offender, already close to you, is moving toward you with hostile intent, don't command that they "Stop" or "Freeze." They may comply and still be too close. Instead, command that they **"Step Back"** or **"Move Back"** or **"Back Off."**

The commands **"Stop"** or **"Freeze"** should be used to arrest an action that will, in itself, result in harm, for example, if an offender is about to assault another person, throw something, or simply run out into traffic, or to shock them into momentary immobility, so that you can effectively deploy a weapon to stop their threat.

CHAPTER 54

Across the Spectrum of Anger

All of the de-escalation techniques outlined in this section are for an offender between 20 – 95 on the aggression scale. They are contraindicated with an enraged offender who is between 95 – 99.

Figure 54.1 Strategies for Angry Offenders Versus Enraged Offenders

To Underscore: Strategies used to de-escalate angry people don't work with <u>enraged</u> offenders. In fact, they will very likely further escalate the situation. Imagine trying to "validate" a berserk methamphetamine intoxicated psychotic, "I see you want to rip my brains out of my skull and smear them on the walls. You've been having a rough day today."

Conversely, using strategies that are suitable for enraged offenders (control tactics) with angry offenders will flame them upwards *into* rage. Imagine coming home and your spouse tells you that he or she is not happy at all that you forgot the groceries in the trunk of the car, and you say, "Step back. Give me five feet right now!"

In any case, the PO must first center themselves before stepping into the center of the conflict and establishing control of the situation and the offender. (If you have properly trained in the procedures in Section III, centering is an almost instantaneous act.) Once the offender is under control and their anger has cooled, you can attempt to resolve the situation that led to the aggression.

If you don't establish safety for yourself and others, you can be of no assistance to the offender, or anyone else. This does not mean that you should cease talking with, reassuring, or negotiating with the offender. What the authors mean is that everything you do must have a tactical basis. In the sections that follow, the reader will be introduced to a variety of de-escalation techniques, some of which may appear to be polar opposites of each other. Some are applicable over a wide range of circumstances, whereas others may only be useful in very specific situations. Think of them like the scales and octaves of music that must be mastered so that you can improvise freely.

Remember, de-escalation is about resolving everyone's problem, which obviously includes you and the offender. Your problem is the agitated offender, while their problem is attempting to obtain a goal of some sort. After all, offenders become angry and violent because they want something. Successful negotiations will work to solve everyone's problem, although the offender is not likely to achieve exactly what they want at the moment.

Mentally ill offenders present a somewhat different problem regarding de-escalation as opposed to "regular" offenders, because their fears, concerns, and outbursts may be due to their mental illness, and not necessarily their desire for something. In other words, their problems are internal, although at the moment of crisis, this may be difficult to distinguish. Here are some guidelines for handling the angry mentally ill offenders:

De-escalate, and then solve the problem. Your focus should be on what the offender is doing, and not the cause of their anger. You can't solve a problem with an angry person. Remember, the offender sees the conflict as a win-lose proposition. He/she will view any negotiation or agreement as a loss of power. For this reason, first eliminate the anger, and then engage in problem-solving.

Officer presence. The POs presence, especially in the field or at a residential treatment facility, can be enough to calm an offender down. "Presence," however, does not merely mean that you are "there." It means that you have established through your stance and demeanor, an authority that can't be ignored.

Watchful waiting. A crisis always requires a moment-by-moment decision on the best course of action. Sometimes, all that is necessary is that you remain centered and ready, as the offender calms himself or herself without any assistance from anyone else. This does NOT mean that you ignore them, but from time to time, the best control tactic is letting them control themselves.

Trust your hunches. As the authors have noted several times throughout this book, POs should pay attention to their intuition and "gut feelings." If you have a vague sense that something is wrong with the offender, you are probably right. Pay close attention to the offender's behaviors, both verbal and non-verbal, and simultaneously, undertake an on-scene threat assessment. What do you see? How is the offender interacting with other people? Have they been having any problems recently? What is different now from the way they act normally?

One point of contact. When de-escalating an offender, only one person, preferably their assigned PO, should be communicating with them. This becomes more relevant the angrier they become. Trying to talk to two or more people at once, particularly if *they* are not in complete agreement, will cause the angry offender to become more and more confused, as well as making him/her feel surrounded and overwhelmed.

Be what you want them to be. Speak calmly, control your breathing, and maintain an upright and non-threatening posture, all the while remaining ready to respond to any attack. Your intention is that the offender will template to your behavior and demeanor. This is not an unattainable goal. In a crisis situation people tend to mirror the behavior of the most powerful individual with whom they are interacting. If the PO is out of control, the offender will feel even more threatened, and become even more aggressive. If you are calm, however, you can imbue the situation with that calm.

Tell me—don't show me. As elementary a suggestion as this might sound, the following illustrates the power of this intervention. An offender, very upset, begins swearing at a PO on the phone. She replies, "Al, it is absolutely clear that you are upset. Furious! And I am able to help you with this. But I can't and won't do that when you swear at me. You can tell me why you are upset; you don't need to show me."

Demonstrate empathy. Empathy is not the same as sympathy, that feeling of sorrow for the person's plight. Empathy simply means that you understand, approximately, what other people are feeling based on their physical organization, what they say and how they say it. Use phrases such as, "I understand you are…." or "What you are saying really makes sense." Or "I imagine I'd feel the same way…." We thereby demonstrate that we grasp what the offender is experiencing without necessarily agreeing with it.

Figure 54.2 Caution
Don't overuse this, or you will sound like a parody of a therapist. Like everything else we have discussed, it is a tactical communication to be used sparingly at just the right time. Consider such a statement, perfectly timed, during an interrogation.

Be professional. Some officers act in far too friendly and informal a manner. Professional distance gives the subject of your attention a clear understanding of the true nature of your relationship with them. POs should not allow people to call them buddy, pal, dude, babe, or any other form of casual address that implies a friendship or intimate relationship. Conversely, the officers should address offenders with the respect they deserve. Use their name, not just "Hey you."

Team up with them. Incorporate them into your "team" by using the word "we." When they accept this unconsciously, they begin to feel that they are working with you, not against you. Such statements as listed below are helpful in teaming:
- "Let's you and me sit over here."
- "Yes, we do have a problem. Let's see what we can do to figure this out."

Give praise for their good ideas and/or positive acts. Don't be over-effusive, but highlight any positive moves the offender makes. Seriously, many of your offenders have had so little positive feedback in their lives that they can perceive a little praise as a major thing. This will encourage them to offer more productive solutions. However, praise is not a "put up," to make them feel good, as if a few mere compliments will solve everything. "Ride" the praise into a problem-solving solution. Note the examples listed below:
- "I like that idea! I think we can make it work. You have a few phone calls to make."
- "I like how you decided to ignore that guy in the waiting room. You are making some good decisions lately. If you can bring that attitude home with you, you'll not get angry at your son and this probation will go pretty smoothly. Honestly, if you can handle the kind of grief that guy was trying to give you, you can handle your kid."

Humor. This is the ability to see a situation from another perspective, can sometimes work like magic. However, you must be very careful; it only is helpful when the offender is at low levels of escalation—irritation—rather than strong anger. If they are too upset or agitated, their response to a joke or humorous comment is likely to be, "You are making fun of me," or "This is serious. You think this is a joke?"

Figure 54.3 One Author's Experience

Many years ago, one of the authors was a member of a mixed-race group when one of the men, an ex-con with a history of assaults, started singing a little song, "I got a bullet here for every white man here, because everyone should die." I smiled at him and said, "That won't work on me. I can only be killed by a silver bullet, followed by garlic and a stake through the heart." I looked at him blandly, and he gave me a momentary hard stare. Then we both broke into laughter, and the atmosphere in the room lightened considerably.

Distract. Particularly with young or cognitively impaired offenders, it is often best to simply distract them. Their anger is driven by feelings and sensations, rather than by what they are thinking. If you can change the focus of their attention, their anger often dissipates.

Honesty is golden. In any interaction with any offender, POs must be honest and forthright, never making promises (or threats) that can't be kept. This is especially true when de-escalating an angry and potentially aggressive offender. Don't try and fool the offender or agree to their demands in the heat of the moment. If you do suggest a solution, be clear as to what the limitations are, and exactly what your legal responsibilities are as their PO.

The last thing you should do is leave the offender feeling betrayed after the incident has been resolved, particularly if they are taken into custody and lodged in jail. In fact, should the offender be taken into custody, the PO has a responsibility to advise them of the violation process (after the crisis has been resolved safely, or perhaps during an interview with the offender in jail), and of any recommendations he/she will make for evaluations, treatment options, or transfer to an appropriate residential facility.

If you think of de-escalation as negotiation, then you have the opportunity to achieve a compromise solution to the problem. Since the offender is unlikely to realize their original goal you can offer them a secondary goal or solution. However, since many offenders take negotiation as concession, believing they will get everything they demand, you must be absolutely clear with them, "You want X, but X simply can't happen, so how about Y?"

Keep in mind that with de-escalation at this stage of aggression, you are not trying to intimidate the offender into compliance or capitulation, but rather to have the offender *choose* a second or third option because they eventually realize that they are not going to accomplish their original intentions through violence.

Don't try to win—try to establish peace. As the ethical PO will be honest and forthright when de-escalating an offender, so too should they be magnanimous following the successful resolution of the event. Regardless of the offender's motivations, POs should allow the offender to save face. Try to resolve the situation so that the offender can separate with pride intact. Even if they have not achieved their original goal, the offender should at least have a certain amount of respect for the professional way that his PO handled the situation. If they subsequently feel cheated or betrayed they will likely be non-compliant in the future due to the personal animosity they feel for the PO.

Another point the authors would like to make here is that word of your behavior as a PO travels quickly through the offender community and the jail. Never forget that your offenders talk to each other: all the time. If you treat an offender in a disrespectful manner, lie to them, or go back on your word, your reputation will precede you when dealing with other offenders, leading to confrontational relationships before you ever meet. The contrary is also true. Indeed, one of the authors can recall a number of occasions when, on meeting a new offender for the first time, had said, "yeah, I heard about you" or something to that effect.

Figure 54.4 Important Note

When we use the phrase "Do not try to win—try to establish peace," we are, of course, talking about the de-escalation of anger, NOT a combat situation. In the latter, your intention must be, "I will win."

A private space. As a general rule, de-escalation is best accomplished without an audience, although this is sometimes unavoidable. Whenever possible, the offender should be escorted to a more private area in the office (although your fellow officers should be close by and ready to respond to any threats or actual assault), free from the view of any onlookers, such as a waiting room full of offenders. If this is not possible, then the waiting room should be cleared until the situation is resolved.

- Disorganized offenders may be frightened by onlookers.
- Enraged or more predatory offenders may become excited by the crowd or begin to attack others who are present.
- "Bluffers" may be afraid they will lose face. Therefore, in front of others they feel they have to remain aggressive or obstinate.
- Manipulative offenders will use the crowd to their own advantage, by acting out to an even greater degree in an attempt to turn the onlookers against you. Of course, in the field, the PO may not have the authority or the ability to clear away onlookers, and you certainly don't want to isolate yourself with an angry offender in their residence. At times like these, POs should remove themselves from the residence and either return with appropriate backup, or call 911 if a police response is necessary.

CHAPTER 55

Diamonds in the Rough—
Essential Strategies for De-escalation of Anger

Codes for Living: Following the Access Route

Offenders, perhaps even more so than others, have a code, or a series of codes by which they live. Some of those codes are based on the culture into which they are born, and others are based on the culture or lifestyle they adopt. Some of these codes are passed down within a family, or offenders may create a code in reaction or resistance to the codes they were bequeathed, while other offenders develop their own credo, unique to themselves. Mentally ill offenders may develop an eccentric set of rules congruent only with their mental illness or character disorder.

The heart of their code is often a phrase or two words that sum up their deepest values. When people talk about themselves, their codes of living are often woven throughout their speech. This is especially true with an angry person, whose reason(s) for their outrage is often their belief that their code is being threatened or compromised:

- They perceive that others are demanding they violate their code.
- They believe they are facing a choice that forces them to violate their code.
- They take offense when others don't conform to their code.
- They think another's actions require them to respond, lest they violate their code.

Figure 55.1 Examples

Offender 1. "I'm a man. He can't talk about me that way."

Offender 2. "Think of how I feel. If someone did that to you, wouldn't you be upset?"

Offender 3. "Are you saying I'm not going to get paid? I did the job and you owe me. Whether you like it or not isn't the issue, you owe me!"

Offender 4. "I was standing there all alone. Everyone was looking at me. Talking about me!"

Angry offenders will very often proclaim their values and code for living in their explanation or tirade, and POs should be able to identify their core metaphor in 1 or 2 words or phrases. What is most important to each of these offenders in the above examples? Offender 1's is pride. Offender 2's is caring or empathy. Offender 3's is mutual obligation. Offender 4's is fear of being shamed.

<u>Use the code to reach the offender</u>. When you incorporate their code in your response, you are recognizing the offender's values (however misguided or anti-social). This is what the offender often means by "respect." This connection, however tenuous, allows you to work with the offender toward a resolution. Take note of the following:

- If you discern that personal integrity is a core issue of concern to a male offender, frame your responses and suggestions with the same theme. "I wouldn't want people talking about you as a man who can't control himself."

- To the young offender who believes someone treated him with disrespect (an enormous source of conflict and violence within the offender community): you can say "Man, I can see how angry you are. I'd be angry too if someone said that to me, but if you try to hurt him, you'll end up losing. You'll lose your freedom, and end up back in jail. Yeah, I know you think he *disrespected* you, but if you assault him, you would be letting him *own* you. He says three words, and your response means you lose your home, your job, and your kids, is that what you want?" Because the issue of respect is a common cause of violence, especially among youthful offenders, POs should impart upon their offenders the wisdom of English clergyman George Herbert (1593-1633), who stated that, "Living well is the best revenge."

- Sometimes a core metaphor is situational, something as ostensibly benign as the weather. "Look, Frank, it's a hot day, I'm tired, and I guess you are too. I don't care who's right here, really. I just want to finish this paperwork so you can get that appointment with your psychiatrist. The computers are down, so we have to figure out some other way to get through to them. Gosh, these days are nasty. Here we are, all stressed out just because we're both hot and tired."

- A mentally ill offender can get so focused on an issue that they get "tunnel vision," and it is all they can think about. In effect, the problem defines their existence at the moment. "You are absolutely right, those meds are disgusting. They must taste terrible, but if they didn't work so well, your doctor wouldn't ask you to take such foul tasting things. But they do work, don't they?"

Break the Pattern

POs often find themselves in the same argument(s) over and over again, and often with different offenders! In order to detect any patterns or behaviors that may have negatively affected your communication with an offender, you can easily perform personal After Action Review of your actions and responses in past disputes, noting "hot buttons," as described in Chapter 17. An honest attempt at self-reflection will hopefully reveal any patterns of behavior, personal style, even *your* personal codes, that may have had a detrimental effect on your relationship with a particular offender, or group of similar offenders. As with any occupation, POs can get "caught in a rut" that only deepens with prolonged interaction with criminal offenders, especially those who are mentally ill.

At times however, you may be forced to more dramatically break the pattern of interaction between you and an offender, by doing or saying something that makes continuing the dispute absolutely impossible. In many cases, you will use a dramatic voice or display somewhat uncharacteristic or unexpected behaviors. This technique is not recommended for "routine" episodes of de-escalation, and most definitely not as an opening in any encounter. However, breaking the pattern can be effective because many offenders expect their victims, including law enforcement personnel, to react in a somewhat predictable manner to their displays of anger and/or violence. By reacting in an unanticipated manner, you can throw the offender off balance. This tactic can work with very angry individuals. It sometimes takes the fight out of the interchange like suddenly letting out the air from a tire. Here are a few examples of breaking the pattern from one of the authors:

Figure 55.2 Author's Experience

A very aggressive, manic individual, after capering around my office while verbalizing very dangerous fantasies, whirled around and said to me, a grin of delight on his face, "You are scared, aren't you?" I blurted out, "Yes, I am," (this statement, from a story early in my career, was clearly a mistake I would not make today). He then started to stalk menacingly toward me. Realizing I was in danger, I jumped up, and yelled in a dramatic voice "You know what I'm scared about? I'm scared what's happening to kids today! They are being murdered in wars throughout the world. But we don't even have to go that far! They are cutting school lunches and little children who go to bed hungry are not even being fed in schools!!!!! I'm scared about what's happening to kids today!" With a look of shock on his face, he dropped into a chair, and said, "I like kids. What are we going to do about that?"

Figure 55.3 Author's Experience

A man came into a clinic, drunk and belligerent, looking for a fight. I came out and said, "Man, WHAT have you been DRINKING? Me, I like Ten Canes Rum. Whoa, <holding up two hands and yelling boisterously> Not your turn yet! I'm talking about my rum! Ten stalks of sugar cane for one bottle of rum. It is SWEET as sin and gold as a tiger's eye. What have YOU been drinking?" He blearily looked at me and said, "Whiskey." I said, "What KIND of whiskey. I need to know WHAT you have been drinking! Man, I love my rum. I go home, take two ice cubes and put them in a glass. When the rum hits that ice, I hear a crack as clear as the bell in a church and I know everything is going to be alright!" Within 5 minutes, we were sitting on 2 chairs, laughing and talking about our favorite drinks.

Figure 55.4 Example of the Use of Humor to De-escalate

An offender appeared at the office intoxicated. His PO placed him into custody upon which he called her the word that, more than any other makes many women incensed. With a look of puzzlement on her face, she said, "Jimmy, do you spell that with a "K" or a "C."

"K," he replied.

She answered, "Jimmy, if you are going to use big boy language, you should at least know how to spell it. It starts with a "C."

He responded "It does? Damn, they didn't teach me that one in school."

Determining the time and necessity of breaking the pattern may seem like magic, but instead, this is a highly intuitive skill that is developed with time and experience. Because future behavior is unpredictable, POs can't prepare an array of specialized catch-phrases ready to disarm an aggressive offender. This technique is pure improvisation, grounded in the same strong and powerful calm that we have written about throughout this manual. If you consciously try to be overly creative, or if you are excited about what a cool funny thing you are about to say, you may indeed say something witty, but it will be at the wrong time, to the wrong offender. When you are in control of yourself, with the mainline skills of de-escalation at hand, such improvisation will simply emerge.

Some Guidelines for Limit Setting

As soon as you draw a line, it will become the main focus of your interchange. Don't ever set a limit that you cannot enforce or one that is not reasonable and simple to understand.

Beleaguered by mental illness, struggling with substance abuse, beaten down by poverty or unemployment, offenders often experience their lives fragmenting into pieces. When the rules shift, they can become profoundly anxious. When dealing with such people, limit setting is a kindness rather than oppression.

- Your tone of voice should be matter-of-fact, rather than critical. Simply remind them of the rule or set a proper limit (a new rule, so to speak).
- Only set reasonable limits that the person can do. If you can't explain clearly why the limit is necessary, at least to your peers, and then it's not a good limit.

The following will help in setting a "full stop" limit:
- **Give clear directives with no wiggle room.** For example, you say in a confident, commanding voice, "Billy Jo, lower your voice."
- **Give praise if Billy Jo complies.** Give him a brief mark of "approval" and continue with the verbal control
- **If he does not comply with the directive, depersonalize the reiteration.** "Billy Jo, you are required to lower your voice. "Don't say, "I expect you to…." The individual should experience what you are saying as the "law," an institutional command or policy, rather than a personal issue between them and you.
- **Don't get them caught up in manipulative word games.** Don't respond to professed ignorance, excuses, or confusion. You are using this tactic because there is no ambiguity regarding the transgression and no ambiguity what the consequence will be.

Silence

Sometimes, the most powerful thing you can do is to be silent. Be sure that you are not being passive-aggressive, fuming in silent anger, or appearing to ignore or dismiss the offender. Instead, you should wait, quietly and powerfully. Such silence can evoke curiosity, anxiety, or a desire for a response. Keep your facial expressions calm, your posture centered, and carefully listen. Nod your head calmly as you listen, doing so slowly and intermittently. In many cultures, including the United States, nodding your head too rapidly indicates that you want the other person to hurry up and finish, or worse, just shut up.

Silence, however, is not that easy, particularly for the person who is suffering the brunt of another's anger. There are three ways to listen silently, and two of them will make people very angry.

Contemptuous silence. You are tired of the dispute, or tired of the offender. You fidget, you sigh, and most significantly, you roll your eyes upwards to one side, and twist one corner of your mouth. In almost every culture, this facial expression and behavior express an attitude of contempt, and is guaranteed to provoke anger or rage.

Stonewall silence. When you stonewall, you ignore the offender, or otherwise make it clear from your demeanor that you have no interest in what they have to say or why they are saying it. You can to do this inadvertently by entering case notes into your computer while the offender is talking, or by taking a phone call during the interview. On the other hand, some stonewall deliberately. Such dismissive behavior can evoke anxiety or anger in the offender who wants to get through to you, only to find that there's a "wall" in the way. As a result, the offender will do anything to get through to you, including trying to tear down that wall.

In addition to upsetting the offender, such indifferent behaviors on your part will also increase risk, and decrease your ability to defend yourself from attack because your attention is improperly focused on your computer screen or your telephone conversation, instead of where it should be, on the offender. POs are encouraged to take short notes on a piece of scrap paper or the offenders report form, and transcribe more detailed notes of the interview into the case file after the offender has left the office.

Interested silence. This is the right way to listen silently. When you have been listening quietly, the offender often interrupts to ask, "Aren't you going to say something?" or "Don't you have any ideas?" If they don't stop, and continue to talk and talk, *you* may have to interrupt them. Do this by advancing a hand slightly at waist level or a little higher, fingers curved, palms down (you don't want the offender to interpret your hand movement as a "shut up" gesture). You should also lean toward the offender slightly, indicating that it's your turn to speak. If they don't notice your hand gesture, put both hands up in front of you in a "fence," and tell them to stop a moment, in a voice that is loud and holds a little humor. "Joey, Joey, wait a minute. You 'gotta' give me a chance to say something! Listen to me a second!"

After interrupting the offender, the first thing you should do is to sum up your understanding of what he or she just said. This proves that you were indeed listening to them, and are interested in solving their problem. Once you have summed it up, you can either go into problem-solving mode, or, if they are still heated, shift into "tactical paraphrasing" (Chapter 56).

CHAPTER 56

Tactical Paraphrasing—
The Gold Standard With Angry Offenders

What is paraphrasing?

Paraphrasing is perhaps the most important technique for calming **angry** offenders. You sum up in a phrase or sentence what the angry offender has just said in a paragraph. If you paraphrase accurately, you have established that you have "gotten" it that far, so they don't have to repeat it, or try to say it in other words. It is like peeling off a single layer of an onion so that you can be shown the next layer. If you don't show that you "get" it, the offender will feel compelled to repeat and/or elaborate that layer of the problem with more and more intensity. As they get more intense, they usually get more irrational, and their ability to communicate breaks down even further. The wonderful thing about paraphrasing is that you don't have to be "smart" and interpret anything. You simply have to listen carefully.

Figure 56.1 Paraphrasing versus "Mirroring" or "Active Listening"

Many people refer to this method as "active listening" or "mirroring." We have chosen another phrase to describe it to highlight some important differences between the proper use of this method in a law enforcement context and that of many others.

- Mirroring often entails repeating word-for-word what the offender is saying. This can be experienced as taunting or mocking.
- As for active listening, this term often carries a certain ideological baggage—many counselors, following a particular theory of healing, try to establish a nurturing relationship with their client, thereby either making them "feel better," or in the safety of such "validation," allowing them to emote freely. This is, in a subtle way, manipulative. By talking to another person as if they were fragile, they may feel so, or they may feel that you are *trying* to make them feel fragile. In either event, this can elicit "contact regression," where the person becomes childish or further angry or even enraged. Unfortunately, this mode of communication has spread far beyond that one sector of counseling theory. We have both heard POs try to use this with mentally ill subjects, and it hasn't gone well at all!

Returning to our image of an onion, as you peel off each layer, the offender gets to the next layer that is driving them. They might start out complaining about their PO who was late for an appointment at the front desk, and that paraphrased, tells you that they lost their job, and that paraphrased, tells you that their wife left, and that paraphrased, starts talking about suicide.

Paraphrasing establishes that you are truly listening and have understood what they have said. There is another component where we also take a slightly activist approach. We *select* what we will sum up from the complex, multi-faceted communication that the offender has just given us, choosing the healthiest aspect of what they have just said.

This method is "self-correcting," whereas passive summation can make things worse. If you sum up an angry offender's worst impulses, they will find themselves in agreement with you. You have lined up with that which desires destruction. If you sum up an aspect of what they have said that is in the direction of conflict resolution, you will draw out of them that which does wish to resolve the conflict. On the other hand, if they are, in fact, bent on mayhem, they will correct you by escalating what they are saying, believing that you are not getting the message. Remember, they are trying to communicate! All you have to do is sum up what you understand from what they said. When you get it right, they go to the next layer.

Figure 56.2 Example of Correct and Incorrect Paraphrasing

Angry Father. I am so mad at my daughter that I could just wring her neck!"

Incorrect paraphrase: "You want to murder your daughter."

Correct paraphrase: "You are *really* furious with her!"

If you have, in the second example, accurately paraphrased the meaning of the angry father's intention, you will naturally go on to the next layer of his complaint.

Angry Father. "You won't believe what she did. I come home and find her on the couch lip-locking that punk from down the street. You know, the kid who epoxies his hair in corkscrew spikes?"

If, however, the second example is *inaccurate*, the angry father will correct you with more vehemence.

Angry Father. "No, not 'really furious.' I honestly want to loop a belt around her neck and slowly strangle her. Seriously! She better not be home when I get back from your office."

Why not simply ask the person what's going on? If they want to tell me, why don't they just answer the questions?

Asking questions is usually not a good idea with really angry offenders. They already believe you have to "get" what they are saying, and a question shows that you do not. Still angry and now frustrated at their failure, this makes them try harder, albeit with less organization and coherence than before. Over and over, they experience failure, because they can't get through to you! When anger is combined with a sense of powerlessness, the offender feels like he is "losing" to a more powerful other. In essence, they experience a question, a demand for an answer, as putting you in a dominant position in regard to them.

Figure 56.3 Example: How Irritating Questions Can Be

Imagine coming home after a bad day. You are hot, tired, and frustrated. You walk into your house, drop your gear on the floor, sigh loudly, and walk toward the shower. Your spouse says, "Did you have a bad day?" Isn't this irritating? Isn't it *obvious* you've had a bad day? After all these years together, and he/she doesn't know when a bad day just walked into the house! On the other hand, imagine your spouse observing you and saying, "Bad day, huh?" You continue walking towards the shower, and say, "I don't want to talk now. I just want a shower. I'll talk to you later." You are not "forced" to explain yourself.

How to Use Paraphrasing Successfully

It is very important that your voice is strong. You speak to the offender as someone who has the power within to take care of himself/herself and their problem, not as someone who is fragile or volatile (even if he/she is). You must contact the strong aspect of the offender, the future looking side, that which is striving for strength, looking for integrity. If you contact the weak, or the insecure, you may foster regression to a less mature level of action. Childish action is often impulsive or violent. Sometimes, you can use a dramatic summation: "You are really ticked off!" Here, you sum up the offender's mood with your voice and posture, in addition to what is being said.

Figure 56.4 Example A Successful Use of Paraphrasing

Johnny. "I never get enough sleep."

PO. "You look really tired."

Johnny. "I don't know how I look, but I feel exhausted!"

When you are inaccurate in your summation, the other usually corrects you. He is not arguing with you, just tuning up the signal.

PO. "You've been up late the last couple days, waking early, and now you are really tired, aren't you?"

You can include extra information that sums up the experience the other is having. This is for the purpose of steering the individual toward problem-solving while not giving advice. It also allows you to assess how responsive he is to you. In other words, if you add a little something, is he even able to hear it?

Johnny. "I am not tired at night."

PO. "You can't fall asleep when you go to bed, huh?"

Notice the tag lines like, "huh?" or "aren't you?" These are not really questions. They follow statements and give the other an <u>invitation</u> to correct you or give you more information.

Johnny. "I don't even bother going to bed. I just lie there looking at the ceiling if I do."

PO. "It seems like a waste of time, and then you wake up early anyway. It'd be fine if you weren't tired."

The second sentence by the officer is an attempt to sum up what he believes are Johnny's feelings about his sleep cycle. It is also another assessment—he offers Johnny something to agree with or correct.

Johnny. "Yeah, I'd be fine if I wasn't tired. I'd just sleepless and do more. But I'm too tired for that. I wonder if I need to talk to Dr. Montour about my medications. I think I need something to help me sleep."

Imagine that Johnny is a young man who is very resistant to talking about his medications, and one who usually gets in lots of trouble when he doesn't take them. If the PO had responded to his initial statement about being tired by suggesting he go to the doctor immediately ("problem-solving"), Johnny might have angrily stopped talking or argued with him. By listening and showing step-by-step that he understood him, the PO got Johnny to find the "deeper layer" of his concern by himself.

Figure 56.5 Example of Successful Use Paraphrasing With a Mentally Ill Woman (Who often becomes suicidal when frustrated)

Shoshona. "I can't believe it. He is so stupid!"

PO. "You are really upset!"

Shoshona. "No! I'm really furious!"

Note: When you sum up imprecisely, the other usually corrects you. This is as if she were tuning up the signal rather than arguing with you.

PO. "I haven't seen you this mad in a long time."

Note: You can include extra information ("in a long time," for example). This is for the purpose of steering the person in a positive direction slightly. It also helps to assess how responsive she is to you. In other words, if you add a little something, is she even able to hear it? In this case, you are validating that she hasn't been angry in a long time—in essence, that she has shown that she is able to maintain control of herself.

Shoshona. "I know. But nobody's ever done anything like this to me!"

PO. "This is something new, huh?"

Shoshona. "Yeah, I asked him out last week, after my NA meeting, and he said "yes," and then, in front of everybody, he said he was just joking."

PO. "You must have been so embarrassed!"

Shoshona. "I was ashamed. It was just like when my mom left. I felt like I wasn't good enough for anybody."

You just got the story without a single question. She even trusts you enough to tell you something real about her past. Now you are in a position to do a threat assessment, to determine if she is either suicidal or has aggressive intentions towards the guy who shamed her.

Using Paraphrasing to Communicate with Severely Mentally Ill Individuals

Paraphrasing can be remarkably effective for communication with severely mentally ill offenders. Given the internal chaos that people experience when psychotic, manic, or disorganized, it is essential that we don't add to their sense of confusion by barraging them with questions or attempting to solve their problems by taking over and telling them what they should feel or do.

Figure 56.6 Example of Tactical Paraphrasing With a Severely Psychotic Individual

After Murray didn't show at the office, his PO visited his home for a welfare check, and found him in a decompensated state

He said there are pink rose petals flying all around his head—clouds and clouds of roses. The PO could have asked him lots of questions in order to have him explain what he meant, but instead, he summed up the only thing he did grasp. (Notice the progression from one layer to another).

PO. "Pretty confusing, huh?"

Murray. "You are darn right it's confusing. How'd you like to be in my head?"

PO. "I wouldn't want to be in a confused head. It must be hard to think."

Murray. "Hard to think and scary. The roses turn bloody red, and I fly apart."

PO. "You can't keep things together."

Murray. *(nodding)* "In the fear, it feels like blood."

PO. "Feels like blood, huh? I don't see any blood out here though."

Murray. "In my head, only. Where the fear is."

Notice the officer's last sentence. Realizing that they have reached a "core point" of Murray's concern, he intervenes more actively to validate his perception ("I don't see any blood out here, though.") and, at the same time, base him in reality. If, near the end, the PO had asked, "Is anybody hurt?" Murray might have been overwhelmed. Murray might think that the PO seems worried, and he could start thinking of all the people whose feelings he has hurt over the years, and wondering if he hurt someone and can't remember, etc. By making a matter-of-fact statement, the PO takes a lot of psychological pressure off the offender, and it is easier for him to re-organize enough to be able to communicate.

Remember, though, that paraphrasing is self-correcting. Murray might have replied, "There's no blood out here. She's lying in the back. That's where the blood is."

Core

We know we have reached the core level when there is no more "progress." The offender "spins his wheels." They may use different words, but they say essentially the same thing over and over again. Other offenders express relief at being finally understood. Some offenders exhibit an intensification of emotion, because you have reached that which is most distressing. When you reach core, and it is clear that you are on the same wavelength, you can begin problem-solving. This can be:

- Further paraphrasing, where you show greater and greater understanding about what they are upset about.
- A summation of the core problem, followed by a puzzled "why?" For example, "You trusted him, and let him stay in your home. He came on to your daughter and stole money. I can understand why you'd be so furious at him. What I am confused about is if you do break his arm, he wins. He gets hurt, sure, but you will be violated and go to jail, and no one is home to protect your daughter. We have to figure out a way that you can really win without getting into trouble."
- With some offenders, you have, by paraphrasing them every step of the way, established that you are a person of trust. In some cases, you can now be quite directive, because people often are willing to accept advice or even instruction from people we trust.
- With others, we are ready to engage in a collaborative process of problem-solving, trying to figure out a way to solve the situation that is in the best interest of everyone involved.

Don't Waste It

Paraphrasing is almost a cliché, so much so that we can imagine some of you rolling your eyes when you read the title of this chapter. This technique is too important to abandon, and at the same time, it must be used carefully, i.e., *rarely*. If mentally ill offenders are used to you using paraphrasing as your primary method of discourse, they will cut you off, because you will appear to them to be giving nothing back, except mirroring. It is "cold fare" compared to a rich dialogue, a combustible exchange of views, or a lush conversation. <u>If the individual is not getting angry and requiring you to use de-escalation tactics, don't use paraphrasing. Simply talk with them.</u>

If there is a crisis, however, and the offender does *not* believe they are understood, *now* paraphrasing comes into its own. Paraphrasing can have an almost electrifying effect with an angry individual. Imagine the feeling when you try to pull a splinter from under your fingernail, and after ten long minutes of aggravating struggle, you get a hold of it finally and pull it out of your nail bed. That is the sense you get when, angry and desperate to be heard, you realize that the other person "got it."

Figure 56.7 How to master paraphrasing

As you as you view paraphrasing as a 'specialized,' pseudo-counseling technique, you probably won't want to do it—and you won't be good at it anyway. When you are hit by adrenaline, dealing with an angry, perhaps mentally deranged offender, you will stumble over your words if you try to remember to say things like:

- "So what you are sharing with me is . . ."
- "What I hear you saying is . . ."

Don't do this! Many people will find you irritating, and you will be in your head at a time where you must be aware of what's going on in front of you.

You are, in fact, a master of paraphrasing. You do it all the time simply keeping a conversation going, saying things like:

- "Your kid flunked out, huh?"
- "You're not getting a raise."
- "You hate that guy."
- "She's the one."

In short, the natural statements you intersperse in any conversation are perfect paraphrasing. However, because you do this unconsciously, it's hard to tap into as an *emergency technique*. It's easy to perfect, however. Consider this—how many conversations do you have a day? Twenty? Thirty? Forty? <u>In each and every conversation, at an arbitrary moment of your choosing, decide to paraphrase the next thing they say.</u> Just once. Your conversational partner won't even notice. But because you made a conscious decision to do this, your brain notices. That means you have practiced that skill twenty to forty times a day. Consider how good your take-down or hand-cuffing skills would be if you do twenty, thirty, forty perfect repetitions every day—it would become automatic! Similarly, if you do this every day, you will be able to step into crisis oriented paraphrasing without hesitation. It will be so natural to you that you do not even have to think about it.

CHAPTER 57

Big Mistakes That Seemed Like Such Good Ideas at the Time

Unlike report writing, where the PO has ample opportunity to refine and edit their work before submission to the Court, de-escalation requires on the scene improvisation, in a very fluid and dynamic setting, often with volatile and unpredictable offenders. In such a highly charged atmosphere, where clear communication is necessary to prevent any misunderstandings that may worsen the situation, POs must think quickly, but calmly, before speaking.

By maintaining a professional emotional distance, and not reacting personally to anything the offender may say, you will be less likely to escalate an already heated situation. Conversely, POs must not be obsequious, or claim to relate personally to the offenders' problems, as any personal comparisons will just anger the offender further.

Many mistakes are very obvious, and the moment something leaves your mouths you think, "Uh-oh. I shouldn't have said that!" Fortunately, this can be prevented rather easily by taking a moment to gather thoughts before responding to what the offender has said. Sometimes holding up your hands to give them pause will give you time to gather your own resources, and then reply.

Some mistakes are subtler. On certain days, you may be tired, not feeling well, or be distracted by family matters perhaps, and de-escalating an angry offender is the last thing you wish to do. Not surprisingly, risk increases when you are at less than your optimum ability and awareness, and you are more likely to make a mistake in your communications with the offender at these times. You actually need to be more alert, and in control of both yourself and the immediate situation when you are not at your best.

The following topics are areas the authors feel POs should take special note, so as not to make innocent blunders that may lead suddenly to escalating encounters with angry offenders:

Ingratiation. Don't try to ingratiate yourself with the offender; don't pretend that a potentially aggressive situation or encounter has not developed by continuing to engage the offender as you would normally; and, don't ignore the aggressive behavior or language while calmly going about your business in the hopes that the offender will eventually tire himself or herself out.

One of the paradoxes of ingratiation is that POs who belie their professional integrity by allowing the offender to control their interactions often present themselves as having a "special rapport" with an offender who, in fact, intimidates them. Oddly enough, these same officers, who try to avoid conflict, or "make nice," are often suppressing a lot of anger at being controlled. They displace this on those who call them on what they are doing. Thus, one of the first signs that the PO is ingratiating himself or herself is an attitude of self-righteousness, a defense mechanism that enables them to avoid questioning the violations of their own integrity. The following factors are also signs of ingratiation toward the offender:

- You worry about "how things are going" between yourself and the offender, and act or react accordingly.
- You are sometimes ashamed of your actions, or believe that you act in a cowardly fashion in the way you interact with the offender.
- You believe you are caring and nice, so you react with shocked outrage when an offender is unkind, cruel, or aggressive toward you, as if you and the offender have made some sort of transaction that they have now betrayed.
- You allow the other offender to speak to you in overly familiar or rude terms, such as dude, buddy, pal, babe, sweetheart, etc.

The mistake of mind reading. Sometimes, POs will try to connect with an offender by telling them how they must feel, by confessing to having the same issues, or claiming to have gone through a similar situation. As noted elsewhere, personal comparisons normally make the offender even more indignant at your assumed familiarity. Statements like, "I know how you feel," "I know you love your son," or "When I...." are statements that the angry offender may not agree with at all. They then decide to prove you wrong by demonstrating that they are NOT what you just said they are.

The mistake of allowing venting. Pure venting is an expression of energy, such as going for a run chopping wood until fatigued, so that you can "let go" of an unpleasant incident, or just a bad day at work. In Chapter 14 we referred to letting an offender "get something off their chest." This is not the same as venting. The purpose of the former action is to get finished with something by talking about it—the purpose of the latter is to stoke oneself up into higher levels of aggression. Generalized aggression expressed verbally in front of others (tantrums), or aggression expressed about one person to another is also designated by the same term. And tantrums by adult offenders can be life-threatening.

Many people have a false idea about aggression, and imagine it to be some kind of psychological fluid that builds up pressure inside of us. When we vent (hence the word), these people believe that we get rid of the anger and then become peaceful, similar to a valve releasing pressure from a water line. Aggression, however, is not a fluid; it is state of arousal. Just like any other state of arousal—sexuality, happiness, excited interest—additional stimulus elicits more arousal. When you shout, yell, complain, kick things, or the like, you are stimulating yourself to greater and greater aggression. Therefore, if you allow an offender to vent angrily, rather than helping them to calm down, the more angry they will become. This only makes de-escalation more difficult.

Don't attempt to parse any distinctions between venting directed at other people, and either anger or rage. Simply consider it for what it is: aggression. When you let an offender vent about other people, they perceive that you are giving implicit approval to their verbal complaints and abuse. If you listen to their venting silently, without de-escalating or controlling their verbal escalation, they believe you are on their side. However, when they get so angry that they start to become dangerous and *then* you object, they will turn on you, feeling betrayed. <u>If an offender begins to vent, de-escalate and control them.</u>

Obvious mistakes we shouldn't make but do anyway. Although some of the items included in the following list have been discussed elsewhere in this book, they are repeated here as a reminder to the reader of the seemingly minor, yet crucial, details of de-escalation. POs should not:

- Make threats or promise consequences you can't keep. False promises or implied threats, which the offender may know the PO is incapable of keeping, will lessen your credibility. The failure to follow through on promises made or consequences threatened will also serve to undermine your authority with the offender after the incident has been resolved.
- Bombard the offender with choices, questions, and solutions, as this will only overwhelm the offender, especially if they are suffering from mental illness.
- Ask an upset offender "why." Asking a "why" question demands an answer or an explanation from the offender, something they may be quite unwilling, or unable, to do. "Why" questions should only be used when you have used paraphrasing to reach the core problem successfully (Chapter 56).
- Talk down to the offender as if they were stupid or ignorant, or, conversely, in an overly solicitous manner. Don't roll your eyes or sigh heavily while the offender is trying to communicate with you. Don't interrupt as they speak, particularly to correct what they are saying. On the other hand, interruption of aggressive verbalizations or pointless monologues on the part of the offender IS the right thing to do.
- Analyze their behavior while de-escalating. Problem-solving and evaluations can be completed after safe de-escalation.
- Share the offender's private information in front of others.

Figure 57 Concerning Offender's Privacy

Be mindful of "hallway consultations" and consider who may be within earshot of your conversations, either with other offenders or with your fellow officers. If offenders overhear you discussing the details of another offender's case they may think, "If they talk about that person like that, they are probably talking about me in the same way."

- Take things personally when the offender attacks your character or professionalism. The measure of the true professional is NOT taking things personally.
- Allow the offender to trespass on your personal boundaries, or violate theirs. The safety issues inherent in personal spacing issues are quite obvious. Safety is enhanced when one enforces a strong, professional hierarchical relationship with the offender.

- Touch, push, or try to forcefully move the offender from one place to another, or point at them in a threatening manner. In fact, POs would be well-served to limit any personal contact with all offenders to the obligatory handshake, and even that minimal contact is not necessary. The only time POs should lay their hands on an offender is when they are defending themselves physically or taking the offender into custody.

- Adopt an authoritarian or demeaning attitude, particularly in front of their   peers or other on-lookers, including fellow officers. Authoritarian attitudes and behaviors are some of the most common precipitants of assault by offenders.

SECTION X

Communication With Mentally Ill and
Emotionally Disturbed Youth

CHAPTER 58

Working With Potentially
Aggressive Youth

> ### Figure 58.1 A Note Concerning Youth
>
> Generally speaking, you will use the same de-escalation strategies with youth as are outlined in the rest of this book. The differences are often more on nuance than on major details. We have, however, "sub-divided" youth in some general categories based on behavior that will help both in understanding young people as well as using the best strategies to help stabilize and calm them when they have become aggressive or are otherwise in crisis.

General Concerns

The youth described in this chapter are young *now*, but they will grow up to be adults, perhaps living in your community. Understanding them will aid you—and them—in the coming years. Youth today don't just face "coming of age" growing pains. Despite all the prosperity and opportunity in our society, youth face many dangers. Drugs are everywhere, and not only do they affect children directly, but also, far too many have been affected *in utero* by their parents' drug abuse, and not just by their mother: there are questions about genetic changes in the sperm of male drug/alcohol user as well. Furthermore, when one's parents use drugs and alcohol, their attentiveness and caring towards their children is lessened in the "best" of such circumstances; abuse of all kind increases exponentially in drug/alcohol abusing homes.

Gangs metastasize within a community, just like cancer. There is a putrescent vitality to gang life that is both charismatic and compelling. Despite the terrible things one may do, the gang offers solidarity, and a life committed to something bigger than oneself, however damaging that might be. Once initiated, one crosses a line that is hard to cross back over. This charisma, by the way, is not only attractive to children from broken or abusive homes; the vitality of a warrior culture, no matter how violent and destructive to both its victims and its own members seduces children from loving families as well. It is only when "the good" has a power and charisma greater than that of gang culture that youth find it easy to turn away.

Youth and young adults manifest mental illness in much the same manner as adults. If a young person is displaying psychosis, mania, latency, or any of the other behaviors described in Section VI, the strategies offered there are fully applicable. In this section, we will be describing the character traits that are often related to aggression in youthful offenders; you can view these traits as the youth's fundamental attitude towards the world. A reader might reasonably ask when dealing with an aggressive sounding youth, how could one tell what mode they are in?

View each chapter in this section as a quick step-by-step process. If the approach on impulsive youth, Chapter 59, does not work, quickly move on to the next. Once you are familiar with that particular youth, you will know exactly where to start. Furthermore, it is quite likely that you will, intuitively, grasp that a youth is in one or another mode, and start with the tactics appropriate to that behavior. At any rate, this section will take things as a quick (matter of moments) step-by-step process. [18]

Figure 58.2 The Effect of the Presence of Family on the Youthful Offender

Some youth are far calmer in the presence of their parents, or other family members. Others escalate when their parents are there, and are much more manageable when they leave. Quite often the parents' behavior is the proximate cause of the youthful offender's aggression. POs should note how the youthful offender acts while in the presence of family members and make a tactical decision whether to include or exclude them in any meetings.

CHAPTER 59

No Brake Pads: A Consideration
of the Impulsive Youth

Children in the United States have been allegedly plagued by an epidemic of Attention Deficit Disorder (ADD)/Attention Deficit Hyperactivity Disorder (ADHD) diagnosis. Per orthodox theory, attention disorders come in two major forms. In the first type, the main manifestation is a short attention span. In the second type, hyperactivity is also present. Although beyond the scope of this book, the issue of ADD/ADHD diagnosis deserves more debate than it is currently receiving in both the media and clinical sources. (We have listed two books that provide that needed contrarian viewpoint).[19]

Figure 59.1 Note on ADHD

This type of problem is not only endemic in America. One of our colleagues wrote to us that in Northern Ireland, "There are various allowances payable to parents of kids diagnosed with ADHD so many parents even lie to their doctor to get the kids on the various drugs, or at least, get the diagnosis."

In any event, let us here consider the impulsive youth, as one who tends to act before he or she thinks. Below you will find some examples of actions by impulsive youth.

- He is in a store and sees a video game he wants, and without considering the consequences, shoplifts it right in front of the security camera.
- She gets in an argument with one of her friends and, her feelings get hurt, she assaults her friend right in front of their teacher.
- Another boy bumps him in the hall and he stabs him in the hand with his pencil. He is as surprised as the victim, both of them looking at the bloody pencil tip with their mouths open in shock.

Due to their difficulty in deriving satisfaction by methodical step-by-step work, as opposed to the thrill of immediate gratification, many impulsive youth engage in disruptive or thrill-seeking behaviors. Aside from any long-term interventions, from educational and vocational planning, to cognitive therapy or medication, impulsive youths need an activity that consumes their interest. They are able to focus with remarkable intensity when something interests them. This activity gives purpose and meaning to their lives, a touchstone they can use to help them manage those more difficult situations where they don't feel at home.

The impulsive young offender gets angry or aggressive for the same reasons as any other person, but they get particularly upset and frustrated when someone interferes with the gratification of an impulse. Swept away by their anger, they find it difficult to stop themselves. Impulsive youths hear very little of what you say, particularly when they are angry, upset, or confused. With such outbursts of anger, tactical paraphrasing (Chapter 56) is particularly valuable, as you prove that you understand their desire and frustration, rather than argue with them. (NOTE: This is a tactic, just as is done in crisis negotiation, *not* approval for their outburst).

Impulsive youth track very little of what you say, particularly when they are angry. If they are too escalated for paraphrasing, it is not the time for explanations, attempts to elicit empathy for the other person, or moral preachments. What usually works best is a calm demeanor and simple short commands.

Figure 59.2 Review: Dealing with Impulsive Youth

Until proven otherwise, when dealing with an upset or aggressive youth, assume that he/she is in "impulsive" mode. How would you know that they are not merely impulsive or upset? If the following strategy doesn't work, go on to the next strategy. Remember, we are talking about an approach that takes only a few moments. This is NOT a counseling session! Do the following:

- Paraphrase what they are saying.
- Give them firm, brief commands
- Help them regain control by directly telling them what to do.

CHAPTER 60

Conduct Disorder: Fierce Youth

> **Figure 60.1 Expanded Definition of Conduct Disorder: Fierce Youth**
> Conduct disorder is a term that delineates behaviors in children and youth that, in someone over
> the age of eighteen would merit the diagnosis of anti-social personality disorder, or even psy-
> chopathy. Because the child/adolescent brain is still so changeable, we properly don't give them a
> diagnosis that would suggest that change is unlikely, if not impossible. The majority of children
> who fully merit the diagnosis of conduct disorder don't grow up to be psychopaths. Nonetheless,
> Chapters 39 & 40 on manipulation and psychopathy are essential in considering any youth who is
> conduct disordered. This section focuses specifically on youth who display ferocious, manipulative,
> or predatory behaviors, whatever the cause may be.

This is a disorder of childhood and teen years, and is often, though not definitively, a precursor of criminality, even psychopathy. Such youth often seem to be without conscience or caring for most other children or adults.

The conduct disordered young offender typically displays rage in three major categories: fury, manipula-tion, and predatory behavior (Section XI). Just as with adult offenders, POs must focus on their behavior, particularly in potentially dangerous situations. Conduct disordered character traits can develop from a myriad of reasons, which may be relevant for psychological treatment, but not for the de-escalation and control of their anger or violence.

Attempting to establish a "sympathetic" or "nurturing" connection with young offenders is often a mis-take at any time, much less during a rage state and this is *particularly* true with such fierce youth. They experience these gestures as an attempt to soften their defenses, and/or as a sign of weakness on your part. Children and teenagers with conduct-disorder place extreme importance on protecting themselves from "invasion." They experience any loss of personal control, which is implicit in a softened response to anoth-er, as weakness. They strive to defend themselves against any emotional need or attachments with others, by adopting a callous attitude, one without sympathy for or even understanding of other people's pain.

In the most basic sense, such young offenders are profoundly isolated, without human ties. They are left with an inflated and easily bruised sense of pride, their most important "possession," something for which they will live and die. Pride however, can be considered an access route for communication and de-escalation. The formula for communication with such fierce youth is "respect outweighs sympathy."

In other words, enforce the rules with calm gravity and strength, and never try to ingratiate yourself, as this will invite contempt. However, if you manifest yourself as a strong and dignified professional who does not make it personal when giving advice or setting limits, you will sometimes draw their attention and curiosity. Imagine the following questions within such a young offender, considering his PO "How come she has nothing to prove? Why, even though she isn't frightening or even trying to frighten me, is she not weak? Why isn't she, like so many others, sucking up to me, trying to please me? What IS this power she has?" If there is hope for such youth, it lies in their fascination with power. You present to them a world unimaginable, one where power and decency can exist within the same body, and that one actually acquires more power through treating others with respect and human decency. If you don't behave in this manner yourself, such a young offender will be unreachable.

Figure 60.2 Review: Dealing with Fierce Youth

You first approached the youth as if their aggression is impulsive and you tried to exert authority over them. That didn't work: instead, the youth becomes more focused and directed in his/her aggression towards you. In this case do the following:

- Let them know where they stand, that anything you are enforcing isn't "personal," that you are doing your job and dispassionately enforcing your authority.
- Respect before sympathy! Don't try to prove you care.
- Deal with them on a professional, slightly disinterested basis.

CHAPTER 61

Dynamite Under a Rock:
Explosive Youth

The hallmark quality of these young offenders is that once their fiery tempers are unleashed, it is very hard for them to stop. They rage and rage. Despite their explosive personalities, many of these young offenders don't necessarily have attention or impulse problems, and they can pay attention just fine when they choose to do so. Others, such as the child with Fetal Alcohol Spectrum Disorder or a history of head injuries can't pay attention very well in the best of circumstances, quite apart from their explosive tempers. Regardless, they are the kids of whom one says, "Billy lost it again today," and everyone nods, imagining the explosion at the judge, along with slung chairs and thrown fits, the young person raging for over an hour *after* they were restrained in hand cuffs.

If you are still at a stage where you are trying to control them verbally, don't yell out commands, as that doesn't work well with these youths. In fact, they may view such commands as further provocation, heightening their anger instead of calming them. The watchword, instead, is containment. You *do* give commands, but your voice must be very firm and calm, even quiet. The command is to get their attention to focus everything on one being: YOU. In favorable circumstances, you can escort this young person to a quiet area where they calm down on their own, with your task being to monitor them so that they don't injure themselves or damage property. You can't, however, problem-solve or otherwise work things out while they are still enraged. If you are unable to accomplish this, you should avail yourself of the strategies in Section XI, particularly Chapter 67 on Hot Rage, or at still higher levels, physical control.

Some youth, particularly those with neurological damage, will shift suddenly into an "organic rage," apparently unmediated by cognitive processes. However, these kids often show small micro-changes of behavior right before assaults. With youth who you have an ongoing relationship with, you should definitely do what you can to learn these signs, in order to help them shift gears into another activity or process, thereby heading off the explosion. This is something you should raise with the youth's treatment professionals and family as well. For example, a girl in a group home had enacted a number of apparently sudden severe attacks against other residents. We found that when she focused on an intellectual task too long, she would begin scratching at her forearm. The "sudden" explosion of aggression followed a few minutes after this "tell." Another youth would knit his brows and glower in a stubborn manner when he didn't understand a conversation. He interpreted this as people "making me feel stupid," an attack in his view. This facial expression was a clear sign to slow down, lighten up, or change the subject.

Figure 61 Review: Dealing with Explosive Youth

You are dealing with a young person and attempt to exert authority, and then, when that doesn't work, you try the professional respect, command presence, and distance that you use with the fierce youth. If such a youth continues to ramp upwards into further aggression, assume you are dealing with an explosive youth. They get more and more aggressive as if they don't have a "circuit breaker" that helps them turn off. They become very reactive to just about anything you say or do.

- Rage is usually explosive. They often have no fear of harm when in an explosive rage state.
- Don't get flamed up yourself, no matter what they say (which will frequently be pretty bad!).
- If you speak at all, use paraphrasing (See Chapter 56).
- Silently, implacably, take them somewhere safe, where they are contained and unable to harm anything. Wait them out, so to speak.
- Containment is the watchword. Thus, the back of a patrol car is often a great "quiet room."

The behavior of "explosive youth," in particular, may necessitate physical control.

CHAPTER 62

Opposition-Defiant Youths: "Even if You Force Me,
I'll Still Make You Miserable"

Oppositional-defiant behavior (OD) is considered a behavioral disorder of childhood. OD usually develops with upbringing typified by poor boundaries (too invasive, too lax, or both). Aggression is typically against family members and those familiar to the child. Dictatorial parents, in an effort to "break" the child to their will often "create" OD youth among those who are too strong-willed to submit. Parents, who are not consistent nor enforce reasonable discipline, being either overly permissive or chaotic, also elicit such behaviors, and the child, almost instinctively acts in ways that demand the limit setting that they are not receiving. In many cases, however, the parents have not raised their children poorly, but their child has bonded with other poorly disciplined children, or they may be trying to imitate behaviors they absorbed from television, movies, and/or video games. Furthermore, experimental drug or alcohol use, and subsequent abuse, can easily transform a well-behaved and respectful youth into an oppositional and defiant one.

Negative Reinforcement

This involves primarily giving attention for negative behavior. This will elicit more negative behaviors. Reinforcement through punishment that is out of proportion or inconsistent teaches the child that discipline is an attack, that the parent is unpredictable, and that acting out at least garners parental attention. In their own way, these youth have discovered that their defiant behaviors give them a sense of power over adults, be they parents, teachers, or their PO, because they know they can make you react to them, even if that reaction comes in the form of punishment. Once power is acquired in this manner, the youth adopts a grandiose sense of his/her own importance, and frustrating and defying adults becomes its own reward.

Oppositional and Argumentative

Such defiant youths are surpassingly argumentative, fighting over fine-points, and claiming to be misunderstood. They appear to thrive on conflict, and they look for any pretext to continue the argument, trying to knock you off center. Such behavior is not a search for truth or understanding: it is simply a power tactic. They hold in contempt adults who take this overly seriously, but unconsciously seem compelled to test over-and-over again if you are worthy of respect. If you are losing your temper, they are winning. This need to argue, at its extreme end, seems related to Obsessive-Compulsive Disorder; their brain, apparently, won't "let go" of their place in the argument. Right-and-wrong does not matter, only their definition of "right" at the moment.

Although OD youth can sometimes be violent, it seems engendered by resistance to authority, and perhaps an unconscious desire that a clear, trustworthy, and consistent authority be exerted upon them so that their place in the world is well-defined. Perhaps the most important recommendation the authors can make is that professionals working with such youth must maintain consistent boundaries and rules with NO deviations. The oppositional youth will test these boundaries over and over again to see if the limits have changed.

The watchword when dealing with these young offenders is to pick your battles. Don't waste energy arguing about anything that is not important. When something is important, be implacable. While they put energy in their argument, you respond with a calm, yet unwavering resolve. As an adult, you should never argue with such a youth as an "equal;" instead, you tell them what will be, with no negotiation whatsoever.

These youth are used to a lot of attention when they argue or resist. Because this drains so much energy from those responsible for them, they are often ignored when they are not making trouble, much less acting positively. Therefore, be sure to notice when they are acting with integrity, agreeableness, or respect, so that they experience positive attention for these actions.

Figure 62 Review: Dealing with Oppositional-Defiant Youths

These young people argue for argument's sake. Their reward is the negative attention they require and get from adults, and the sense that they have you—at least your moods—under their control. They believe they've won if they anger you or get you upset. Pick your battles—those not worth arguing, disengage, change the subject, or ignore. Don't argue; require them to follow your instructions. Be like gravity: there's no argument with that. Whenever possible, give extra energy (positive attention) when the young person is doing something worthwhile or worth respecting.

CHAPTER 63

Post Traumatic Stress Disorder in Youth

For both children and young adults, post traumatic stress disorder, including either experiencing or witnessing acts of severe violence, is often physically enacted rather than verbalized. Young men in particular, who would adamantly deny ever experiencing trauma, seem to live by Nietzsche's adage of, "that which does not kill me makes me stronger."

There is not a unique de-escalation method for use with traumatized youth, as they can display aggression and violence in a variety of modes, from terrified and chaotic rage to purposeful predation. If you were to examine any aggressive or violent episode by such a youth, you will have, in symbolic form, the story of their own trauma, not only what happened to them, but also what was created *within* them by the trauma. Traumatized children, in particular, often display Terrified Rage (Chapter 67). The more predatory or furious rage states that some children and teenagers exhibit is a kind of reaction formation; they have found a way to cease experiencing the pervasive dread of the victim. Tragically however, this often results in their only feeling safe in the role of the victimizer.

There is increasing research and evidence that demonstrates the efficacy of a form of therapy called Eye Movement Desensitization and Reprocessing (EMDR) when working with traumatized children and adults. If you are working with traumatized offenders, juveniles or adults, referring them to therapists familiar with this method may be beneficial.[20]

Finally, circular breathing (Chapter 18) contains a method that you can, on occasion, teach to traumatized youth that can help them turn their trauma (lived experience) into memory (past experience). Circular breathing is particularly useful with those who are guarded against both therapy and help from others because it is a "does it yourself" procedure, which allows them to feel that they continue to be in control. You can, quite honestly, introduce it as a martial arts technique to control the mind rather than a therapy method, the latter being something the youth may resist.

Figure 63 Review: Dealing With Traumatized Kids
- Whatever their history, de-escalate based on their behavior at the moment.
- Don't let them "off the hook." Hold them to the highest standard of behavior.
- The damage from trauma is curable if they get help! These are youth who desperately need good therapy. With it, they will heal, and will likely not return through the years as criminal adults.

CHAPTER 64

Pseudo-Nihilism

By definition, nihilism means a general rejection of customary beliefs, and the belief that there is no meaning or purpose in existence. Such a youth affects a posture that includes boredom, self-destructive behaviors, or disinterest. Juveniles who adopt this outlook feel a sense of power when they horrify, disgust, or offend others. Nihilistic youths may also display an aloof callousness, with a distinct lack of sympathy for the feelings and emotions of others. By making themselves outcasts, they are inviolate vis-à-vis the larger society and its goals. Taken further, they achieve power when they experience themselves as untouched by other people.

When interacting with these young offenders you should not be emotionally bland, distant, or apathetic. Instead, pay attention to what the youth presents and offer them a human reaction. If you try to make yourself impervious, pretending that their provocative behaviors don't affect you, they may escalate until they do evoke a reaction. If you do succeed in "stonewalling" them, all you have succeeded in doing is establishing that you don't care. Beyond a "human reaction," you must demonstrate that you are inviolate, but not in the sense of becoming disinterested or uncaring. You demonstrate that you don't *need* them to change, and that you are, in your own way, free. One of the most striking things about rebellious youth is how they clump with others assuming the same fashion. Your ability to be unique embodies what they profess to desire.

Of grave concern with youth of this type is their attempt to suppress all emotions of caring or understanding. Despite their outwardly indifferent persona, these young offenders are in need of an adult to be a fair witness to their world, able to provide feedback in a way that they won't feel compelled to resist. They need someone with more life experience to talk with, someone who is not going to abuse them, abandon them, or treat them unfairly. Therefore, public safety is served when such youth have a PO they can respect, and look to for alternative viewpoints and opinions to their issues and dilemmas.

Figure 64 Review: Dealing with Pseudo-Nihilism

These youths are cut-off. They may be aggressive, but their primary goal seems to **NOT** make a link communicating with you. Other youth may be very much at odds with you:they may even rage or curse at you. One way or another, these kids try to cut themselves off from you.

- Don't try to make them change or "feel better." In particular, don't follow the "self esteem" model, that all they need is someone telling them nice things.
- They may try to repel you with what they say, or what they say they have done. Give them a human reaction, but not an over-reaction. In other words, a Great Dane doesn't bark when a little dog is yapping at him/her.

They are most dangerous when left alone to stew in their own juices. Be the adult that they almost surely don't have in their life, so they have a moral touchstone.

SECTION XI

Managing Rage
and Violence

CHAPTER 65

Preface to Rage and Violence

Rage and anger are not merely different in degree; they are different modes of being, just as water, once past the boiling point, becomes steam. Frustrated offenders posture or otherwise act angrily to establish dominance, or to force agreement or compliance from others. If nothing else, their goal is to communicate their feelings, although, due to their lack of interpersonal skills, their mental illness, or the effects of drugs and/or alcohol, they often resort to anger in an attempt to make themselves heard.

The reader will recall that anger is denoted as falling between 20 – 95 on the aggressiveness scale (Chapter 48). This represents a very broad range of arousal, ranging from mildly irritated to truly irate. Rage however, occupies a much smaller fraction of the scale, from 95 – 99, with 100 signifying an act of violence. When in a state of rage, the offender desires to commit mayhem, i.e., the destruction of property or physical violence. Enraged offenders are in a "threshold" state, their anger and rage escalating until they have overcome any moral or personal constraints that may prohibit them from committing the ultimate expression of rage—violence.

Therefore, all of the strategies described in the previous chapters dealing with the angry offender are more or less useless with one who is truly enraged. Sometimes the only viable option for the PO is to remove him/herself from the situation until reinforcements can be summoned, especially if the encounter is at the offender's residence or elsewhere in the field. In the office setting, the enraged offender should quickly elicit a response from the rest of the staff. In fact, the authors would hope that the PO will have already called for assistance through the use of code words or other early warning systems as the offender becomes noticeably angrier. At the very least, raised voices and angry outbursts should draw a crowd of POs to the interview room well before the offender is actually enraged.

There are various types of rage, and POs need to recognize what type of rage the offender is expressing, because there are different verbal control strategies to deal with each type. Fortunately, an enraged offender's behavior is quite obvious, and after reading this section of the book, you will be able to identify what type of rage the offender is exhibiting rather easily, allowing you to employ the appropriate strategies to control them.[21]

Figure 65 IMPORTANT CAUTION

Here, and in several other areas of this book, we have used animal symbols to aid in the understanding of various types of rage or other behavior. For example, we use the image of a leopard or a shark in describing predatory rage. These are thought devices, and are not intended to be used in either paperwork or communication to describe such offenders. In our hypersensitive times, such a reference to a specific offender may be misconstrued as stigmatizing an individual as "being an animal." Nothing could be further than the truth – the images are to assist in understanding modes of behavior, not character. Nonetheless, such images should remain aids of understanding, not terms of reference.

CHAPTER 66

Chaotic Rage: A Consideration of Rage Emerging from Various Disorganized States

Chaotic rage is typified by profound disorganization of cognitive and perceptual processes, and can be engendered by severe psychosis that has "crossed over" into a delirium state, mania, intoxication, drug withdrawal, severe intellectual/developmental disabilities, senile dementia, overwhelming emotions, or as a result of brain injury or trauma. Enraged disorganized offenders are often very impulsive and unpredictable, striking out in all directions. They may not be coordinated in their actions, but they are fully committed, meaning that they have no fear of injury or consequences to hold them back. They are also often indifferent to, or unaware of, pain or injury to themselves. Particularly with trained fighters, combative reflexes are almost instinctive, and thus, even though they are cognitively shattered, in a state of complete incoherence, they can still fight, throwing punches and kicks with accuracy.

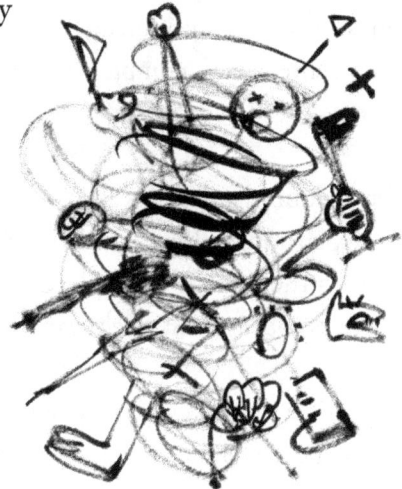

Unlike a classic psychosis, the most salient characteristic of chaotic rage is the near impossibility of establishing *any* lines of communication with them. Offenders in this state often can't logically string words together, communicating in ways that are comprehensible only to themselves. They may utter cascades of words making no sense whatsoever, or grunts, moans, and mumbling. Others make sentences based on rhymes, puns, or cross-meanings, their brains capriciously linking words together based on sounds, not meanings. Delirious offenders may laugh or babble, completely at variance to the seriousness of the situation. They may speak in repetitive loops, fixating on one subject, which could be real, hallucinatory, or such a manifestation of their disorganization that you don't even know what they are talking about.

Delirious offenders can easily become quite frightened or irritable, especially if they are overwhelmed with stimuli, such as a large number of onlookers or the presence of several POs or law enforcement officers. They may begin yelling, screaming, lashing out physically, or engaging in self-injurious acts such as scratching and gouging their own flesh, or striking themselves repeatedly, or banging their head against the wall or ground. Such behaviors should be considered medical emergencies, and proper medical attention must be summoned as soon as possible. Ideally, they should stage nearby while the PO, and possibly other law enforcement, are establishing the safe de-escalation and resolution of the crisis. Chaotic rage can be a sign of a life-threatening emergency, and offenders manifesting it must be transported to a hospital as soon as possible. Disposition afterwards may range from further hospital treatment, a residential facility or incarceration.

De-Escalation of Chaotic Rage

Disorganized or delirious offenders are among the most difficult to de-escalate verbally, because comprehension and coherent cognitive processes are among the first faculties chaotic offenders lose. Because of their impulsiveness and unpredictability POs must be on guard against a sudden attack. Therefore, knowledge of any triggers that might have set them off in the past is very useful.

One person, usually the supervising PO, needs to take command and control of the situation and direct other officers as to what they should do, i.e., clearing the room of others, providing site security to prevent others from entering the area, phoning for police and emergency medical assistance, etc. Inform emergency dispatch that the individual is displaying chaotic rage, describe the most salient behaviors and request that they activate the protocol for "excited delirium" (see below).

Use calm movements, and a firm but reassuring voice. Chaotic offenders often experience poor motor control, vertigo, disorientation, etc. Slow movements and soothing tones of voice help orient them physically and emotionally. Use simple, concrete commands with no more than a single "subject" in each sentence, as complex sentences or detailed instructions will be confusing, overwhelming, and/or threatening to the offender. Repetition is always helpful.

Disorganized offenders in chaotic rage states are sometimes susceptible to being deflected to another topic, although this is unlikely when they have entered fully into chaotic rage. You can sometimes fabricate a theme that catches their attention and seems to engage higher thought processes, delaying their outburst of rage until help can arrive.

If possible, the arrest process should be worked out beforehand, even if an alert is made at the last minute from the secretary or the supervising officer that the offender seems agitated. Only the arrest team or those POs who responded to the initial incident should be present. All other extraneous personnel and onlookers should be removed from the area if at all possible.

Figure 66.1 Example of Deflection: Dealing With an Offender in a Chaotic Rage State

A paramedic approached a delirious man who was standing on the edge of a highway, and said, "Ike, what are you doing here. I haven't seen you since high school." As he kept rattling off fictitious memories to the man, whose name was *not* Ike and whom he had never seen before, the delirious man gazed into his eyes in confusion, rocking back and forth in rhythm with the paramedic's words. The paramedic was successful in capturing the man's attention, which kept him from dashing into traffic, until police could arrive. To illustrate how dangerous this situation was, the moment the police tried to physically ease him back from the highway, the man exploded into a violent attack, requiring a number of police officers to subdue him.

- Use tactical paraphrasing to validate and acknowledge their confusion and/or fear. For example, use phrases such as, "Really scary, huh?" Or "You are really worried, aren't you?"

- One of the last things we "retain" is our name, so use their name, repetitively, interspersing it frequently in your commands in order to get their attention before initiating attempts to redirect them to another activity. This can be very helpful with combat veterans experiencing a "flashback[22]

- Be very cautious about touching chaotic offenders, as this may be experienced as invasive, or even as an attack. POs should make physical contact only as a means of self- defense, to take the offender into custody, or to prevent the offender from harming themselves or any other people present.

- Use simple, concrete commands with no more than a single "subject" in each sentence. Repetition is almost always helpful. Use only one thought at a time, as complex sentences will be confusing, and thus threatening or irritating. For example, say slowly, "Sit down, William. Sit down. Sit down. William, sit down."

- Minimize such distracting behaviors on your part as extraneous body movements. Your movements should be calming and also only be those useful in helping the person understand what is going on.

- Because of their difficulty in attending to what you say, non-verbal communication is a paramount concern. A calm reassuring presence, manifesting both strength and assurance is your best hope of helping to stabilize an offender in chaotic rage.

Figure 66.2 WARNING

Disorganized offenders are among the most difficult to de-escalate verbally because words and coherent cognitive processes are the first thing that they lose. You must, therefore, be prepared to evade a sudden attack, and further, be prepared, throughout, to use physical control tactics to ensure your safety as well as that of others.

Catatonia – Special Considerations

Catatonia is a very rare, very bizarre condition in which an offender stays in a fixed posture, not congruent with injury or seizure. Catatonia is caused either by mental illness (schizophrenia) or an organic condition, for example, drug use. The catatonic offender's posture may be quite awkward or twisted, seeming to require great flexibility. A classic symptom of true catatonia is "waxy immobility," whereby if someone else moves the catatonic's body or limbs, he or she maintains the posture into which they were moved. Such offenders will often be totally unresponsive to speech, touch, even pain, and there seems to be no way to establish any communication with them.

Considerable caution is needed in dealing with immobile offenders, for several reasons. First, they may be injured or having a seizure and are in need of

medical attention. A second consideration is safety. One way to regard catatonia is to view the individual as exerting one hundred percent of their will to <u>not</u> interact with the outside world. Trying to help, you may be tempted to make physical contact, clap your hands in front of their face or speak forcefully in an effort to get them to respond when they are unsecured. This can be a disastrous mistake. Imagine the incredible exertion of will required to maintain immobility for hours, even days, without movement, without response, without even blinking in some cases. Now imagine disturbing this equilibrium. The result is what is clinically called "catatonic rage," a state that really can be considered one form of excited delirium (below). The catatonic offender shifts from one hundred percent stillness to one hundred percent explosive motion. One of the authors can recall an incident where a law enforcement officer's career was ended by such an individual who, all of one-hundred-ten pounds, grabbed hold of his arm and yanking as if he was cracking a whip, ripping through all the ligaments of his shoulder and shoulder blade.

Although you may think the offender is unaware, they *can* hear you. Therefore, speak calmly and respectfully. Offenders can have very long memories of being shamed, and if you speak about or treat the catatonic offender as an object rather than as a person, you may evoke a terrible sense of humiliation. In their frozen state, they may not be able to respond immediately, but months or years later, someone or something may trigger an episode of postponed rage, and they may express it on the body of another PO or even a totally uninvolved individual. Beyond that, everyone, even a person in a coma, deserves to be treated with respect. Even if it seems that the person can't hear a word that you are saying, act as if they are listening to every word.

Whenever an offender is immobile and unresponsive POs should summon medical attention. If you have any suspicion that the offender may be catatonic, have them placed in restraints and transported to a hospital where they can be evaluated safely. To be sure, there are protocols in handing over care of an individual to emergency response personnel. Nonetheless, do everything in your power to ensure that EMS are aware that they are dealing with someone who is very likely catatonic and that they should not disturb them any more than is necessary when they are, as yet, unsecured. Testing reactivity to pain, light or noise, for example, should not occur until the individual is safely in restraints. When you move them to a gurney, make sure you have sufficient numbers to safely manage them, just encase they were to explode suddenly while being moved.

Excited Delirium Syndrome

Excited delirium is a rare condition at the extreme end of the hyper-aroused wing of the delirium spectrum. Etiology can be varied, but it is most commonly associated with long-term use of stimulants; particularly cocaine and methamphetamine. Single doses of such drugs as PCP, Ketamine, pyrovalerones such as methylenedioxypyrovalerone (so called "bath salts"), and very rarely, psychedelic drugs such as "magic mushrooms," can cause chaotic rage states. It is also associated with extreme manic or psychotic excitement, and can be precipitated by a variety of purely medical conditions. It is typified by some, if not all of the following: a sudden onset of extreme agitation; pervasive terror, often without object; chaotic, sudden shifts in emotions and disorientation; communication difficulties, including screaming, pressured incoherent speech, grunting, and irrational statements; aggression to inanimate objects, particularly shiny objects like glass and mirrors; hyper-arousal with unbelievable strength, endurance, and insensitivity to pain; hyperthermia accompanied by stripping off clothes; and most notably, violent resistance to others, before, during, and after arrest or restraint.

Accompanying their almost unbelievable level of physical arousal and resistance to both physical and mechanical restraints is possible respiratory and cardiac arrest. These people die! The usual pattern is that they struggle with incredible power and then, suddenly, they stop moving. Or sometime after becoming quiet, either in a stupor or in seeming normality, they succumb to cardiac arrest. Excited delirium can look remarkably similar to a seizure, also a very dangerous syndrome.

If they haven't been already called, get an emergency medical team on the scene immediately! Correct protocol demands that EMS should be staged, and ready to intervene medically the *instant* the subject is physically subdued. Furthermore, POs (or police) should NOT transport the person either to the hospital or jail, unless there is no other option. Ensure that EMS transport. If the individual dies in your car, YOU will be deemed responsible! The only time you should transport such a person is when it is proven and documented that EMS was not available, and no other means but your vehicle was available.

Such individuals can be appallingly dangerous both to others and to themselves. We can't emphasize strongly enough that this is a medical emergency manifesting as physical danger, and usually requiring police and emergency medical intervention to secure the offender so that they can be treated.

If they are not presenting an immediate assault risk, make the attempt to verbally de-escalate and control them, using the principles delineated above. You may be able to de-escalate them. You may also be able to gain partial compliance that makes it easier to take them into physical custody. If nothing else you will "buy time," allowing sufficient emergency personnel to muster, making the restraint that will be necessary to get them help more feasible. By getting the subject focused on you, they often stop moving. This will make it substantially easier to deploy less-lethal means than if they are running amok.

Figure 66.3 Excited Delirium or Chaotic Rage

Most offenders who go into chaotic rage are not in an excited delirium, but given the ever-increasing abuse of stimulants (methamphetamine, cocaine, etc.) that are the most common precipitants of this condition, it is important that you are familiar with the signs, symptoms, and "best-practice" interventions. Furthermore, we strongly urge local law enforcement, emergency rooms, paramedic organizations, and 9-1-1 dispatches to become fully familiar and trained to deal with individuals suffering from this syndrome. A joint training of all who may be involved in the restraint and treatment of such individuals is imperative. There needs to be an established protocol to ensure public safety, law enforcement safety, AND the safety, as best as you can accomplish it, of the delirious subject.

Greater knowledge about this syndrome has led to several new problems.

- The protocol for excited delirium is to subdue the offender as quickly as possible in order to get the medical attention they need, as well as protecting everyone else from the violence this type of offender may enact. As most mentally ill offenders, including severely disorganized offenders, are NOT in excited delirium states, this protocol can seem to directly contradict the model of verbal de-escalation we have offered here. In brief, with most mentally ill offenders, take extra time to talk them into compliance; with those offenders manifesting excited delirium, subdue them as quickly as possible. However, a careful reading of this text reveals a graduated set of interventions, including how to approach a disorganized individual, even one manifesting chaotic rage. As we have emphasized throughout the text, assessment is behaviorally based, and any dangerous behavior on the part of the offender should elicit a well-practiced physical response.

- Because excited delirium has finally begun to be recognized by the medical community as a genuine medical syndrome, this complicates things for officers. Psychosis, unlike schizophrenia, is a general term. Therefore, it is usable. However, if an officer uses the term excited delirium, he/she can be accused of diagnosing the offender. Therefore, we recommend the use of the term **Chaotic Rage** describe such individuals. It is fully descriptive, encompassing both the disorganization AND the agitation that such individuals display. Furthermore, the officer is not required to make a distinction between a person with genuine excited delirium, a mushroom intoxicated naked man running down the street or a distraught grief-stricken individual in a chaotic state. All parties, from police, corrections, EMS, and dispatch can use this descriptive term without running the risk of being either over-specific or diagnosing in the street.

The term "chaotic rage" will help POs, on a behavioral basis, to distinguish it from either lower levels of disorganization or psychosis so that best practice interventions can be used.

CHAPTER 67

Terrified Rage

> ### Figure 67 Terrified Rage and Chaotic Rage
>
> Be aware that the line between terrified rage and chaotic rage can be very fine. The terrified offender, overwhelmed, can shift into chaotic rage. When facing an offender in a state of either pure terror or terrified rage, be prepared, therefore, to shift to protocols suitable to assisting individuals in chaotic states (Chapter 66).

What Terrified Rage Looks Like

Terrified offenders believe that they will be violated or abused. They appear apprehensive and furtive, looking halfway ready to run, halfway ready to strike. Their voice can be pleading, whiny, or fearful, and their eyes are often wide-open or darting from place to place. Wide-open eyes don't always indicate fear however. When fearful, the muscles under the eyes are slack, giving the face a pleading look. Even through the terrified offender is looking in your direction, they don't, usually, look *into* your eyes, nor do they want you to look into theirs. The enraged, aggressive individual with wide-open eyes, on the other hand, displays tension around the eyes. Furthermore, they do, often, look penetratingly into your eyes, or stare *through* you.

The mouths of some terrified offenders gape open slightly, as they breathe in panicky, short gasps, while others press their lips together in a quivering pucker. Their skin tone is often ashen or pale. Some make threatening gestures with a flailing overhand blow, while others primarily use a fending off gesture, as if trying to ward off attack. Their body posture can be described as concave, as they pull away from you or hold themselves tightly in fear. Terrified offenders also exhibit heightened levels of physical arousal, accompanied by panting, sweating, and/or trembling. They may back themselves into a wall or corner. They also may yell, seeming to be threatening and pleading simultaneously, using such phrases as, "Stay back! You get away from me! I will hit you!! You stay back!" There is a hollow, pleading quality to the voice as if there is not "foundation." This is due to the tightening of the abdomen and diaphragm, so that not only breathing, but also speech is high in their chest.

Causes for Terrified Rage

Severely frightened offenders often suffer from paranoid delusions, fear of the unknown or terrifying hallucinations. At other times, they are afraid of a loss of control or of being laughed at or humiliated. Some are afraid that they are in terrible trouble with some agency, be it police, the courts, or mental health professionals. Finally, for any one of a number of reasons, they are simply terrified of you. Imagine a snarling wolf cornered, backed up against a cliff face. It is a frightened animal with fangs. Do you think that what it really needs right now is a hug?

De-Escalation of Terrified Rage

Reduce the offender's sense of danger. Maintain a safe, distance, and relax your posture. Make sure your movements are unhurried, and that your voice is firm, confident, and reassuring. If direct eye contact is reassuring for the offender, do so; if intimidating, don't. How will you know? Notice if their body relaxes or tenses in response to your eye contact or its lack. Of course, you should never take your eyes *off* of them. Just don't look penetratingly into their eyes if they are terrified by the eye contact.

Initiate a litany of reassuring phrases, speaking slowly, with frequent pauses: "I know you are scared, that's okay. Put down the chair, you don't need that. I keep it safe here. You can put it down now. I'm way over here. Go ahead. Sit down. I keep it safe here." Don't say, "I'll protect you" or "I won't hurt you." Many offenders who go into terrified rage have been hurt by people who said those kinds of phrases. However, when you say "I keep it safe here," you are telling them, "This is my territory and no one, including you, will be hurt on my territory. I am taking responsibility, and because of me, you will be safe." Furthermore, by saying something similar to what they expect to hear, yet somehow different, you cause a "glitch" in their thought process. "What did he say?" He didn't say, "I'll keep you safe." "What's different in what he said?" By getting the offender questioning what you said, you cause him to "re-engage" the parts of his brain that actually thinks things through as opposed to just reacts.

The offender's body language will also indicate that they are calming down. Their breathing will get a little shuddery or be expressed in short high-pitched gasps. They may slump into a chair or onto the floor as if physically exhausted, even beginning to weep. Maintain your reassuring litany, and slowly approach them. If they show signs of becoming frightened again, pause, move back slightly, and continue to speak to them reassuringly.

As you approach the offender, move in "half steps." For example, move the right foot a full step, then bring the left foot *up* to the right foot—pause. Move either right or left foot forward, and then bring the other foot forward *up* to the lead foot—pause. The advantage of moving this way is that you stay balanced, in case the offender attacks suddenly. Additionally, if the offender becomes startled or reactive, you can ease backward, creating more space between you.

CHAPTER 68

Hot Rage

> **Figure 68.1 Some Good Advice**
> "Hot rage explodes when officers can't calm the offender down for a variety of reasons, didn't take the time to calm them down, or the officers themselves were so pissed off that they got the subject into that stage. One out of three is not our fault. Three out of three become our responsibility."
> Quote from veteran officer.

When you think of an offender who is on the edge of violence, hot rage usually comes to mind. Imagine being faced with an individual who is yelling and screaming, brandishing their fists or another weapon, and threatening to do harm; they throw things, tip over desks, and engage in other forms of violent behavior. Such behaviors are often thought to be instinctual, a product of our primitive "flight or fight" response to danger. However, instinctual aggression is usually uncoordinated and flailing, and falls under the category of terrorized or chaotic aggression.

Hot rage, however, is coordinated: a learned behavior, trained through repetition, learned through modeling, and reinforced through success. This doesn't mean that hot rage is the equivalent of the actions of a professional fighter, who coolly and calmly prepares his line of attack and focuses his aggression on his opponent. Instead, hot rage should be considered a pseudo-instinct, a deeply ingrained combination of primitive drives and trained actions. Such pseudo-instinctual behaviors are actions that have either been repeated so often, or are so ingrained in powerful early experiences that they function almost like reflexes. Over-arousal also leads to deterioration in judgment, and at higher states of arousal, even of basic cognitive processes, leading the offender to fall back on these behaviors that function, to some degree, automatically. For example, some offenders with long histories of abuse lash out in rage whenever frightened, with no ability to evaluate whether or not they are currently in danger. At the same time, they target where best to hit, and frequently, choose a time and a place where they believe they have the best chance of success.

On a more functional level, a good street fighter who loses his temper does not necessarily lose his coordination. He does his best to knock his opponent senseless, but he automatically takes a stance with chin tucked in, shoulder rolled forward, and punches with his entire body lined up so that the power of the blow is amplified by his body weight and the torque of his hips.

General Information About Hot Rage

The more often someone goes into a state of hot rage, the more comfortable he/she is with their rage, and the easier it becomes to be violent. Hot rage is often a behavior that has led to short-term success in the past, such as scaring and beating a selected victim either for criminal gain, or just for the fun of it. In a state of rage, such an offender has no concern about longer-term consequences, much less guilt. For some, there is a sense of liberation, even a paradoxical kind of joy when they peak into rage. All one's fears and insecurities disappear, and one is left with only the ecstasy of the pure act. For this reason, some desire rage, because that ecstatic state is, to them, the best thing they ever feel.

Displacement. This is a common factor of hot rage, meaning the offender's anger is displaced, at least temporarily, toward an inanimate object instead of you or another individual. This also includes picking things up and slamming them down, throwing things, punching or kicking walls, furniture, or other nearby objects. More predatory offenders use displacement as a tactic to make the target of their aggression more fearful, while warming themselves up for an attack.

Peer group influence. Hot rage is also associated with peer group influence and masculine display, a primitive attempt to dominate access to or eliminate perceived competition, status, or other objects of desire. This can be especially problematic if the offender begins acting out in front of a group of onlookers, friends, or family, where to save face, they must act aggressively toward anyone representing authority.

Frustration. Some therapeutic professionals claim that hot rage is a result of frustration, but frustration alone does not usually elicit rage in normal people. When frustrated desires are coupled with something personal, as when the offender believes another person is impeding them, they are more likely to become enraged. Hot rage can be a "transference" in which the PO is a representative or stand-in for someone else who frustrated or controlled them. In their mind, you are the emblem of everyone who ever controlled them or put them down, an agent of an oppressive society, or simply a legitimate target to express hatred and violence.

There are various types of hot rage, each typified by almost unendurably intense feelings. We distinguish 3 subtypes: Fury, Bluffing, and Aggressive-Manipulation. These 3 subtypes will be discussed later in this chapter.

Figure 68.2 Example: Hot Rage Escalates Into Violence

A man is walking down the street and sees a father slap his child's face. He intervenes, saying, "That's just a child. Be easy on him." The angry father shoves him and says, "Mind your own business, or I'll give it to you, too."

The man later describes hearing a high pitched noise, and his vision turning black-and-white. He comes to himself astride the man, pounding the face of the abusive father with his fists.

General De-Escalation of Hot Rage: The Ladder

The primary method of de-escalation for hot rage is called "The Ladder." This is an ideal technique for someone who is beginning to get threatening. It is used only for rage, that gray zone between anger (even extreme anger) and violence. The offender is no longer trying to communicate with you, and they are right on the edge of assault—in a sense, doing a war dance to work out inhibitions to committing violence.

Figure 68.3 CAUTION

The Ladder should only be used with an enraged offender. Using this technique with an angry individual, even an extremely angry offender, will cause them to escalate into rage. In most cases, de-escalation tactics suitable for dealing with an angry offender are sufficient.

Figure 68.4 Safety is Your Primary Concern

Don't hold back from any action to keep yourself and others safe if the offender does become violent. Escape, evade, and fight back, if that is what you have to do.

The technique itself is simple. Identify the most dangerous behavior and repetitively demand that it cease. Use short sentences and easily understood commands. Once they stop that particular dangerous behavior, identify the next problematic behavior and use the same technique; continue until the offender is de-escalated. **This technique is only effective right before, during, and after the peak of the crisis** because it is a control tactic rather than a "Lining Up" de-escalation tactic. Control tactics will provoke rage in a merely angry offender, someone we might have over-estimated, due to his loud tone, or dramatic behaviors. As described earlier, facing an enraged offender causes us to experience fear in a way that anger does not. The danger is NOW, not merely a possibility should the situation continue to deteriorate.

Establishing a Hierarchy of Danger

The general hierarchy of dangerous behaviors, from most to least, is as follows:
1. Brandishing an object or a weapon in a menacing way (NOTE: If they are too close, or are trying to use the weapon, this is violence, not rage.);
2. Approaching or standing too close to you with menacing intent;
3. Kicking objects, punching walls, or throwing things (displacement activity);
4. Pacing, stomping, and inflating the body in an aggressive manner (posturing);
5. Shouting or talking in low, menacing tones;
6. Using language that is intended to violate, demean, or degrade.

The Ladder is not merely a verbal intervention. Like any other control tactic with an aggressive offender, you must move as needed to maintain the optimum space to both defend yourself, and exert maximum influence upon the aggressor. If they are very close, or threatening, not only should your hands be up, prepared to ward off any attack, but also as a gesture that is both calming and dominant. On other occasions, you should, as previously described, clasp the wrist of one hand with the other hand. On still other occasions, you should have your hand on your weapon, or your weapon drawn, in your hand.

Give the offender a straightforward command to stop their most dangerous behavior. By keeping things so simple, you can use your mind to look for escape routes, where weapons might be, or how to get help. By holding to a demand that the most dangerous behavior cease, you are displaying clarity and strength to the aggressor, as well as helping him focus his mind on the most problematic thing he is doing. You should not scream or shout—that won't get through, and will increase their aggressive energy. Rather, your voice should be strong, low, and commanding (Chapter 53).

After a couple of repetitions, always add, "We'll talk about it when you...." followed by the same command. Once that behavior is stopped, pick the next most problematic behavior (the next "rung" of the ladder), and command/require that it stops. If the aggressor does calm down and stops all the aggressive behaviors, including assaultive language, THEN set a firm and direct limit.

This is not the time to try and think of something brilliant or life changing to say. By keeping things simple, you can continue to look for escape routes, identify potential weapons, and attempt to get help. You should intersperse your sentences frequently with their name, using this to pace and break the rhythm of your commands, as well as "calling them back" to a more personal interaction. In addition, by holding to a demand that a specific behavior cease you are displaying clarity and strength to the offender, as well as helping him or her focus the mind on their most problematic behavior, then the next, and on down the rungs of the ladder. Continue working your way down the rungs until the offender is no longer in a state of fury. If the offender re-escalates to a higher and more dangerous activity, simply return to that rung of the ladder and begin again. Remember to stand and use your voice as described in the previous sections.

The last "rung" is probably swearing or other obscene language. Remember, some offenders swear as punctuation, without any hostile intent. They may be crude, but they are not trying to be verbally violent. If that kind of language offends you, it is something you will deal with at another time, during moments of calm. However, if the swearing is an attempt to violate you, it must be dealt with in proper order. However, don't focus on the language, no matter how vile, if the person is *doing* something dangerous. Remember that predatory offenders will use language to shock, distract, immobilize, or terrorize. Their behavior is far more dangerous than anything they are saying.

Figure 68.5 CAUTION
Remember, the Ladder should only be used with an enraged offender. Using this technique with an angry individual will cause them to escalate into rage. In most cases, de-escalation tactics suitable to dealing with angry offenders are sufficient.

Figure 68.6 Witnesses

All witnesses will have heard your commands. Because you will have calmly repeated the same order in a strong, non-abusive voice, there is a better chance that they will be <u>good</u> witnesses should this situation deteriorate further into a physical confrontation. You will have been heard, repeatedly, commanding the person to comply with an order that they repeatedly ignored or refused.

Figure 68.7 Example of the Ladder

Your voice is firm, low pitched and commanding, as you "descend" down the rungs. In the following scenario, each statement is, of course, in response to something the aggressor has done or said. Don't talk too fast. Command presence, not hysteria!

1. "Step back. Step back. Robert. We'll talk about it when you step back. Robert. Step back. Step back, Robert. We will talk about it when you step back."
2. "Stop kicking things. Robert. Stop kicking things. We'll talk about it when you stop kicking things."
3. "Robert, I can't follow you when you pace around. Sit down and we can talk. Sit down, Robert."

Notice the paradoxical message, that you can't "follow" him. Of course you could, if you wanted to. This is another example of what we call a "brain glitch," the same as we do with the individual in Terrified Rage, when we say, "I keep it safe here." You are trying to catch their attention as they try to make sense of what you said. We want them thinking again, trying to figure out what you said and why you said it. We want the part of the brain that thinks things through taking over from the part that is driving them towards violence.

Imagine they have stepped forward again, thus ascending to a higher "rung" on the ladder

1. "Step back! Robert! Step back and we'll talk. We will TALK about it when you step back, Robert. Step - - - - -back."
2. "Sit down Robert. We will talk about it when you sit down. We can't talk when you are walking around. We will talk about it when you sit down."
3. "Lower your voice. I can't hear you when you yell that loud. Lower you voice and we will talk."

Here is a second paradoxical communication, of course, you can hear an aggressor who is shouting loudly. Once again, you are trying to create a "glitch" where he tries to figure out what you mean when you say you can't hear him when he is yelling.

"Talk to me with the same respect that I talk to you. We will talk about it when you stop swearing. Stop swearing. Robert. We will talk when you talk to me with respect, the same way I talk to you."

Remember, people often swear as punctuation. They have no hostile intent whatsoever. If the individual is swearing in this manner, it is not a problem. For example, "Officer, I'm sorry, I was just mad at my f**king daughter, and s**t, you happened to arrive at just the wrong damn moment."

However, if the swearing is an attempt to violate you, it **must** *be dealt with in proper order. However, don't focus on the language, no matter how vile, if the aggressor is doing something dangerous. Remember that predatory individuals will use language to shock, distract, immobilize or terrorize. What they are* **doing** *is far more dangerous than anything they are saying.*

Hot Rage Subtype #1: Fury

What does fury look like? Furious offenders are very tense, looking as if they are about to explode. <u>If they are of big stature, think of a grizzly bear, if they are smaller—think of a wolverine.</u> In either case, the image suggests an animal that will tear you to pieces if it perceives danger, if provoked, or if cornered. Many offenders, both with a mental health diagnoses and without, display fury, and it is particularly common among those who have suffered head injuries. Furious offenders may show some of the following physical manifestations of their rage:

- Their skin tone is flushed as they become angered, turning red or purplish in color. As they become even more enraged however, their skin blanches, and they turn pale or gray (depending on their skin tone), as the blood pools in the internal organs.
- Their voice, whether loud, or low and quiet, has a menacing and belligerent tone.
- They often pace, inflate their upper body, hit or kick objects, or strike their hands together ominously, punching one fist into the other hand.
- They tend to stare into your eyes directly, glowering from under their brow, with a furious and hostile look on their face.
- Their eyes will appear red or inflamed; usually their eyes are wide open, with tension around the eye sockets and facial muscles.
- Physical arousal, blood pressure, and muscular tension all increase. You may notice veins popping out of the skin, particularly around the neck.
- They may display a smile that shows no humor or joy. Others snarl, or compress their lips with a twist, as if they have a foul taste in their mouth. Still others bare their teeth, or clench their jaws so tightly that the muscles stand out in bunches.
- They are very impulsive, and unconcerned with possible consequences.
- Their breathing is often loud and strained.
- They may claim to be disrespected, humiliated, or shamed. Others will allege that they are not getting their questions answered and their problem solved, or that no one listened or cared. They

may rant about "the system" and claim that they are out of alternatives or solutions.

- At their most dangerous point, they may become calm, break off eye-contact, or adopt a thousand-yard stare.

When confronting a furious offender your posture and tone should be confident, commanding, even imposing. Maintain direct eye contact, and frequently use their name. Stand directly in front of the offender, using a blade stance, but out of range of an immediate blow. This best prepares you to escape along tangents to his attack, to ward off blows, and if necessary, to fight back. With the blade stance, you are already "chambered" to do this. As described earlier, your hands are either up in a fence, or the wrist of one arm is clasped in the hand of the other in front of you at waist level.

Stand too close and you will appear to be challenging them, too far and you will be seen as fearful—a potential victim. You may have to move forward or backward to maintain this spacing. In either event, move smoothly, without flinching on the one hand or any sudden or threatening gestures on the other. When you move with a relaxed body, you are more ready to protect yourself, yet you don't appear as if you are trying to initiate a physical altercation.

Your voice is strong and forceful. Don't, however, shout. Instead, keep your voice low-pitched and calm, dropping it into your chest where it resonates, as enraged people, in particular, react violently to threatening or angry vocal tones. The only time you would shout is a "battle cry," the lion's roar of outrage and strength that you use only when you are trying to stop an actual attack.

You will use the Ladder in its most orthodox form—with your voice pitched low and powerful. You should feel it vibrate in your chest. The offender will exhibit one of only three actions:
- They keep on coming—you will do what you have to do ensure safety.
- They get close and when you tell them to step back, they say, "make me"—you will do what you have to do to ensure safety.
- They comply—when individuals in hot rage comply with the command to step back, they usually do so yelling and screaming—"you can't tell me what to do."

Once you have them de-escalated, you must maintain control. This can mean anything from an arrest to simply "reading them the riot act" and putting them on notice that they came dangerously close to either being hurt or arrested. Only after setting very strong limits would you shift into problem-solving, even with a mentally ill individual. Otherwise, they will assume that the best way to get a reward—your attention or help—is to abuse you.

Hot Rage Subtype #2: Bluff Aggression

In keeping with the animal analogy when describing the furious offender, the aggressively bluffing offender is like a gorilla beating his chest, a display of aggression designed to keep you at a distance. There is a sense of bluster rather than the pent-up pressure of the enraged offender. However, their manifest behavior appears much the same as the individual displaying fury, hence the terrifying image of the enraged gorilla. At 50 yards, could you tell the difference between a charging gorilla and a charging grizzly bear? Both are huge, hairy beasts that apparently mean you harm. In all likelihood, the gorilla would prefer to be left alone, rather than engaging in combat, but he postures as if he wants nothing more than tear you to pieces. If he perceives no other alternative, he will do so.

How can you tell the difference between a furious offender and a bluffer, if their behaviors are so similar? When facing a furious offender, fear is your natural and likely response. You instinctual mind, that part of you that places survival above all else, demands your immediate attention, and it uses fear to accomplish this. An aggressive bluffer, in a state of hot rage, may also elicit fear, but this fear will be accompanied by another emotion. You will find yourself irritated, thinking how stupid (yet potentially dangerous) this incident has become, and that if the bluffer was not with his friends, or in another case, if his wife had not chosen to taunt him as being less than a man, this dangerous situation would never have developed.

The enraged bluffer *often* displays aggression for the benefit of friends or family. On many occasions their friends or family members have provoked them to "prove" they are tough. *In reality, they are actually frightened that they will be found out as being frightened, intimidated, or succumbing to authority.* Perhaps they are trying to impress others or convince them that they are someone to be taken seriously. These offenders can become quite violent if they feel a strong sense of peer pressure to resist your commands and efforts to de-escalate them. Because they are performing in front of an audience, afraid of losing their "street cred" as someone to be reckoned with, they will often attack to protect their image. Sometimes bluffers are alone, but they still have an audience, an image inside their own head to which they believe they must conform. You will often hear this in their self-talk as they amp themselves up. "You don't know who you are talking to. Do you believe this guy? Do you have any idea who I am?"

Many bullies, having a long record of violence, actually function day-to-day in "bluff mode." They are in a perpetual quest to prove to others, and even more so, themselves, that they are not frightened or insecure. As a result, they repeatedly solicit situations where they must either intimidate others or resort to violence. POs must short-circuit this behavior before it escalates into violence. Obviously, the best way to achieve this is to separate the offender from his or her audience; a relatively simple matter in the office setting. In the field however, you may be unable to isolate the offender safely (remember, you don't want to be *totally* isolated with an enraged offender without sufficient back up on the scene), and your only recourse is to withdraw and return later.

One thing which lone POs simply shouldn't do is to try and "out tough" the offender by refusing to back down or leave the scene. *This is bluffing behavior on your part*, and the offender's audience will only amplify their calls for the offender to be even more resistant. As the authors have stated many times throughout this book, don't personalize any of your encounters with your offenders, and if professional prudence dictates that you should retreat, then do so!

POs need to recognize that the aggressive bluffer is not really in confrontation with you; they are *pretending* that they are, usually for an audience, but sometimes they are trying to stand up for their own self image. These offenders remain quite dangerous because they may believe they need to prove themselves by refusing to back-down. Another aspect of bluffing is that when frightened, the bluffing offender will move forward, toward you, so that no one will see how frightened they truly are.

If you can't simply retreat, de-escalate and control using the Ladder, much as you would with an individual in fury, but with a much more matter-of-fact tone. Your eye-contact, too, is matter-of-fact, as if you are having a conversation rather than a confrontation. Rather than having your hands in front of you (either clasped or in a fence position), open your hands, slightly to the sides, palm up. You can still protect yourself just as easily, but your posture appears non-threatening, more open and relaxed. Your body language expresses, "there is no fight here." Remember, these offenders will attack out of the fear of being "found out" by their peers. Your task becomes one of helping them to save face, rather than issuing forceful commands and instructions. In doing so, you will greatly reduce the risk of violence. However, POs can't allow the offender to win the encounter with concessions or agreements, and there must be some form of consequence subsequent to the resolution of the crisis. The imposition of punishment or consequences can come at a later date, especially if the offender is not taken into immediate custody.

Figure 68.8 The bluffer's strut
When you tell them to step back, aggressive bluffers often strut back with a smirk, sometimes glancing around and making eye-contact with onlookers. This is for the benefit of the audience, and their own self-image. They are trying to show that they are not afraid, and in control of the situation.

When exerting verbal control on the enraged bluffer:
1. Don't point out their fears in front of others. They will feel the need to defend their honor.
2. Don't try to be more forceful than they are, or appear overly domineering or condescending, as their self-image may require them to strike out.
3. If they are not responsive to a more low-key approach and continue to escalate, you may have a furious offender (see above) who happens to be in front of other people or a bluffer who has

shifted into fury. In this case, you "turn up the dial," adopting a more powerful tone and stance, and shifting into the more forceful version of the Ladder technique for the furious individual.

4. Remember, the offender's audience is what makes them dangerous. If possible, removing them from their audience will often result in the offender calming down on their own. For this reason POs should prohibit offenders from reporting to the office with a retinue of friends and family. In the field, POs should note the presence of others in the home or neighborhood before interacting with their offender and act accordingly. One PO notes, "We actually have a sign in our lobby that states, 'Your Probation Officer will be meeting with you alone. Please have your family members and/or ride wait outside.' People tend to take it less personally once they realize that we ask this of everyone, not just specific offenders' family/associates."

Figure 68.9 Speaking to a person who was in bluff-rage after you have them under control:

"Bernard, I'm glad this worked out with no one getting hurt. Had you not chosen to sit down and talk, you very likely would have ended up being face down on the floor. No. Listen to me for a minute. I'm not disrespecting you—that's why you and I are over here talking instead of in front of them <indicating the onlookers>. I'm telling you, it was a very near thing. Again, I'm glad this has worked out that you and I are standing here talking."

"Next time, though, don't do this in front of them" (referring to his friends or family for whom he was on display, and actually put a little *contempt* in your voice when you say the word 'them' as if to indicate that Bernard is better/cooler/stronger than those people he is trying to impress.)

"Come to me and talk to me one man to another" OR "one woman to another" ("one adult to another" in male-female conversations). "You shouldn't put your personal business in front of them." You will observe him "puff up," feeling himself to be flattered. You then continue, "Okay. Are we clear for next time? Good. Now as for this time...." Then set the same types of limits as you did with the individual in a state of FURY, which will often include the phrase, "You are under arrest." They can take the message in when their ego is built up enough to take the hit.

Hot Rage Subtype #3: Controlling Aggressive Manipulation

Aggressive manipulation looks like. Aggressive manipulation is a *strategy*, not a symptom of illness. Such offenders are calculating, trying to monitor the effects of their actions. They are not constrained by feelings of honor, integrity, or pride; their goal is win any way they can. Sometimes, you can tell when you are being manipulated ("played") because you are confused about why the offender is upset, or the purpose of his argument. The aggressive manipulator changes either his mood or the subject of the complaint frequently, displaying some or all of the behaviors of manipulative and psychopathic individuals (Chapters 32 & 33).

Aggressive-manipulative offenders may have a long history of losing control, particularly when their desires are frustrated, or when they believe they are not given what they feel they are entitled. They frequently have a history of various character disorders (habitual behavioral styles that make others miserable).

These offenders may approach you with flattery, or a plea for something, explaining their dilemma in great detail with talk of their suffering. Once their request is denied, however, they blame or criticize you for their troubles, inferring that your refusal will result in furthering their suffering or cause them irreparable harm. They might try to make you feel guilty, or begin to demean you, shifting to subtle threats of violence. They may talk in an arrogant manner, trying to make you look incompetent to others or stupid to yourself. They often claim to be victims, basing this on either real or imaginary issues. Furthermore, they may use their "status" as a member of an oppressed or victimized class of people as a means of intimidating others, making their demands in a whiny, accusatory voice. Such offenders will recall past grievances, adding their current crisis to the list of prior accusations. They will tell you how you are just like someone else who wronged them. They ask frequent or repetitive questions. They try to frighten you or make you feel uncertain of yourself.

Manipulation does not mean false threat, and manipulative offenders will often harm others. The difference between an aggressive-manipulator and those in a state of pure fury is that the furious offender's inhibitions are swept aside by their rage. You will often hear terms like "He just lost it" to explain such behavior. The aggressive-manipulator, on the other hand, attempts to monitor your responses and the situation as a whole to assess if his actions and behaviors are successful. Although the offender's behavior may be calculating, that does not mean he is in control. As he becomes more and more agitated, his judgment deteriorates, and he may concoct a rationalization for violence that makes sense to him in the moment.

Control tactics for aggressive manipulators. Offenders who use this strategy attempt to twist your feelings and emotions, making you doubt yourself, making you ashamed or scared, for example, to get what they want. Don't buy into it. <u>If you recognize this strategy early on in your interaction with the offender, cut it off at the onset.</u> If, however, the manipulative offender begins to escalate his or her strategies, you may have to use the Ladder as a means of control and de-escalation. In this case, however, your tone of voice should be matter-of fact and slightly detached.

Making eye contact enables another person to truly see you as you are, and in return, see them as well. Aggressive-manipulative offenders don't care about you, and they use apparent feelings of contact and intimacy to "read" you and control others. They are interested in gaining information that they can use to their benefit. Similarly, they will use their own eyes to create a false sense of trust or intimacy, as it suits them to confuse you, misdirect your attention, or dominate you. Therefore, when they are just building up towards rage, rather than making eye contact, look past one ear.

Figure 68.10 Don't Look Away

Don't look away. While looking past an ear, you can still see what they are doing. If you look away, you will be assaulted and not even know it is coming. This disengaged look, done properly, indicates that you won't participate in the degradation that manipulation creates.

Ladder for aggressive manipulators. If your attempts at control and de-escalation of their manipulative strategies are unsuccessful, the offender may escalate into a rage state. What distinguishes this from pure fury is that, even now, they continue to read and monitor you for advantage. Are they intimidating you; have they succeeded in distracting or throwing you off balance so that you are open to an attack; have they got you trying to "bargain" your way to safety? At the same time, they begin to "lose it," as it becomes more apparent that their strategic application of intimidation is unsuccessful. Furthermore, they get increasingly frustrated because they believe their manipulation *should* be working, primarily because it has worked so well for them in the past.

In essence, aggressive-manipulative rage is a merger of hot rage and predatory rage (see other Chapters in this section). When dealing with such offenders POs should:
- Stand relaxed and ready to evade a blow and counter the attack.
- Express flat disinterest in their demands, accusations, and complaints.
- Use the repetitive commands of the ladder technique. Your vocal tone should be flat. Don't negotiate. Don't discuss other matters as long as the manipulative behavior continues.

Figure 68.11 IMPORTANT: LOCKING EYES (THE LOOP)

If the offender escalates into *fury*, or if they continue to be otherwise non-compliant, turn from looking past the ear to looking right in their eyes, accompanied by a firm command to stop what they are doing. When you turn your head to look directly in their eyes, roll it slightly up and then down as if sighting a weapon. Speak powerfully and directly, just as you do with the offender who is in a state of fury. If you have ever raised a teenager, you have almost surely done this. In essence, once you make eye-contact with the aggressive-manipulative offender, treat them as you would the furious type.

Several things can happen with the aggressive-manipulative offender when you attempt to control their rage:
- Your flat disinterest indicates that they can't "get to you." After trying several different avenues, they give up, leaving in frustration, shifting to another strategy, or sagging in defeat.
- In more heated situations, they will flare into a fury (or pseudo-fury).
- When you "lock in" eye-contact, they may "bounce" off into another tactic—sudden tears for example.

- If the behavior does not stop immediately upon being "hit" with your eyes, this means that an attack is imminent. You will shift into the de-escalation techniques used for controlling fury, or take appropriate action to ensure your safety in the event of violence.

CHAPTER 69

Predatory or Cool Rage

Thankfully, this type is rather rare. Offenders with this type of rage are intimidators who threaten with vague innuendoes or explicit threats. Their aggressive behavior is calculated, but unlike the manipulator, violence is often their first choice rather than one of many options. The predatory offender may deliver threats in cool, dangerous tones, often *after* a clear and strongly stated demand. Then they offer you a chance to avoid injury if you comply. A variant tactic is to pretend being out of control. This is in contrast to a genuine attack, an action that they are eminently capable of and willing to carry out. Our symbol for them is either a leopard or a shark, depending on if they present as "warm-blooded" or "stone cold."

While these offenders seethe with hostility and/or contempt for others, they have developed these emotions as a deliberate weapon of terror, perhaps even enjoyment. Paradoxically, their physical arousal is often low. Their heart rate can actually go down and they can be charming and engaging, even as they prepare to commit an act of violence. This disconnect between appearances and intentions can cause POs to lower their guard because they may have a hard time believing that such a seemingly nice guy is ready and willing to terrorize others psychologically, or hurt them physically.

These offenders actually have no inhibitions regarding their aggression other than tactical calculation or self-interest. They have no capacity for sympathy or remorse, and many experience low levels of anxiety in situations that would frighten ordinary people. Every time they intimidate someone successfully, their behavior is reinforced, and they view non-action on your part, either during the confrontation or afterward, as either weakness or of tacit approval, thereby increasing the likelihood of similar behavior in the future.

The best response is a combination of overwhelming force and respect.[23] Under ideal circumstances, you will never be in a situation where you are vulnerable with such an individual. "Respect" means, simply, that you make your control "institutional," not "personal." When you are dealing with them, they should not have a problem with you, personally: their problem is between themselves and society, whose rules they are breaking. As a law enforcement officer, you are merely society's agent.

What to Do When You Don't Have Overwhelming Force

Your basic task is to demonstrate that you are not prey, that you are not a ready victim, and that the offender's attempts at intimidation will simply not work. Most predatory offenders don't wish to interact with someone whom they *don't* intimidate or otherwise control through emotional abuse or physical posturing. Instead, they seek more conciliatory and subservient victims, where their chances of success are great. When engaging a predatory offender POs should remember the following:

- Stand or sit ready to move. Be poised, but don't appear fearful or too defensive.

- Avoid gesturing or expressive movements. Fear often causes your movements to be awkward, and the offender will see this as confirmation of their control over you.

- Be open and strategic in everything you do: the way you position your body, your voice, and your posture. The predatory individual is well-versed in reading body language and assessing weakness. Protect yourself openly, and don't change your actions based on what they say, i.e., their efforts to put you at ease or promises of compliance. Another tactic the predator may use in these circumstances is to use anything you do against you, either deriding you or pretending that you are out of control, paranoid, or acting strangely. Ignore all that, and openly act to keep yourself safe.

- Don't make explicit or unrealistic threats, such as "If you come near my family, I will kill you!" To the predator, that tells him what you won't do. In his mind, if you really meant it, you would do it now. An explicit threat is an empty threat.

- Don't over-react to vague threats, or he/she will interpret your reaction as a victory. If however, the offender makes an explicit threat to harm you then they should be taken into custody immediately or shortly after the encounter (after you have removed yourself from the situation safely and returned with sufficient force). POs can't allow any offender to threaten them with physical violence without the swift and sure response of incarceration and an appearance before the Court.

- Don't comply with any of the offender's orders or demands that you should not carry out your professional duties and responsibilities.

Cryptic Consequences

Keep your voice matter-of-fact, and give clear and direct statements of *potential* consequences. If you can, smile. These consequences are of a special type, clear, but cryptic, i.e., "You know what would happen if you did hit me." In this case, don't tell him what would happen. Let his imagination take over. These vague consequences are a mirror of his own method of intimidation, and he may likely react to you as "not prey, not edible, not worth the trouble." If he says, "What are you talking about?" you should reply, "You know exactly what we are talking about." When the predator responds to your cryptic consequence with questions or with confusing statements that would make your statement illogical, simply say, "You know what is going on here. You know what is happening." You may have to intersperse your vague consequences with ladder commands if he escalates his behaviors. You can sometimes make things even more cryptic. Imagine he says, "Well, suppose you spell it out." You reply, "No need for spelling lessons. We both know how to spell, and we know what time it is too." This is deliberate semi-nonsense, where the predator, trying to figure out what you really mean, gets increasingly confused and off-balanced.

Try to minimize eye contact. However, you need to look directly at him, so look between his eyes, or look at him with a flat stare. Your eyes are flat, with no attempt to "penetrate" or make contact: flat as buttons. You should make sustained eye-contact only if in a fight for your life. Then, you must shift focus, trying to penetrate his eyes as if you were a laser beam.

Don't over-react to threats, or he/she will interpret your reaction as a victory. As soon as you have achieved your goal of separating yourself from the predator, get reinforcements and arrest them. If you and your family have been threatened (whether the tone is velvet or harsh), you must do what is necessary to keep everyone safe (See Chapter 73). You may have to be on your guard for a long time. Such incidents are often just words, or a one-time incident, but on other occasions, they can go on for a long time, with further threats, stalking, and/or other dangerous behaviors that require you to muster all professional skills and assistance to ensure that you and your family are safe.

Figure 69.1 CAUTION

You ONLY use this strategy with the openly predatory, that most rare of people, and ONLY when they are escalating into predatory rage, and only when you don't have sufficient force or backup to place them immediately under arrest. In other words, it should never happen, but you need to know what to do if it does.

Figure 69.2 Example: Interaction with Predatory Individual

Predator. "Look, this is very simple. I think you and I can agree that you misinterpreted what I said about punishing my child. I don't know where you got the idea that I said I beat her. Look, I understand. You must have been having a bad day, and you over-reacted. This can be fixed very easily. Just call the DA and tell them that you didn't quote me accurately, that you've been overworked lately and misjudged the situation. See, I bet you love your family as much as I do. You've got your child in a good school over at Echo Lake. Actually, it's amazing, that's one of the last schools in this area that still lets the kids out for recess. Oh, sorry, I'm a little off track. What I'm saying is that I bet you would be devastated if anything happened to your family. I'm the same. The problem is that what is happening to my family is you! And this is a problem you could fix, unless you are really sitting there telling me that you want to destroy my life and that of my child. IS THAT WHAT YOU ARE SAYING??!!!!"

PO. *(With a little smile and a strong, confident voice)* "I am really glad we are having this conversation, because it's good that we both understand each other."

Predator. "So you'll make the call."

PO. "Oh, you know what's going to happen."

Predator. "Suppose you tell me."

PO. "There's no need to do that. You know exactly what's going on."

Predator. "Are you threatening me?"

PO. "I don't know where you got that idea. In fact, we both know the situation here."

Predator. *(Walking away)* "You think this is over. You better watch your back."

To reiterate, you don't have to prove that you are bigger, tougher, or more dangerous. Merely establish that you are on to his game, you are not someone who will be victimized, and that there will certainly be consequences for their actions. Predatory offenders are likely to disengage if you don't react to their threats as they wish.

CHAPTER 70

De-escalation of Developmentally Disabled Offenders

Developmentally disabled offenders present a special situation. The preferred de-escalation tactics are not remarkably different for developmentally disabled offenders, but one must be aware of their cognitive deficits. If you use language that is too sophisticated, either in terms of meaning or nuance, you may elicit more frustration and anger within the offender by making them feel stupid. In addition, many developmentally disabled offenders are subject to magical thinking, and their beliefs about the world, and their own powers and vulnerabilities often don't conform to reality. Sometimes, POs can use these beliefs to help calm this type of offender, just as you would with a child. On other occasions, one must be aware of these beliefs to keep the situation from escalating out of control.

If you try to control a developmentally disabled offender based on their physical age and appearance, say a 250 pound, 35-year-old male, for example, things can go wrong very quickly. Most of our associates have found that once we make eye-contact, we can usually estimate the emotional age of the developmentally disabled person very quickly: small child, young kid, pre-teen, or teen. Then you can speak to them at their emotional age.

However, regardless of the offender's emotional age, you can't permit their apparent childishness to compromise your physical safety. As with children, developmentally delayed offenders can be quite impulsive and unpredictable. Unlike a child however, they have the physical strength of an adult, and even more dangerously, may not recognize their own strength. For this reason the tactics for evasion, self defense, or taking the offender into custody are unchanged.

POs can still use tactical paraphrasing (Chapter 56) with an enraged developmentally disabled offender. Particularly with more severely developmentally delayed individuals, however, don't just sum things up calmly. Use a more dramatic voice, and over-emphasize certain words. For example, "YOU are RE-ALLLLLY upset about having to go back to court! You really don't want to go!" Your tone is a combination of drama and enthusiasm. In essence, you are trying to catch their attention with charisma, a kind of energy in which you change the dynamics of the relationship through your voice and demeanor. Your dramatic voice validates how important the situation is to the offender. They will find themselves in interaction where there is no "fight" coming from you. Rather, you draw them in to a dynamic where, although conflict is absent, the relationship is still of compelling interest.

Following the crisis, which was undoubtedly frightening and confusing to the developmentally disabled offender, POs can certainly acknowledge and validate their feelings. For example, "Mark, that was really scary. I'm glad that's over. I want you to sit in this chair now. Yeah, know you were scared, but it's over now." A detailed critique or discussion, however, may be a mistake. Developmentally delayed offenders are often cognitively impaired, and this also affects their memory. They are unlikely to recall or retain detailed information. Emotionally, they may react to your debriefing as a new attack. Your concern should be behavioral stability (no new attack) and reassurance because they are very likely afraid that you will punish them for their behavior.

Figure 70.1 Author's Experience

A developmentally disabled woman once grabbed my finger, trying to break it. I neutralized her attempt by shifting the angle of my hand as she yanked, and as she was at the emotional age of about eight years old, rather than commanding her to "let go!" I said, "I know you want to hold my hand. You don't have to twist my finger. We can hold hands as much as you like. Sure, we can hold hands." She suddenly let go and dropped to the floor, crying.

Figure 70.2 Review: De-escalation of the Developmentally Disabled Person

Speak to them at their emotional age, not their chronological age. Use tactical paraphrasing, summarizing not only what they are apparently thinking, but what they are doing.

CHAPTER 71

Mob Rage: Feeding Frenzy

Figure 71.1 Rage State and Possibility of Violence

This discussion covers both the rage state and the possibility of violence. Pack behavior can easily escalate and therefore, it is impossible to separate rage from violence in this discussion. The discussion here concerns situations where you don't have sufficient forces to manage the mob.

Mob behavior increases hot rage exponentially, with one person's behavior and arousal amplifying that of those around them. The more people there are, the more likely that they will coalesce into an enraged mob, a beast of many heads, with one terrifying, destructive mind. Individually, members of a mob will display any or all of the types of rage that have been discussed throughout this section. An aggressive bluffer may try to entice those he/she is trying to impress into violence. Sometimes, mob frenzy is created and stoked by one predatory offender who uses the mob as a weapon or distraction. When faced with such a situation the best possible solution is to escape and summon help from the police. However, if escape is impossible attempt the following to control the mob:

1. **Overwhelming force**. Quite simply, the most powerful method of de-escalation is a demonstration to the mob and its members that they will be stopped. Each member of the mob suddenly feels alone—"the first to go down." We are aware that this is the extreme end of the spectrum, but all the possibilities must be named when considering such a terrible situation.

2. **Isolating the leader as the one individual who will face the consequences**. All of your psychological energy should be focused on the leader. This is particularly effective when the leader is hiding behind the power of the mob. If you perceive that the leader is manifesting manipulative, bluff, or predatory rage, make it clear that whatever happens, they won't emerge unscathed. The goal is definitely not to shame them, especially before the mob. Instead, presenting yourself with a quiet, grave, yet powerful calm and allowing the leader to save face are essential if you have any hopes of causing him to draw his forces back.

3. Build up the leader's ego by clearly identifying them as one worthy of conferring with. This is for the purpose of either drawing him away from the group, or appealing to his grandiose narcissism. If his goal is to appear important in the eyes of his mob, you may have given him what he really wants, without the need for violence.

4. Break the pattern, as Discussed in Chapter 55, you do something so unexpected or outlandish that none of the individuals in the mob knows how to react.

Figure 71.2 Author's Experience

About forty years ago, while hitchhiking, I was malevolently dropped off in a very dangerous area of a city during a very volatile period of racial strife. A crowd began to coalesce around me. I grabbed a stick I found on the ground, began cackling and shrieking like I'd lost his mind, and began dancing and whirling down the street, attacking moving cars with my stick. Everyone pulled back. I continued for about ten blocks until I reached a safer area.

To review, the best option when facing a mob is to escape and summon police assistance. If you do intervene, be aware that you may have to fight for your life. Your best hope, were this terrible situation to develop, and go "berserk." Fight like a wolverine in a trap with teeth, claws, and anything else you can use, tear your way free; trying to maim your attackers as savagely as you can. The goal is to become so violent yourself that each member of the group wants to get away from you. As they recoil, hopefully, an escape route opens up.

CHAPTER 72

The Aftermath: What happens to the Aggressive, Mentally Ill Offender After an Aggressive Incident?

Rage and even more so, violence, are exhausting experiences, both emotionally and physically. Many people get the "shakes" after such an incident. So much blood has "pooled" inside the core of their bodies to prepare for combat that they feel cold and start to tremble. Most individuals have a significantly impaired ability to remember what happened in sequence. They may have a patchy memory of a few events. Much of the rest of the incident is a blur. Although they may be remorseful, they usually don't remember what happened, how it started, or who was responsible. Even more drastically, they can lapse into a state of defensive confusion where they no longer recall what happened at all, or they distort the incident in their memory completely, thereafter taking no responsibility whatsoever.

Others may feel profound guilt. This might be positive, were it to lead them to reflect on their own responsibility, but for most people, this guilt is so noxious that they project responsibility onto the person who "makes" them feel guilty. Thus, they soon shift to resentment and begin to blame the other person.

Humiliation, the feeling of having one's faults or vulnerabilities involuntarily or forcibly exposed to others, is quite common, and here, too, many people become defensive. People describe humiliation like being flayed alive. Many respond by becoming enraged all over again. Their thinking seems to be, "If I feel this bad, someone must be doing it to me." What is almost universal is a post–crisis fatigue, a combination of the depletion of energy stores in the body and the cumulative effect of all the mood and cognitive changes described above.

Managing Risks Post-Crisis

In some situations, consequences or punishment will be unavoidable. In this is the case, POs must clearly convey the processes and procedures of their arrest and detention to the offender. Dependent on the nature of the arrest, POs must try and arrange for the transfer of the mentally ill offender into a residential facility as appropriate, or for an evaluation within the confines of the jail.

As noted in the opening section of this book, incarceration is almost always detrimental to the mental health and well-being of the mentally ill offender. A developmentally delayed offender is unlikely to equate his/her behaviors with consequences, or understand the need for them. So, unless they have committed a serious crime, these offenders should be stabilized and returned to a community treatment program as soon as possible.

Once the crisis has been resolved and the offender is stable and willing to talk, clear and unambiguous limits regarding future behaviors must be imposed. Without the imposition of limits and the reiteration of consequences for violating those limits the offender will simply repeat their aggressive behavior. Through de-escalation you have established control over the offender, and you can't relinquish that control simply because the crisis has passed. Reassure the offender that you are not out for revenge, but neither will you pretend that nothing serious happened nor are you going to reward them just because the aggression is over.

Consequence must be imposed swiftly, and can include more restrictive reporting and treatment stipulations, an actual court appearance, or detention in jail. This depends on the nature of the actual incident, the original stipulations imposed by the Court, and the judgment and discretion of the supervising officer.

If the offender is really frightened or devastated by what happened, the first priority is <u>reassurance and orientation</u>. For offenders who are disorganized, psychotic, or otherwise in a fragile mental state, you may have to explain to them what has happened, what is going to happen, and why. With offenders who don't have the mental capacity to really understand the details or implications of what happened, the best approach is to be calming and reassuring, and not detailed attempts at problem-solving.

If the offender has the cognitive ability to understand, then an <u>educative follow-up</u> is necessary. Of course, this may be delayed until the offender has been released from custody, or a long-term treatment program. Still, the incident should be reviewed with the offender in order to clarify and reiterate the consequences of similar behavior in the future. Discuss with the offender what other tactics they might have used to get what they desired, assist them in recognizing patterns that lead to aggression and how to avoid such situations in the future, and return the offender to a sense of dignity and integrity.

Consolidation of Gains

Another important factor is to consolidate whatever gains you made. Just because the offender seems to be listening doesn't mean they understood or even heard what you said. There are several strategies you can use to ensure that your statements are heard and agreement established.

- Paraphrase their understanding; "So, John, we've agreed that you will … and I will …"
- Have the offender repeat your instructions back to you.
- Have the offender read and sign a written copy of the instructions and stipulations of their supervision plan. Although the offender will have signed a copy of the rules and regulations at their initial interview, the recent incident may call for a modification of that plan.
- Establish a time frame for compliance and follow through with any promises you may have made, such as helping them secure housing or placement in a treatment program. Failure to uphold your end of the bargain will lead to feelings of betrayal, making future de-escalation more difficult.

CHAPTER 73

Managing Threats to Your Family

Anyone working in the field of law enforcement and corrections is much more concerned with, and disturbed by, threats made toward their family than they are with threats toward themselves. By threatening your family, promising to attack when you are not there, offenders can create a sense of helplessness and desperation on your part. The threat is usually empty, made in the heat of the moment or as means of additional defiance when being arrested and meant to terrify you. You must, however, take any such threats seriously, because it is almost impossible to know when the threat is real or not. And, truth be told, a bit of preventative planning, and educating family members as to their need to be mindful and aware is never a bad thing.

The basic safety concepts outlined in Section II of this book are easily transferrable toward enhancing the safety of your home and family, although the authors have also expanded that list with the recommended strategies listed below. Remember, as in the work environment, the development of a safety plan is not enough, and your plan should be reviewed regularly with your family.

- **Inform your family** of any threats and of the need to take protective action. In regard to children, your responsibility is to explain everything they *need* to know, but no more. Furthermore, if you display your own fears excessively, you will only frighten your family members. To this end, we strongly recommend that you acquire two books by Gavin de Becker: *The Gift of Fear* and *Protecting the Gift*.[24]
- **Inform local law enforcement**. Police officers will assist you in drawing up a safety plan as well as considering what, if any, action they can take on your behalf.
- **Review home security**. Are you a soft target or a hard target? A soft target is easily accessible, predictable, and unaware of danger. A hard target is not easily accessible, or predictable. Adequate lighting and the use of quality locks, doors, and windows will limit the ability of an intruder to enter your home. Consult with your local police department as to how to make your home more secure. Some departments will be more willing than others to send an officer out to walk through and around your home to inform you of security gaps. There are also excellent books on home security available. Consider having a home alarm system installed.
- **Concerning firearms**. Should you decide to purchase a firearm for home security, each member of your family must attend a firearm safety and instruction course. Firearms should be stored and cared for as delineated in the course.
- **Concerning dogs**. In many ways dogs are a better security option than a firearm. Unlike humans, a well-trained dog, particularly certain breeds, won't hesitate to act when they perceive a threat. Dogs will also provide you with an early warning system, detecting sounds and smells that

you can't. Further discussion of dog breeds and training is well beyond the scope of this book. A good dog can be one of the most important aspects of home security.

- **Scan your surroundings**. Your family members must learn to scan their surroundings and note anything out of the ordinary. Remind family members to report suspicious people and cars.
- **Inform employers and schools** so they are aware of the identity of the potential assailant. Make clear to school officials exactly who is allowed to meet or pick-up your children.
- **Change your routine**. As much as possible, travel by different routes and at different times. Be unpredictable.
- **Safety in numbers**. Neither you nor any of your family members should be the last to leave their workplace or school. Enlist co-coworkers, coaches, teachers, etc., to be part of a team.
- **Notify your office and family of travel plans**, and ask that they not reveal any travel plans or other schedules.
- **Be careful about giving out personal information**. This can be difficult with children, as they happily exchange information with their friends or others. Remind them to be careful of strangers, and to report any such inquiries. Don't forget about social networking sites such as Facebook and MySpace, and other dangers of the Internet.
- **Plan an escape route**. Figure out the best ways to escape from your home and rehearse this with family members. You can combine this with fire drills—something the children are already familiar with from school.
- **Plan how to ask for help if in public and how best to call for help if needed**. If your children are alone and there are no nearby police cars, the best stranger to ask for help is a *woman*, as women are far less likely to be a threat. Of course, this is not the case if a woman is the threatening offender.
- **Teach your children a code word** or challenge that must be answered by strange individuals. This includes neighbors, and in some cases, relatives. For example, a person approaches your child after school and says, "Tasha, your mother and father were injured in an automobile accident. The police told me to take you to the hospital! Please come with me now." Your child should have been taught to keep her distance, looking for escape routes as she asks "What's the word?" If the person does not reply immediately the child should run to a safe haven and describe the individual as best they can.
- **Post emergency numbers** near each telephone in your home. Establish safe havens to escape to in times of danger. If possible, enlist your neighbors in your safety plan.

CHAPTER 74

Conclusion

Due to the economic downturn of 2007, the future of governmental funding for criminal justice and law enforcement needs is uncertain. Therefore, policymakers must consider alternative solutions to crime control that will keep communities safe while making the best use of scarce public funds. To that end, administrators and professionals at all levels of the criminal justice and treatment communities must identify and initiate long-term strategies related to the supervision and treatment of mentally ill offenders. Vital to the achievement of this goal is the realization that the missions of public safety and public health overlap, and strong professional partnerships must be established between probation officials, law enforcement agencies, corrections officials, judges, prosecutors, defense attorneys, and community-based treatment providers. Only by working together can these stakeholders develop cost effective strategies that increase public safety, reduce recidivism, and improve outcomes for the mentally ill offender.

As we enter into the second decade of the twenty-first century, POs will find themselves busier than ever before, supervising an ever growing number of offenders, many of them with undiagnosed or unaddressed mental health and/or substance abuse issues, increasing the chances of a violent encounter significantly. In addition to increasing caseload sizes and workloads, the financial crisis of 2007, which continues to reverberate throughout the economy, will result in fewer available resources in the community upon which probation and parole agencies can depend for treatment and services for their offenders. Given the inevitable increase in the number of untreated offenders under supervision, the ability to recognize, confront calmly, and de-escalate aggressive behavior safely is a necessary tool for today's PO.

With that in mind, the authors hope they have met their original intent, which is to offer the PO a comprehensive, "one–stop-shop" guidebook designed to increase safety and reduce risk. The authors also hope that by taking into consideration the office and fieldwork security tactics presented in this book you will reduce the opportunities for aggression greatly, and thereby the need to employ the accompanying de-escalation techniques. Of course, the development of a safety mindset is not something that can be accomplished simply by reading the material presented in this book, and POs are encouraged to attend any and all of the safety and self-defense trainings offered by your agencies. Officers who are mentally and physically prepared to perform their duties are much more likely to ensure the compliance of their offenders, reduce risk, and increase public safety.

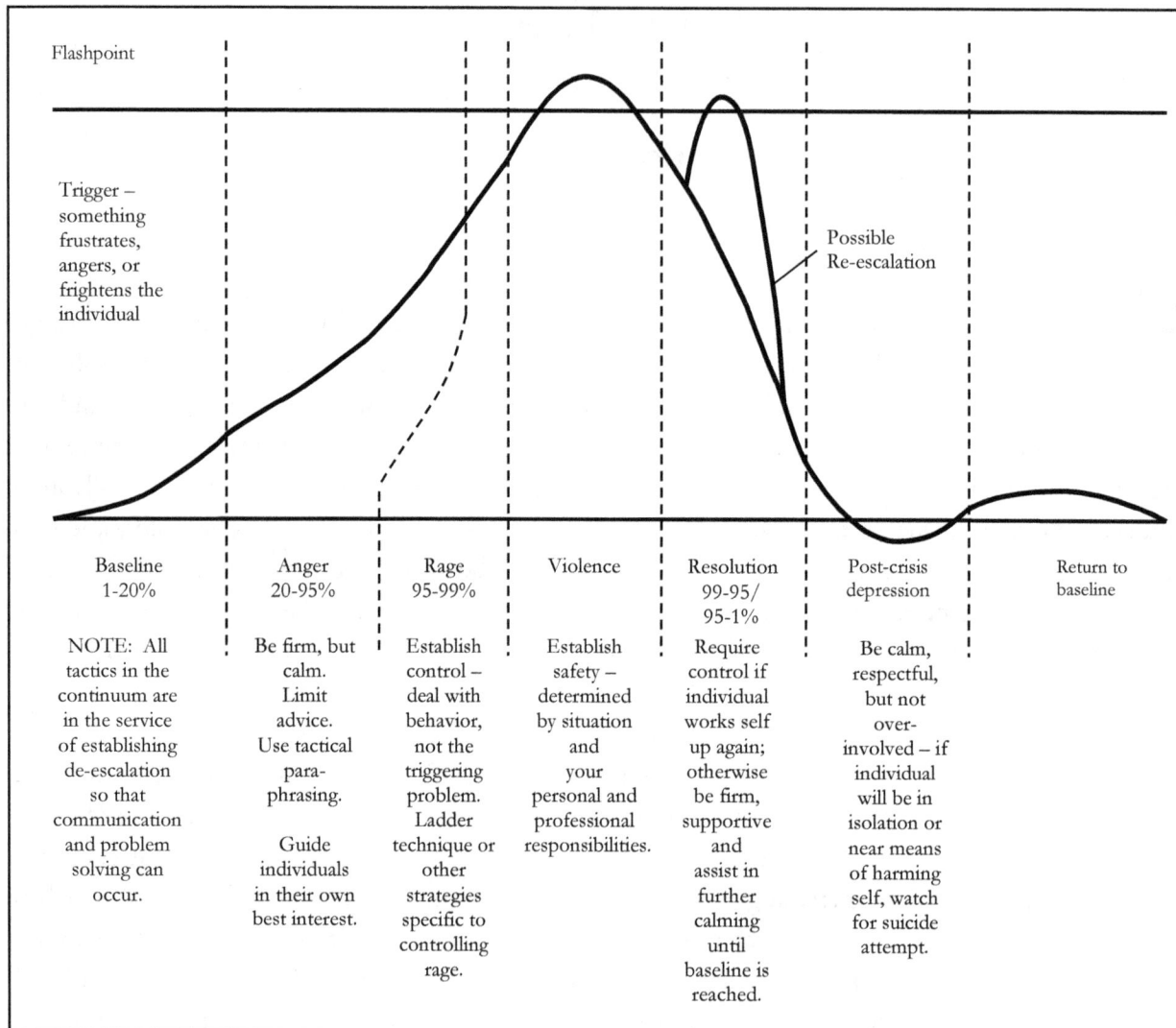

Flashpoint

Trigger –
something
frustrates,
angers, or
frightens the
individual

Possible
Re-escalation

Baseline 1-20%	Anger 20-95%	Rage 95-99%	Violence	Resolution 99-95/ 95-1%	Post-crisis depression	Return to baseline
NOTE: All tactics in the continuum are in the service of establishing de-escalation so that communication and problem solving can occur.	Be firm, but calm. Limit advice. Use tactical para-phrasing. Guide individuals in their own best interest.	Establish control – deal with behavior, not the triggering problem. Ladder technique or other strategies specific to controlling rage.	Establish safety – determined by situation and your personal and professional responsibilities.	Require control if individual works self up again; otherwise be firm, supportive and assist in further calming until baseline is reached.	Be calm, respectful, but not over-involved – if individual will be in isolation or near means of harming self, watch for suicide attempt.	

References

Alschuler, A. W. (2003). The changing purposes of criminal punishment: A retrospective on the past century and some thoughts about the next. *The University of Chicago Law Review, 70*(1), 1-21.

American Bar Association. (2008). *Criminal justice system improvements.* Retrieved January 7, 2009, from http://www.abanet.org/poladv/transition/2008dec_crimjustice.pdf

American Psychiatric Association. (2004). *Mental illness and the criminal justice system: Redirecting resources toward treatment, not containment.* Retrieved January 3, 2010, from http://archive.psych.org/edu/other_res/lib_archives/archives/200401.pdf

Arieti , S. (1974) *Interpretation of Schizophrenia* (2nd ed.). New York: Basic Books.

Austin, J., & Fabelo, T. (2004). *The diminishing returns of increased incarceration: A blueprint to improve public safety and reduce costs.* Retrieved January 3, 2009, from http://www.jfa-associates.com/publications/srs/BlueprintFinal.pdf

Beckett, K., & Sasson, T. (2004). The politics of injustice: Crime and punishment in America.

Bloom, J., & Krishnan, B., & Lockey, C. (2008). The majority of inpatient psychiatric beds should not be appropriated by the forensic system. *American Academy Psychiatry Law, 36*(4), 438-442. Retrieved January 1, 2010, from http://www.jaapl.org/ cgi/ content/ full/36/4/438

Burrell, W. (2004). *Trends in probation and parole in the states.* Retrieved January 4, 2009, from http://www.appa-net.org/eweb/docs/appa/pubs/TPP.pdf

Council of State Governments Justice Center (2009). *Improving responses to people with mental illnesses: The essential elements of specialized probation initiatives.* Retrieved November 11, 2009, from http://consensusproject.org/jc_publications/probation-essential-elements/Improving_Responses_to_People_with_Mental_Illnesses_-_The_Elements_of_Specialize_Probation_Initiatives.pdf

Daniels, P. (2004). *U.S. prison boom creates an Orwellian world.* Retrieved January 3, 2009, from http://www.wsws.org/articles/2004/may2004/pris-m13.shtml

Ekman, P. (2003). *Emotions revealed.* New York: Times Books-Henry Holt.

Goin, M. (2004). *Mental illness and the criminal justice system: Redirecting resources toward treatment, not containment.* Retrieved September 11, 2010, from http://archive.psych.org/ edu/other_res/lib_archives/archives/200401.pdf

Haney, C., & Zimbardo, P. (1998, July). The past and future of U.S. prison policy: twenty-five years after the Stanford prison experiment. *American Psychologist, 53*(7), 721.

Justice Policy Institute. (2008, April 1, Press Release). *Jailing communities: The impact of jail expansion and effective public safety strategies.* Retrieved January 16, 2009, from http: //www.justicepolicy.org/content.php?hmID=1811&smID=1581&ssmID=73

King, R., Mauer, M., & Young, M. (2005). *The sentencing project: Incarceration and crime: A complex relationship.* Retrieved December 16, 2009, from http://www.sentencingproject .org/doc/publications/inc_iandc_complex.pdf

Liptak, A. (2008, April 23). U.S. prison population dwarfs that of other nations. *International Herald Tribune.*

Marion, N. & Oliver, W. (2006). The *public policy of crime and criminal justice.* Upper Saddle River, NJ: Pearson/Prentice Hall.

Maxwell, S. (2005, August). Rethinking the broad sweep of recidivism: A task for evaluators. *Criminology and Public Safety, 4*(3).

Merriman, H. (2000). *Robbing ourselves blind: The economics of getting tough on crime.* Retrieved November 14, 2009, from http://www.oberlin.edu/news-info/01may/robbingblind.pdf

New York Times. (2008). Not winning the war on drugs. (Editorial) Retrieved September 20, 2008, from http://www.nytimes.com/2008/07/02/opinion/02wed1 .html?_r=1&oref=slogin

Perlstein, Rick. (2008). *Nixonland: The rise of a president and the fracturing of America.* New York: Schribner.

PEW Center on the States. (2008, February). *One in 100: Behind bars in America* (Public Safety Performance Project). Washington, DC: The PEW Charitable Trusts.

PEW Center on the States. (2009, March) *One in 31: The long reach of American corrections.* Washington, DC: The PEW Charitable Trusts.

PEW Center on the States. (2011, April). *State of Recidivism: The Revolving Door of America's Prisons.* Washington, D.C.: The PEW Charitable Trusts

U.S. Department of Justice. (2006). People with mental illness. Retrieved January 2, 2010, from http://www.cops.usdoj.gov/files/RIC/Publications/e04062003.pdf

U.S. Department of Justice. (2009a). *Office of Justice programs grants.* Retrieved Sept 14, 2010, from http://www.ojp.usdoj.gov/BJA/recovery/OJPRecoveryFactSheet.pdf

U.S. Dept of Justice. (2009b). *Probation and parole in the United States, 2008.* Retrieved December 19, 2009 from http://bjs.ojp.usdoj.gov/content/pub/pdf/ppus08.pdf

U.S. Department of Justice, Office of Justice Programs, Bureau of Justice Statistics. (1999). *Mental health and treatment of inmates and probationers.* Retrieved Sept 14, 2010, from http://bjs.ojp.usdoj.gov/content/pub/pdf/mhtip.pdf

U.S. Department of Labor-Occupational Safety and Health Administration. (2002). *OSHA factsheet: Workplace violence.*

Endnotes

1. CIT officers are ordinary first response officers with an added certification based on CIT training. In most jurisdictions, there is no specialized "mental health police." Rather, there is a certain proportion of officers on the road at all times who have this specialized training, and when there is a mental health related call *and they are free*, they will respond. Therefore, response from a CIT officer is dependent on who is available. Always ask. If no officer is available, you will get the closest available officer anyway, without delay.

2. See Rhodes, Richard. (1999). *Why they kill: The discoveries of a maverick criminologist*. New York: Vintage, on the work of sociologist Lonnie Atkins, who coined the phrase "violentization," to describe the process in which a victim of violence becomes a perpetrator. Atkins focused on the family, but violentization can also occur later in life.

3. Ibid.

4. One of the authors observed an informal study by a neurologist at a youth detention facility. He noted signs of closed head injury (through neuro-psych evaluation) in approximately 50 percent of the male inmates.

5. See: Skidmore-Roth, L. (2010). *Mosby's 2011 nursing drug reference*. Philadelphia, PA: Elsevier Books.

6. You will sometimes see the same thing with people for whom English is not a first language.

7. An extremely valuable book regarding OCD is: Schwartz, Jeffrey (with Beverly Beyette). (1996). *Brain lock: Free yourself from obsessive-compulsive behavior*. New York: Regan Books.

8. One of the best books on manipulation is: Allen, B., & Bosta, D. (1981-2002). *Games criminals play: How you can profit by knowing them*. Berkeley, CA: Rae John.

9. See: Hare, R. (1999) *Without conscience: The disturbing world of the psychopaths among us*. New York: Guilford.

10. We are grateful to the late Dan Kelleher, former professor of Antioch University, for the image of the "undamaged self."

11. In Greek mythology Sisyphus was a king who, as a punishment from the gods, was made to roll a huge rock up a steep hill, but before he could reach the top of the hill, the rock would always roll back down, forcing him to begin again, dooming Sisyphus to an eternity of frustrations. Today, pointless and frustrating activities are often described as Sisyphean.

12. Other major categories of stalkers are:

    -   **Relational stalkers**. Often an extension of a controlling or violent relationship, this stalker is either keeping tabs on his/her partner, or pursuing them once they have left.

    -   **Obsessive stalkers**. The classic stalker—a hyper-focus on the victim as prey, not necessarily to kill or even harm, but always to control. Like ordinary obsessive-compulsive disorder, this stalker can be well-aware that the victim does not desire contact, and may be afraid of or hate him/her. But just as the germ-obsessed obsessive MUST wash his hands 50 times, despite *knowing* that they are clean, the obsessive stalker has to have the attention of his/her victim.

    -   **Psychopathic stalker**. Such an individual may certainly have been in a relationship with or be obsessed with his/her victim. In addition, there is considerable "ego" involved—this stalker's psychological energy focuses on self rather than the victim. A true predator, he/she is doing something they enjoys—simply because they can (for amusement), or because the victim, in some way, offended them (for revenge).

13. Our thanks to Aaron Fields of the Seattle Fire Department for this example.

14. An actual incident. The engineer was killed trying to jump clear when the manic person wrecked the train.

15. Researchers note that a mixture of alcohol and cocaine is particularly dangerous, as the body synthesizes them together into a new substance, cocaethylene. Retrieved from http://jpet.aspetjournals.org/ content/274/1/215.abstract

16. One of the authors first heard this method presented by author David Grossman. Also see his exemplary book: Grossman, D. (1996). *On Killing: The psychological cost of learning to kill in war and society*. Santa Ana, CA: Back Bay Books.

17. We owe the image of the hands as a fence to Geoff Thompson, who has authored a number of books on his career as a doorman in violent British pubs, as well as exemplary books on self-defense.

18   We are indebted to John Holttum, MD, Child Psychiatrist from Tacoma, Washington. One of the authors attended a presentation given by Dr. Holttum which influenced us greatly in terms of how to "subdivide" the presenting behaviors of youth and how best to intervene with them. We must underscore that any intervention recommendations are ours, and may be at variance to those Dr. Holttum might offer.

19   We recommend the following 2 books: Louv, R. (2005). *Last child in the woods: Saving our children from nature deficit disorder.* Chapel Hill, NC: Algonquin; Sax, L. (2007). *Boys adrift: The five factors driving the growing epidemic of unmotivated boys and underachieving young men.* Philadelphia, PA: Basic (Perseus).

20   See: http://www.emdr.com/

21   The authors owe a debt for some of the basic information in this section to a form of training called Professional Assault Response Training (PART), thanks to a workshop one of us attended approximately 20 years ago. We have made major changes in their basic 4-part schema, as well as adding a significant amount of new data. Therefore, our approach is, in many aspects, quite different, and it should not be confused with PART's procedures.

22   (Sherwin, Cotler, written communication)"

23   See: Salter, A. (2004). *Predators: pedophiles, rapists and other sex offenders: Who they are, how they operate and how we can protect ourselves and our children.* New York: Basic Books. Our gratitude for the formulation of the overwhelming force/respect concept which she presented in a great story during a seminar.

24   See: de Becker, G. (1997). *The Gift of Fear: Survival signals that protect us from violence.* U.S. and Canada: Little Brown; and (1999). *Protecting the gift: Keeping children and teenagers safe (and parents sane)* New York: Random House, New York.

ABOUT THE AUTHORS

Ellis Amdur

Edgework founder Ellis Amdur received his B.A. in psychology from Yale University in 1974 and his M.A. in psychology from Seattle University in 1990. He is both a National Certified Counselor and a State Certified Child Mental Health Specialist. He has written a number of books concerning communication with mentally ill and emotionally disturbed individuals and the de-escalation of aggression, all of which are available through www.edgework.info

Since the late 1960s, Amdur has trained in various martial arts systems, spending thirteen of these years studying in Japan. He is a recognized expert in classical and modern Japanese martial traditions and has authored three iconoclastic books and one instructional DVD on martial arts subjects.

Since his return to America in 1988, Ellis Amdur has worked in the field of crisis intervention. He has developed a range of training and consultation services, as well as a unique style of assessment and psychotherapy. These are based on a combination of phenomenological psychology and the underlying philosophical premises of classical Japanese martial traditions. Amdur's professional philosophy can best be summed up in this idea: "The development of an individual's integrity and dignity is the paramount virtue. This can only occur when people live courageously, regardless of their circumstances, and take responsibility for their roles in making the changes they desire."

Ellis Amdur is a dynamic public speaker and trainer who presents his work throughout the U.S. and internationally. He is noted for his sometimes outrageous humor as well as his profound breadth of knowledge. His vivid descriptions of aggressive and mentally ill people and his true-to-life role-playing of the behaviors in question give participants an almost first-hand experience of facing the real individuals in question.

For more information on books and training by Ellis Amdur, please refer to his website at www.edgework.info

Alan Pelton

After graduating from the University of Pittsburgh with an undergraduate degree in psychology Alan began working for the Allegheny County Adult Probation Department, Pittsburgh Pennsylvania, in 1991. The first 15 years of his career were spent supervising a "regular" caseload in a regional field office, before becoming a supervisor in March of 2006. In the fall of 2007 Alan returned to school and obtained a Master of Science degree in the Administration of Justice and Security from the University of Phoenix.

In addition to his work in the field of Probation and Parole, Alan has also been studying, practicing, and teaching a number of martial arts and self-defense courses since 1984. Over the years Alan has achieved masters rank in Tae Kwon Do, a Korean art, and yondan rank in Aikido, a Japanese art that he currently studies and teaches. In fact, Alan first met Ellis at his Aikido dojo in Pittsburgh some years ago, when Ellis was presenting a martial arts seminar there.

Noting the similarities of both their professional and self-defense backgrounds Ellis and Alan maintained contact over the years. When Ellis approached him about co-authoring this book, Alan eagerly accepted the opportunity to meld Ellis' dynamic approach to mental illness and de-escalation with the very real personal and public safety concerns of today's Probation and Parole Officers.

www.ingramcontent.com/pod-product-compliance
Lightning Source LLC
Chambersburg PA
CBHW081436190326
41458CB00020B/6220